Glob

Phrasal Verbs
Dictionary

Martin H. Manser
Nigel D. Turton
Andrew Betsis

Ideal for learners of English preparing for exams:
IELTS, TOEFL, TOEIC, BULATS, PET, FCE, CAE, CPE

GlobalELT
ENGLISH LANGUAGE TEACHING BOOKS

Contents

Published by GLOBAL ELT LTD, 2013
www.globalelt.co.uk
email: orders@globalelt.co.uk

British Library Cataloguing-in-Publication Data
A catalogue record of this book is available from the British Library.

● *Global ELT Phrasal Verbs Dictionary* - ISBN: 9781904663690
© **GLOBAL ELT LTD,** 2013

Acknowledgements
The authors would like to thank Jeremy Clear, Gwyneth Fox and Susie Turton for their assistance in preparing the manuscript.

Preface

To be fluent in English, you have to be able to use phrasal verbs. This dictionary has been written for intermediate and advanced students who want an easy-to-use reference book that deals with this area of the language. The emphasis is on idiomatic phrasal verbs, whose meaning and use are especially difficult for the student.

The dictionary is a development of the highly successful *English Verbal Idioms* and *English Prepositional Idioms* by the late F. T. Wood.

Great care has been taken to present the meaning and use of each verb clearly, and a system of notation has been devised that shows at a glance how each verb is used in a sentence.

Nigel D. Turton
Martin H. Manser

Phrasal Verbs are very important in English and quite difficult for students to learn. It is necessary for learners of English to be able to both recognise (in Reading and Listening) as well as to be able to use them (in Writing and Speaking).

The 120 common Phrasal Verbs, followed by the Exercises, included in this dictionary serve exactly this purpose.

This dictionary can be used in the classroom, or for self-study purposes, as a general reference book.

Andrew Betsis

Introduction

To understand and use the idioms of a language correctly requires a degree of proficiency that is hard for the non-native speaker to acquire. An area of the English language which presents the student with particular difficulty is the idiomatic phrasal verb.

Idiomatic phrasal verbs

A phrasal verb is a verb which consists of two or three separate parts: *come in, run away, look forward to,* etc. With an idiomatic phrasal verb, the meanings of the separate parts tell us little or nothing about the meaning of the whole. For example, the student may be fully familiar with the meanings of *pick* and *up* as individual words, but this knowledge does not help him when he wants to know the idiomatic meaning of *pick up* in, say, *'Business is picking up'*.

This dictionary has been written to help the learner with this type of idiomatic combination. Non-idiomatic or literal phrasal verbs, which simply combine the meanings of their parts, are excluded.

However, having made the distinction between idiomatic and non-idiomatic phrasal verbs, we must point out that these are merely labels for the opposite ends of a scale: there are many phrasal verbs which are neither fully idiomatic nor fully literal. The guide for selection in these cases has been comprehensibility, so that a verb combination has been included if its meaning is not obvious from its parts. There are two exceptions to this rule: verbs used only in technical or specialised fields are not included, nor are verbs which are no longer in common use. Our intention has been to concentrate on the items likely to be of greatest use to the majority of students.

Grammatical notation

The language learner has to know how to use phrasal verbs correctly in sentences. A very simple guide has therefore been developed, providing the student with a clear visual impression of the grammatical behaviour of a verb without involving him in a long technical description. The basic system is shown below.

① = ●●	Suddenly all the lights *went out*.
② = ●●○	I *bumped into* one of my old schoolfriends today.
③ = ●○●	The examiner *caught* everybody *out*.
④ = ●○●○	He *landed* me *with* the bill.
⑤ = ●○●	They're *bringing* a new book *out*.
or, ●●○	They're *bringing out* a new book.
⑥ = ●●●○	I *don't feel up to* answering their questions.
⑦ = ●○●●○	The mushrooms *brought* her *out in* spots.

① = ●●   ② = ●●○   ③ = ●○●   ④ = ●○●○   ⑤ = ●○● *or* ●●○   ⑥ = ●●●○   ⑦ = ●○●●○

The system employs two symbols: a filled circle and an empty circle. Each filled circle represents one part of the phrasal verb. Each empty circle represents one or more words that the user must add.

① and ②   Consider the first **two** sentences in the above table:

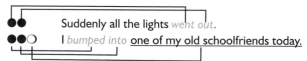

Both *go out* and *bump into* have two parts, so both are represented by two filled circles. However, while *go out* does not necessarily have to be followed by anything, *bump into* must be followed by something, and this is shown by the final empty circle.

③   In some cases, it is necessary to insert an object between the parts of a verb. Again, an empty circle shows where the object must be placed:

Note that when the object is a single word or short phrase, no other pattern may be used. But if the object is of some length, it is also possible to use pattern ② :

② ●●○ The examiner *caught out* everybody who took the exam.

If a long object contains a moveable part, as in the above example, this may follow the second part of the verb:

③   ●○● The examiner *caught* everybody *out* who took the exam.

To reduce the possibility of incorrect usage, only the basic pattern ●○● is shown in the notation.

④   In other cases, it is necessary to insert something between the parts of a verb **and** to follow the last part with something;

⑤ With many phrasal verbs, the user has a choice of word order:

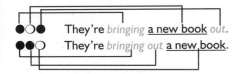

●○●   They're *bringing* <u>a new book</u> *out*.
●●○   They're *bringing out* <u>a new book</u>.

However, when the object in such cases is a pronoun only the first pattern may be used:

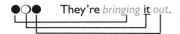

●○●   They're *bringing* <u>it</u> *out*.

On the other hand, if the object is rather lengthy, it is typically the second pattern that is used:

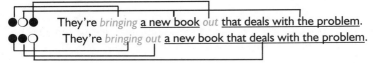

●●○ They're *bringing out* <u>a new edition of the dictionary</u>.

unless the object contains a movable part, such as a relative clause, when either pattern may be used:

●○●   They're *bringing* <u>a new book</u> *out* <u>that deals with the problem</u>.
●●○   They're *bringing out* <u>a new book that deals with the problem</u>.

⑥ and ⑦ There are just two basic patterns for the three-part verbs:

●●●○   I don't *feel up to* <u>answering their questions</u>.

●○●●○   The mushrooms *brought* her *out in* spots.

The following points about the notation system should also be noted:
1. Word order is not necessarily the same for each meaning of a phrasal verb.
   Compare the pattern of *draw up* when it means 'arrive at a place and stop':

●● A car *drew up* and two men jumped out.
   with the patterns used when it means 'compose and write down something in a formal way':

●○● They've *drawn* the contract *up*.
●●○ We've *drawn up* the list of names you asked for.

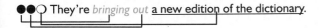

6

In such cases, there is a separate entry for each meaning:

●●   **draw up**[1]
●○●   **draw up**[2]
●●○

2.   Some phrasal verbs may be used with two parts **or** three parts:

●●   I *called in* and saw John instead of going straight home.
●●●○ I *called in on* John instead of going straight home.

Verbs of this type are shown by the use of round brackets:

●●(●○)   **call in (on)**

3. A slash mark (/) is used to show alternatives. For example, '*Come on!* I'm in a hurry!' and '*Come along!* I'm in a hurry!' mean the same. Instead of having two separate entries, pairs of this type are therefore shown in the following way:

●●   **come along/on**

Sometimes the alternatives behave differently. This is true of, for example, *break in* and *break into*:

●●   Thieves *broke in* and stole the jewels.
●●○   Thieves *broke into* the house and stole the jewels.

The pattern of the first combination is therefore shown first, followed by a slash mark and then, beneath, the pattern of the second combination:

●●/   **break in/into**
●●○

Similarly, when the first combination has two or more patterns, these are shown first, followed by a slash mark and, beneath, the pattern(s) of the second combination. Consider, for example, the notation for get in/into[2]:

●●   **get in/into**[2]
●○●/
●●○
●○●○

This notation expresses the following possibilities:

●●	She's lucky to *get in* without the right qualifications.
●○●	Her father must have *got* her *in*; he knows the headmaster.
●●○	How did she manage to *get into* the school?
●○●○	Somehow her father *got* her *into* the school.

4. Nouns derived from the verbs shown in the dictionary have been included, and are signalled by the letter **N** in heavy type in the notation column alongside an example:

N ❐ The first goal came just two minutes after the *kick-off.*

5. Usage is reflected in the examples. For instance, a single example of a passive construction indicates that the verb is typically used in this way:

●●○   **get at.....**

> 4 influence or persuade somebody, especially with a bribe or threat: ❐ *The witness had obviously been got at. He refused to tell the jury what he had seen.*

Style
Most idiomatic phrasal verbs are used by native speakers in everyday conversation, and these have been left unmarked. Occasionally, however, the style-markers *Formal* and *Informal* are used.

Formal is shown against verbs which belong to formal written English, such as business correspondence or to unusually formal spoken English. These verbs will not form part of the spoken vocabulary of the average learner. (It might be helpful to point out here that, in the case of *on/upon* alternatives, the use of *upon* is generally more formal.)

The style marker *Informal* is shown alongside verbs which are used, for example, between close friends or to express the speaker's anger or irritation. Since many of these verbs could cause offence if used inappropriately, the student is advised to treat them with caution.

120

very common Phrasal Verbs

(followed by Exercises)

**All these 120 Phrasal Verbs
are also included in this Dictionary**

be over - Something will be over when it has finished. *e.g. The movie will be over at 9pm if you want to meet for a meal afterwards.*

be taken aback - You are taken aback when you are surprised or confused by something. *e.g. I was taken aback when I found out that Judy had an identical twin.*

beat up - Someone is beaten up when they are punched, hit or kicked violently and repeatedly. *e.g. In some places, if you wear expensive looking jewellery you may be beaten up and robbed.*

blow up (1) - You blow something up when you destroy it with a bomb or other exploding weapon. *e.g. These days everyone is worried that terrorists will try to blow up an airplane.*

blow up (2) - You blow up something such as a tyre or a balloon when you fill it with air. *e.g. I hope you have a pump to blow up that air mattress, otherwise it is going to take forever.*

break down (1) - When machinery breaks down, it stops working. *e.g. I only carry a mobile phone in case my car breaks down on some deserted highway.*

break down (2) - You break down when you lose control emotionally. *e.g. When he heard that his grandfather had died he broke down and cried.*

break into - Someone breaks into a building when he or she enters by force, usually with the intention of stealing or doing mischief. *e.g. Someone broke into the government building and stole important papers.*

break off - You break something off when you end, discontinue or interrupt it. *e.g. Talks between the two countries will break off if they don't reach an agreement soon.*

break out - Violent or disturbing situations break out when they begin, often suddenly. *e.g. I was sound asleep until the fight broke out in the street below my window.*

break out in - You break out in something, such as a rash or sweat, when there is a sudden spread of it on your body. *e.g. She won't walk up the stairs because she is afraid she will break out in a sweat.*

break up (1)- People break up when their relationship or partnership comes to an end. *e.g. Fans can feel very sad when their favourite bands break up.*

break up (2) - You break something up when you stop it. *e.g. The police used tear gas to try to break up the riot.*

bring up - take care of children and educate them *e.g. He was brought up to value honesty highly.*

brush up on - You brush up on something when you refresh or improve your knowledge of it. *e.g. You'd better brush up on your computer skills if you want to get a good job.*

burn down - A building burns down when it is destroyed by fire. *e.g. The protesters attempted to burn down the bank.*

call off sth or call sth off (1) - An event or arrangement is called off when it is cancelled, or stopped [abandoned] after it has begun. *e.g. I'm afraid I have to call off my singing lesson this week because I have a sore throat.*

calm down - You calm down when you stop feeling anxious, upset or angry. *e.g. When you feel angry, sometimes going for a walk can help you calm down.*

carry out - You carry out a task or procedure when you do it, complete it, or put it into practice. *e.g. That's a fantastic idea, but do you think you can actually carry it out?*

catch on - Something catches on when it becomes popular. *e.g. I certainly hope that this style of high waisted trousers never catches on!*

check in - You check in when you arrive somewhere, and let the people involved know that you are there. *e.g. You must check in two hours before your flight is scheduled to leave.*

cheer up - You cheer up when you begin to feel happier or more hopeful. *e.g. Cheer up! Failing an exam is not the end of the world.*

come (a)round/come to - someone who is unconscious comes round or comes to when they regain consciousness. *e.g. I was feeling a bit dizzy; then, the next thing I knew, I came round on the ground surrounded by a crowd of people.*

come across - You come across something when you discover or encounter it without looking for or expecting it. *e.g. He came across a wallet in the park so he turned it in to the police.*

come into - You come into money when you inherit it. *e.g. Since he came into his fortune, he has been spending his time working for several charities.*

come up with - You come up with an idea when you think of it. *e.g. I need to come up with some ways to save money.*

cut down on - You cut down on something when you do or use it less than you did before. *e.g. Don't offer Betty that cake; she's trying very hard to cut down on the amount of sugar she eats.*

cut off - Someone or something is cut off when it is disconnected or interrupted. *e.g. His telephone line was cut off because he didn't pay his bill.*

die out - Living things die out when the whole group or kind dies. e.g. *Many plants and animals will die out in the next ten years.*

do up - renovate something (eg. property) or make it look almost as good as new e.g. *Mr. Brown does up old houses and then sells them for a living.*

do up (2) - You do something up when you fasten, button, zip, or tie it. *e.g. Adam needs to do up his shoelaces or else he may trip.*

drop in - You drop in when you pay a short visit, often without warning. *e.g. I was running errands in the neighbourhood this morning, so I thought I would drop in and see how you are.*

drop off (1) - You drop someone or something off when you take them someplace and then leave them there, often in a vehicle. *e.g. Will you drop this package off at the post office this morning?*

drop off (2) - You drop off when you fall asleep. *e.g. I had to pull the car over and take a nap because I was starting to drop off at the wheel.*

drop out - You drop out of an activity when you take no further part in it. *e.g. If you drop out of school you will have a hard time finding a job.*

fall out - People fall out when they quarrel. *e.g. It is a shame when families fall out over trivial things.*

fall through - A plan falls through when it fails or cannot be achieved. *e.g. Our plan to go on a picnic this weekend will fall through if it rains.*

fill in - You fill something in when you write information in the spaces required. e.g. *Getting a bank account always involves filling in a form.*

find out - discover something you did not know, or learn about it either by chance or through investigation *e.g. I only found out about the exam a few days ago.*

get (a)round (1) - You get round a problem when you solve or avoid it. *e.g. He got round the problem of not having a car by moving nearer to his job.*

get (a)round (2) - You get round, or get around, someone when you manage to persuade them to do something or let you do something. *e.g. Don't worry, my dad is easy to get round; he'll let me go on the trip in the end.*

get away - You get away when you escape. *e.g. The little boy was struggling to get away from his mother and run after the ice-cream lorry.*

get away with - You get away with something illegal or dishonest when you manage to avoid being caught or punished for it. *e.g. I doubt that you will get away with telling people you're a lawyer. What if they ask you a question?*

get over - You get over something such as an illness, shock or disappointment when you recover from it *e.g. I hope you get over the flu quickly!*

get through (1) - You get through to someone when you succeed in contacting them by telephone. *e.g. Oh, I'm so glad I finally got through to you; I need to tell you I won't be at the meeting tomorrow.*

get through (2) - You get through work or a task when you finish or complete it. *e.g. Do you think you'll be able to get through reading the report before the meeting?*

give in - You give in when you admit that you've been defeated, or agree to stop opposing or resisting something and allow it. *e.g. Don't give in to the fashion industry and feel that you have to buy a whole new wardrobe every season.*

give out - You give things out when you give one to each of a number of people. *e.g. They will give out free books to everyone who comes to the lecture.*

give (oneself) up - You give yourself up when you surrender to someone in authority and become his or her prisoner. *e.g. After hiding out for several years, the fugitive gave himself up to the police.*

give up (2) - You give up, or give something up, when you stop trying to do it and admit defeat. *e.g. Tango is a difficult dance, so don't give up if you haven't got the hang of it in the first few lessons.*

give up (3) - You give up something when you decide that you are not going to do it any longer. *e.g. I think my grandfather will give up driving because his eyesight is not very good.*

go down - Something goes down when it reduces, falls or gets lower. *e.g. If your fever doesn't go down by tomorrow, you should call a doctor.*

go for - You go for someone when you attack them, either physically or with words. *e.g. Okay, so I made a mistake. You didn't need to go for me like that and tell everyone what I did and how foolish it was.*

go off - A bomb or gun goes off when it explodes or is fired. *e.g. Don't point a gun at anyone you don't intend to shoot. You never know, it might go off.*

go off (2) - Something, usually food, goes off if it is not good to eat or drink any more because it is too old. *e.g. Does this milk smell like it's gone off to you?*

go through - You go through something such as a room or container when you check its contents carefully. *e.g. I will have to go through my whole desk now because I can't find the paper anywhere.*

go with - Something goes with something else when it matches or suits it. *e.g. I need to buy a belt to go with this dress.*

grow up - to gradually change from a child to an adult *e.g. Jocelyn grew up more quickly than her twin brother did.*

hold on - You ask someone to hold on when you want them to wait. *e.g. Hold on a minute; let me turn off the car's engine before you open the door!*

hold up (1) - You hold something up if you stop or delay it. *e.g. Wearing steel-toed boots can hold you up when you try to go through airport security.*

hold up (2) - You hold up people or things when you use a gun to rob them. *e.g. Did you receive training about what to do if someone tries to hold up your shop?*

lay off - A company lays people off when it stops employing them either permanently or temporarily. *e.g. If the economy does poorly businesses will be forced to lay off hundreds of people.*

let down - You let someone down if you do not do what you promised to do or what he or she expected you to do. *e.g. My friends really let me down when none of them came to my birthday party.*

let off - Someone is let off when he or she is given a punishment that is less severe than deserved, or no punishment at all. *e.g. I will let you off this time but don't do it again!*

let out - You let someone out when you allow them to leave, usually by opening or unlocking a door. *e.g. This neighbourhood gets very noisy around 3pm when the children are let out of school.*

look (a)round - explore something, and try to understand what it is like *e.g. I looked (a)round for months before I decided which car to buy.*

look after - take care of someone (ill) and offer them what they need to be safe and well *e.g. You could tell that the children were not well looked after.*

look back on - think about something that happened in the past *e.g. I spent a lot of time last winter looking back on the previous summer.*

look down on - Someone who looks down on you thinks that you are not very important, or less important than they are. *e.g. Unfortunately, in many countries, economic immigrants are looked down on.*

look for - search for something, and try to find it *e.g. If you need help finding what you're looking for, just let me know.*

look forward to - You look forward to something that is going to happen when you feel happy because you know that you will enjoy it. *e.g. I'm starving; I've been looking forward to having lunch all morning!*

look into - investigate something *e.g. Is Lucy looking into adopting a puppy?*

look over - examine something *e.g. What did you think of the essay that you looked over for Mike?*

look up - look for information in reference books *e.g. Did you find conflicting opinions when you looked the information up?*

look up to - You look up to someone that you admire and respect. *e.g. Tim really looks up to his dad; he imitates everything he does!*

make out (1) - You make something out when you see or hear it, often with difficulty. *e.g. I can't quite make out who that is waving at me from across the square.*

make out (2) - You make out things like checks or receipts when you write the necessary details on them. *e.g. It's been so long since I've used one that I've forgotten how to make out a check!*

make up - People who have quarrelled, make up when they settle their differences and become friends again. *e.g. At the end of the movie, the lovers kissed and made up.*

make up (2) - You make something up when you invent it, sometimes with the purpose of deception. *e.g. When he was a child he made up the most amazing imaginary games.*

make up for - You make up for something wrong that you have done when you do something nice as an apology. *e.g. I'm so sorry I was late; let me treat you to lunch to make up for it.*

mistake for - You mistake someone or something for something or someone else when you wrongly think that they are the other. *e.g. A: "I have no idea who that was waving at me!" B: "He must have mistaken you for someone else!"*

own up - You own up when you admit you were the one who did something that was wrong. *e.g. No one in the office would own up to breaking the computer.*

pass away/pass on - You say that someone has passed away or passed on when they have died. *e.g. Gina is sad because her grandfather passed away last week.*

pass out - Someone passes out when they become unconscious for a short time. *e.g. She was taken to hospital after she passed out and hit her head when she fell.*

pick up - You pick someone up when you stop to give them a lift in your vehicle. *e.g. We need to pick up Sara at her house on the way to the beach.*

point out - You point something out to someone when you indicate it in some way. *e.g. It is not polite to point out when someone has gained weight.*

put off (1) - You put something off when you delay doing it until a later date. *e.g. Why do you put off writing your essays until the night before they are due?*

put (someone) off (2) - Something puts you off when it makes you unwilling or unable to do what you had intended or wanted to do. *e.g. Oh, you've stopped eating! Sorry, did all my talk about worms put you off your food?*

put forward - You put forward an idea when you suggest it for other people's consideration. *e.g. The solution that Tina put forward was so simple that everyone was amazed they hadn't thought of it themselves.*

put on - You put clothes on when you place them on your body, when you dress. *e.g. You have to put on a suit if you want to eat at that restaurant.*

put out - You put out a fire when you extinguish it. *e.g. I panicked when the toaster caught on fire, but my housemate threw a towel over the fire and put it out.*

put through - You put a caller through on the telephone when you connect them with the person they want to speak to. *e.g. I was on hold for twenty minutes before I was put through to the right department so that I could make my complaint.*

put up with - You put up with something unpleasant when you accept it or tolerate it. *e.g. You don't have to put up with being yelled at every day for no reason; I would find a new job if I were you.*

run in - You run something in, such as an engine, when you use it carefully until it is ready for normal use. *e.g. You shouldn't drive too fast in your new car because you need to run in the engine.*

run into - You run into someone when you meet them unexpectedly. *e.g. Michelle didn't go to the party because she didn't want to run into her ex-boyfriend.*

run out of - You run out of something when there is no more of it left. *e.g. If you had told me we'd run out of milk, I would have bought more on the way home.*

see off - You see someone off when you say goodbye to them as they leave. *e.g. She felt sad because there was no one to see her off when she was leaving.*

set off - You set off when you begin a journey. *e.g. When are you planning to set off on your travels?*

soak up - Something such as a sponge soaks up liquid when it absorbs it or takes it up into itself. *e.g. Use the mop to soak up the water on the floor after you have a shower.*

speak up - You speak up when you talk more loudly than before. *e.g. Could you speak up a bit? We can't hear you at the back of the room.*

stand for - An abbreviation stands for a word or set of words that it represents or refers to. *e.g. W.W.F stands for the World Wildlife Fund.*

sth is off (only in the present simple tense) - An event or arrangement is called off when it is cancelled. *e.g. Our economics lecture is off today because the professor is at a conference.*

take after - look like someone (a relative), resemble someone in appearance or behaviour *e.g. Jeremy so takes after his mother!*

take down - You take something down when you make a written note of it. *e.g. Let me take down your phone number just in case Ms. Witsthorpe doesn't have it.*

take in - You are taken in by someone when you are fooled or deceived by them. *e.g. Don't let the dog take you in with her whining; she's not starving. I fed her an hour ago.*

take off (1) - An airplane or a bird takes off when it rises up from the ground and begins to fly. *e.g. The birds all took off and flew away when they saw the cat.*

take off (2) - You take something off when you remove it from the body. *e.g. I always take off my shoes when I am at home.*

take over - You take over when you gain control of or responsibility for something in place of someone else. *e.g. Will you take over steering the boat while I go and get a glass of water?*

take up - You take something up when you start doing it as a regular activity, hobby or job. *e.g. If you are bored, then you should take up a hobby.*

tear up - You tear something up when you destroy it completely by ripping it into pieces. *e.g. Did you tear up the letter because you were angry?*

tell off - You tell someone off when you speak angrily to them because they have done something wrong. *e.g. The neighbours will tell you off if you play your stereo really loudly.*

think over - You think something over when you consider it carefully in order to come to a decision. *e.g. When he proposed to her she was surprised and said she would have to think it over.*

try on - You try on an article of clothing when you put it on to see if it fits. *e.g. I liked this skirt a lot until I tried it on, and then I changed my mind.*

try out - You try something (activity, product etc.) out when you do it for the first time in order to find out if you like it or if it is useful. *e.g. If you've never windsurfed you should definitely try it out; it's one of my favorite sports!*

turn down - You turn someone or something down when you refuse what they are offering or asking. *e.g. That cake looks delicious but since I'm on a diet I will have to turn it down.*

turn into - The act of changing and becoming something or someone different, or making something or someone do this. *e.g. I think I will turn into a very distrustful person if I get robbed again.*

wear off - a feeling, or the effect of a drug, wears off when it becomes less and less noticeable and finally disappears. *e.g. Hopefully her headache will be gone by the time the aspirin wears off.*

wear out - You wear out someone when *you tire them greatly, exhaust them.* e.g. *You will wear your brother out if you make him go running with you in the morning, and then shopping in the afternoon!*

wear out (2) - You wear something out when you use it so much that it becomes weak or broken from use. e.g. *You will wear out you shoes quickly if you wear them every day.*

work out - You work out a problem when you solve it by thinking about it carefully. e.g. *I've worked out that we will save money if we double glaze the windows.*

EXERCISES

for the 120
very common
Phrasal Verbs

Exercise A

Match the first half of the sentence with the second half containing the correct Phrasal Verb.

1. When my brother left for college I went to the airport to

2. It is exciting when you are planning to

3. If you've sprained your ankle it may take a while for the swelling to

4. Mich, since you have the car today, can you

5. Since Jodie's father is ill I think we'd better

6. I wish this horrible party would

7. It's strange; even when inside, he never wants to

8. If you're going to be out in the sun all day, make sure to

9. See that purple speck in the distance? Can you

10. The line is not very good; I think we are going to

11. I don't feel safe in this house; I think we need to

12. Anna is not good at spelling; she needs someone to

13. He brought her a box of chocolates to

14. When you collapsed, I was afraid you were not going to

15. When you wear gloves, all the little buttons are difficult to

16. When some stores are trying to get business, they

17. My mother is the person who I most

18. Secondary school is not a time that I

19. There's someone at the door; could you please

20. By hanging up lots of posters I managed to

1.	
2.	
3.	
4.	
5.	
6.	
7.	
8.	
9.	
10.	
11.	
12.	
13.	
14.	
15.	
16.	
17.	
18.	
19.	
20.	

a. look over her essays.
b. look back on with pleasure.
c. go down.
d. be cut off.
e. do up.
f. drop the children off?
g. come to.
h. get round having to paint.
i. make up for being late.
j. give out discount coupons.
k. put on sunscreen.
l. call off the party.
m. set off on a journey.
n. see him off.
o. take off his sunglasses.
p. hold on a minute?
q. make out what it is?
r. take after.
s. be over soon!
t. look into moving.

Exercise B
Write C or I in the box to the left (Correct or Incorrect) for each sentence using a Phrasal Verb.

1.	The diplomats broke off communication.	1.
2.	They put us on a bus when the train broke down.	2.
3.	They are bringing their children up on holiday.	3.
4.	I need to look up how to spell that word; I can never remember.	4.
5.	Be sure to do up your house each time you go out.	5.
6.	Don't you dare speak up to me like that!	6.
7.	The best friends fell out over a silly misunderstanding.	7.
8.	I can't get through to Betty at home; I hope nothing's wrong!	8.
9.	I can't stand for ice cream, but I really love pizza.	9.
10.	Would you pick up someone you didn't know if their car had broken down?	10.
11.	Can you please take me off at the airport?	11.
12.	The street market is lovely, but it does hold up traffic.	12.
13.	I wanted to get the bridge over quickly because I'm afraid of heights.	13.
14.	He bruised his shoulder and passed out when he hit a chair as he was falling.	14.
15.	She broke out in a new dress for her birthday party.	15.
16.	Can you run in this book to the library? It's due today.	16.
17.	The telephone line has gone dead; we must have been put through!	17.
18.	Have you found out why you keep getting headaches?	18.
19.	At the end of the movie, the two estranged brothers made up.	19.
20.	That novel is off; it is not really worth your time or money.	20.

Exercise C

Fill in the gaps in the text with the correct tense of the Phrasal Verbs from the box below.

- look after - break down - wear out - point out
- be taken aback - break up - drop in - think over
- put off - work out - make up - grow up
- come up with - come into - run into - look round
- come across - go with - try on - look for

Mysterious house

Something mysterious is going on at the house across the street. I can't quite
(1)........................ exactly what it is that is so mysterious, but there is definitely
something going on! I am always tempted to just (2)......................... one day, say
hello, and (3)........................ , but I know that they would be (4)......................... and
that makes me nervous so I (5)............... it .... What I can say is that I can't, for
the life of me, tell how many people are living there! I know a man lives there;
I (6)..................... him regularly around the neighbourhood, though we never speak.
I thought he had a wife, but I don't see her at all anymore. Perhaps they
(7)........................ . Strangely though, it seems like he is (8).......................... several
small children, and they all look alike! And on top of that, they have lived there for
about five years, yet none of the children seem to (9)......................... !
I (10)................... this .... to another neighbour and he (11)......................... the
idea that maybe they are ghosts! I think he may have been making fun of me,
though, for some reason!

Buying a coat

I have just (12)..................... a beautiful coat that I would like to buy. I (13)...............
it .... and it was wonderful. It (14)................................ the rest of my wardrobe
perfectly. I need a coat too, because mine is (15).................... . I didn't buy it though
because it was very expensive, and I have to (16)............... it .... before spending
that much money. To be realistic, unless I (17)......................... a small fortune I think I
will have to (18)...................... something more affordable. Or, maybe, I will just give
in and buy it. But then I will have to (19)......................... an excuse for why I can't pay
the rent - not a good idea! I would probably (20).......................... and cry if I were
kicked out onto the street.

Exercise D

Match the first half of the sentence with the second half containing the correct Phrasal Verb.

1. I haven't spoken French for nearly five years so I need to

2. We are evacuating the building because we think a bomb might

3. If cats or dogs are fighting it is dangerous to try to

4. I'm going to have to go to the corner shop; I think we've

5. When the neighbours' son threw a ball through my window, I had to

6. After only a few minutes of fighting, the smaller child had to

7. He didn't like statistics at all and decided to

8. I haven't smoked for years; I was forced to

9. The murderer felt guilty and scared and decided to

10. I'm tired from preparing for the party; I can't

11. There are lots of firemen near the new shopping centre because of a threat that it may

12. You got caught stealing? It's amazing you were

13. The masked man pulled out a gun and proceeded to

14. Don't waste energy; when you leave the house you should

15. He stopped smoking last year, but now he needs to

16. Even the best thought out plans can

17. After we arrive, we will go directly to

18. His music teacher was the only person that Tom used to

19. Smell the milk before you put it in your coffee; it may

20. When will the next president

1.	
2.	
3.	
4.	
5.	
6.	
7.	
8.	
9.	
10.	
11.	
12.	
13.	
14.	
15.	
16.	
17.	
18.	
19.	
20.	

a. hold up the bank.

b. check in at the hotel.

c. break them up.

d. run out of chocolate.

e. look up to.

f. give himself up.

g. have gone off.

h. put out the lights.

i. drop out of the class.

j. blow up another balloon!

k. take over the Whitehouse?

l. brush up on it.

m. cut down on sugar, too.

n. burn down.

o. give up ages ago!

p. go off.

q. tell him off.

r. let off so easily!

s. give in and stop.

t. fall through.

Exercise E

Write C or I in the box to the left (Correct or Incorrect) for each sentence using a Phrasal Verb.

1. A few pandas have died out.

2. She will get round her dad; he will buy her the toy eventually.

3. He felt beaten up when his girlfriend yelled at him in public.

4. Can I take down a cheque? I don't have any cash on me at the moment.

5. Someone broke into my aunty's house and stole all her jewellery.

6. The car accelerated and passed away around the corner.

7. When her husband left her, she tore up all their old letters.

8. You had better take up cleaning your room when I tell you!

9. It makes me feel sad when you are sad, so please cheer up.

10. You shouldn't give up a task just because it is difficult.

11. I am taller than my little brother so I have to look down on him.

12. When the alcohol wears off, I think she will have a hangover.

13. I hope they never let that vile murderer out of jail!

14. The fire blew up suddenly because it was very hot and dry.

15. His mood turned down when he read the newspaper because there was so much bad news.

16. She put off her jacket because it was warm inside the building.

17. This is fire country; several houses burn down every summer.

18. Boys often look up to famous sports figures.

19. It is extremely rude for guests to go through their hosts' cupboards!

20. That bug is so perfectly camouflaged, that it is easy to mistake it for a stick.

1.	
2.	
3.	
4.	
5.	
6.	
7.	
8.	
9.	
10.	
11.	
12.	
13.	
14.	
15.	
16.	
17.	
18.	
19.	
20.	

Exercise F

Fill in the gaps in the text with the correct tense of the Phrasal Verbs from the box below.

> - take in - drop off - own up - put forward
> - soak up - break out - wear out - get through
> - let down - get away with - fill in - look forward to
> - go for - carry out - try out - wear out - run out of
> - turn into - put up with - lay off - calm down

The pressure takes its toll...

Last Friday at the office there was a huge amount of work to (1)............................. .
We were all already (2)................................ from the difficult week and Natalie was
actually (3).............................. over her keyboard. I suppose everyone blamed me
because I had (4)........................... the idea to do the proposal. I will (5).....................
that I was a bit (6)........................... by the glamour of opening a branch somewhere
in the tropics. It would still be work, but it would also be a chance to (7).................
something new and maybe even (8)............................. some sun! But today we had
dozens of forms to (9)....................... and tasks to (10)........................., and we were
(11)........................... time because the deadline was approaching fast!

I guess it was inevitable that some sort of dispute would (12)....................... because
of the pressure we were under, but I was still shocked when Nancy decided, completely out of the blue, to (13).................... Natalie. "What's this? Sleeping? Why do
those of us who are trying to work have to (14)........................... the others who
(15)................... us .... by trying to (16)......................... doing nothing
all day? You should be (17)....................... for your laziness! "(18)...........................
Nancy!" I said. "You don't need to (19)..................... a little nap .... such a big
deal!" I was (20)............................... the weekend, that is for sure!

KEY

Exercise A

1.n 2.m 3.c 4.f 5.l 6.s 7.o 8.k 9.q 10.d
11.t 12.a 13.i 14.g 15.e 16.j 17.r 18.b 19.p 20.h

Exercise B

1.C 2.C 3.I 4.C 5.I 6.I 7.C 8.C 9.I 10.C
11.I 12.C 13.I 14.C 15.I 16.I 17.I 18.C 19.C 20.I

Exercise C

1. work out 2. drop in 3. look round 4. taken aback
5. put ... off 6. run into 7. broke up 8. looking after
9. grow up 10. pointed ... out 11. came up with
12. come across 13. tried ... on 14. goes with
15. worn out 16. think ... over 17. come into
18. look for 19. make up 20. break down

Exercise D

1.l 2.p 3.c 4.d 5.q 6.s 7.i 8.o 9.f 10.j
11.n 12.r 13.a 14.h 15.m 16.t 17.b 18.e 19.g 20.k

Exercise E

1.I 2.C 3.I 4.I 5.C 6.I 7.C 8.I 9.C 10.C
11.I 12.C 13.C 14.I 15.I 16.I 17.C 18.C 19.C 20.C

Exercise F

1. get through 2. worn out 3. dropping off 4. put forward
5. own up 6. taken in 7. try out 8. soak up 9. fill in 10. carry out
11. running out of 12. break out 13. go for 14. put up with
15. let ... down 16. get away with 17. laid off 18. Calm down
19. turn ... into 20. looking forward to

A, a

② **abide by**
1 accept something without argument, especially a decision or ruling ❑ *Both sides in the dispute agreed to abide by the findings of the court.*
2 obey a rule, regulation, law, etc ❑ *If a member fails to abide by the rules of the club, he has to leave.*

② **account for**
1 provide an explanation for something ❑ *Not one of the girl's teachers could account for her poor examination results.* ❑ *The librarian was asked to account for all the books that were missing.*
2 provide or be the source of something, especially of a geographical area ❑ *The region accounts for almost two-thirds of the world's oil.*
3 consume or be the reason for spending something ❑ *The gas and electricity bills account for a quarter of my salary.*
4 beat, defeat or destroy somebody or something ❑ *By the end of the third day of fighting, over a half of the enemy's planes had been accounted for.*

④ **acquaint with**
make somebody familiar with something ❑ *New students spend the first few days acquainting themselves with the layout of the university.*

② **act as**
perform the function of somebody or something ❑ *Dr Smith will be acting as head of department for as long as the professor is away.* ❑ *The new baby acts as a rather noisy alarm clock.*

⑤ **act out**
perform in real life something that you have thought or felt ❑ *The dream of becoming a famous footballer is one that few boys ever manage to act out.*

① **act up**
behave or perform badly ❑ *Of course, it's always right in the middle of a good programme that the television set starts to act up.*

① **add up**
seem probable or logical, or make sense; usually used in the negative ❑ *She spent a whole year learning French and then went off to work in China! It just doesn't add up.*

⑥ **add up to**
mean or indicate something, especially after all points or details have been considered ❑*What the report adds up to is that the company is spending far too much on advertising.*

② **adhere to**
continue to support or behave according to an idea, rule, plan, etc ❑ *Unless we are all prepared to adhere to the same set of principles, the project cannot succeed.*

② **agree with**
1 suit somebody's health, digestion, character, etc; usually used in the negative ❑ *I can't eat peanuts. They just don't agree with me.*
2 be in favour of something, especially a principle or habit ❑ *I don't agree with allowing young children to buy cigarettes.*
3 be the same as something, or support something logically ❑ *I'm afraid that your calculations don't agree with*

① = ●● ② = ●●○ ③ = ●○● ④ = ●○●○ ⑤ = ●○● *or* ●●○ ⑥ = ●●●○ ⑦ = ●○●●○

mine. ❐ *Except for one minor detail, the defendant's account of what happened agreed exactly with the evidence.*
4 correspond grammatically with something ❐ *I keep forgetting that a verb has to agree with its subject.*

② **allow for**
take something into consideration when making a decision, doing a calculation, etc ❐ *It would be wise to add another ten pounds to the total to allow for price increases.*

② **amount to**
may be interpreted as something, especially after all details have been considered ❐ *Their behaviour amounts to a complete refusal to co-operate.*

② **angle for**
try to obtain something, especially a compliment, invitation, piece of in-formation, etc, in an indirect or cun-ning way ❐ *I think that she was probably angling for compliments.*

① **answer back**
1 reply rudely, especially of a child to an adult ❐ *Answer back once more and you'll go straight to bed!*
③ **2** defend yourself by replying to a criticism ❐ *It's wrong to accuse him when he's not here and can't answer you back.*

② **answer for** **1**
accept the blame or responsibility for something ❐ *Who is going to an-swer for all the damage that's been done?* ❐ *Both governments have a great deal of human suffering to answer for.*
2 guarantee the truth, accuracy, quality, etc, of something ❐ *Knowing very little about art, I obviously cannot an-swer for the originality of these paintings.*

3 accept responsibility for speaking on behalf of somebody ❐ *I know how I feel about the proposal, although I can't answer for the other members of the team.*
4 suffer or pay for your mistakes, sins, etc ❐ *One of these days you'll have to answer for the way you've treated me!*

② **answer to**
1 give an explanation of your actions or behaviour to somebody; often used as part of a warning or threat ❐ *If you are caught with the stolen watches, you'll have the police to answer to.*
2 match or correspond to something ❐ *A man answering to the description in the paper was seen in the park.*

⑤ **argue out**
continue to discuss an issue until a solution or conclusion is reached ❐ *The whole question of responsibility is by no means clear and if the pair of you wish to argue it out, I suggest that you wait until after this meeting is over.*

② **ask after**
ask for news about somebody ❐ *You must go and visit your aunt one of these days. She always asks after you.*

② **ask for**
invite or encourage something un-pleasant to happen to you by your behaviour; often used as part of a warning ❐ *You're asking for trouble if you drink all that whisky.*

③ **ask in**
invite somebody to enter your home, especially for a short visit and without previous arrangement ❐ *They were kind enough to drive us home, so natu-rally we asked them in for a cup of coffee.*

③ ask out
invite somebody to accompany you somewhere, especially for a meal or entertainment □ *If you really like her, perhaps you should* ask *her* out. □ *You can imagine how we felt when they* asked us out *to an expensive restaurant and then left us to pay the bill!*

③ ask over/ round
invite somebody to come to your home for a meal, visit, etc □ *We suddenly realised that we're free tomorrow night, so we thought we'd* ask *you and John* over *for a drink.*

② attend to
give somebody or something your time and attention □ *For the last two months, both doctors have had far too many patients to* attend to.
□ *I suggest that you* attend to *the most urgent matters and let the rest wait.*

B, b

① back down
withdraw or partly withdraw a demand or claim, usually ending a quarrel or confrontation □ *Union leaders are still refusing to* back down *in the dispute with the government over pay.*

⑥① back out (of)
withdraw from a plan or arrangement, often breaking a promise □ *Once you've paid a deposit, it's too late to* back out. □ *Her father will be furious if you try to* back out of *the marriage now.*

⑤ back up 1
give your support to somebody, especially in a discussion, or confirm that somebody's claim or statement is true □ *Before you go and complain to the headmaster, are you sure that the rest of the class will* back *you* up?
2 support something, especially a commercial product, by providing service or additional materials □ *The more expensive models are* backed up *by a guarantee.* N □ *Is there a tape as* back-up *for the course-book?*

② bank on
have confidence in somebody or something, or expect confidently that something will happen □ *You certainly can't* bank on *her help if she is about to leave the country.*

② bargain for/ on
expect and be prepared for something; often used in the negative or preceded by more than
□ *We certainly didn't* bargain for *all this rain when we booked the holiday.*

❐ *Giving birth to twins was more than she had* bargained for.

①/② barge in/ into *Informal*
enter a room or interrupt a conversation in a rude way ❐ *Must you always* barge in *without knocking?* ❐ *He has a bad habit of* barging into *private conversations.*

① be over
something will be over when it has finished ❐ *The movie will* be over *at 9pm if you want to meet for a meal afterwards.*

⑥ bear down on/ upon *Formal*
approach somebody or something quickly or purposefully, especially in a threatening way ❐ *Enemy tanks* bore down on *us so swiftly that there was no time to withdraw.*

② bear on/ upon
be relevant to something ❐ *Everything that was said yesterday* bears *directly* upon *what we decide to do.*

⑤ bear out
agree with somebody or confirm a story, account, etc. ❐ *I'm sure you will all* bear *me* out *that far too much money has been spent on this project already.* ❐ *Her account of what happened is simply not* borne out *by the facts.*

① bear up
not despair, despite misfortune or suffering ❐ *In view of the death of her husband, she's* bearing up *as well as can be expected.*

② bear upon
see bear on/upon.

② bear with
be patient with or tolerate somebody or something ❐ *If you will just* bear with *me for a few moments, I'll explain the reasons behind the decision.*

⑤ beat down
make somebody reduce the price of something by bargaining ❐ *If you think he is asking too much for the car, why not try to* beat *him* down?

③ beat up
someone is beaten up when they are punched, hit or kicked violently and repeatedly ❐ *In some places, if you wear expensive looking jewellery you may be* beaten up *and robbed.*

⑥① beaver away (at)
work busily and steadily ❐ *The organisers have been* beavering away *all week preparing for the exhibition.*

② become of
happen to somebody or something; usually preceded by what or whatever. ❐ *She was worried about what would* become of *her son if he couldn't get a job.* ❐ *Whatever* became of *old John Carmichael? I haven't seen him for years.*

⑤ beef up *Informal*
strengthen or improve something by making a useful or valuable addition ❐ *The first two chapters need* beefing up *a bit with more facts and background details.*

② believe in
1 feel certain that something which cannot be seen or heard nevertheless exists ❐ *Do you* believe in *ghosts?*
2 support or favour a principle, practice, etc. ❐ *They* believe in *going to bed before ten o'clock and getting up at six.*

① = ●●   ② = ●●○   ③ = ●○●   ④ = ●○●○   ⑤ = ●○● *or* ●●○   ⑥ = ●●●○   ⑦ = ●○●●○

3 have confidence, trust or faith in somebody or something ❒ *We stopped believing in the football team after they lost twelve matches in a row.*

① belt up

1 *Informal* stop talking or making a noise; often used in the imperative to express anger or irritation ❒ *For heaven's sake, belt up!*
2 fasten yourself into a car seat by using a safety belt ❒ *He always got his passengers to belt up.*

⑤ bite back

stop yourself from saying something that you are just about to say ❒ *Knowing that she would misunderstand if he told her the truth, he bit back the words.*

① black out ¹

suffer a temporary loss of consciousness ❒ *I felt so faint, I thought I was going to black out.*
N ❒ *If he has another blackout, you really must call the doctor.*

⑤ black out ²

1 prevent light from showing or being seen somewhere ❒ *You could use the kitchen as a dark-room if you blacked out the windows.*
N ❒ *They hoped that the blackout would reduce the number of night attacks by enemy aircraft.*
2 stop television or radio programmes or the release of information ❒ *Both channels have been blacked out all week due to a strike by engineers.*
N ❒ *The military government imposed a complete news blackout.*

⑤ block out

1 draw a plan or outline of something without using details ❒ *Having blocked out the ground floor, they realised that there was no room for a kitchen!*
2 cover or mask something, especially part of a picture or page so that it will not be printed ❒ *The photograph could be improved by blocking out one of the trees.*

⑤ blot out

1 kill or destroy a large number of people, especially in wartime ❒ *During the first hour of the engagement, almost a third of the naval force was blotted out.*
2 hide or partly hide something from view ❒ *The top of the mountain was completely blotted out by a layer of mist.*

① blow in *Informal*

arrive unexpectedly, especially in a casual way ❒ *You can't just blow in when you feel like it. You need an appointment.*

① blow over

pass, especially of a storm or quarrel ❒ *The dispute soon blew over and everyone was happy again.*

① blow up ¹ **1** explode ❒ *The terrorists hoped that the car would blow up just as the officer drove off.*
2 *Informal* lose your temper ❒ *He blows up nowadays whenever the slightest thing goes wrong.*
3 arise or develop ❒ *I shouldn't go sailing today if a storm's blowing up.* ❒ *The present crisis blew up when the question of ownership was raised.*

⑤ blow up ²

1 destroy something by the use of explosives ❒ *They blew up the bridge just as the train was about to come across.*
2 scold or reprimand somebody severely ❒ *Her boss blew her up for losing the contract.*

① = ●●　② = ●●○　③ = ●○●　④ = ●○○○　⑤ = ●○● *or* ●●○　⑥ = ●●●○　⑦ = ●○●●○

3 enlarge a photograph ☐ *If you really like the picture, why don't you have it blown up?*
N ☐ *There's a lot more detail in the blow-up.*
4 make something seem bigger or more important than it really is
☐ *The incident was blown up by the press.*

① bob up
appear or reappear suddenly ☐ *Say hello to Susan for me if she bobs up while I'm away.*

③ bog down *Informal*
overload somebody with work, difficulties, complications, etc. ☐ *Please don't bog me down with any more of your problems.* ☐ *If you get bogged down, ask Paul to help you.*

⑥⑦ boil down to
may be reduced to something ☐ *His reasons for not wanting to go all boil down to the fact that he doesn't have enough money.*

① boil over
1 reach a crisis and become violent or uncontrollable ☐ *The government is afraid that the growing political unrest will boil over unless something is done quickly.*
2 *Informal* lose your temper or be very angry ☐ *He boiled over when his wife drove their new car into the wall.*

① boil up
arise or develop, especially of quarrels and arguments ☐ *The latest row to boil up is over the train-drivers' refusal to work overtime.*

① book in ¹
register your name, address, etc, especially at a hotel ☐ *Always insist upon seeing your room before booking in.*

⑤ book in ²
reserve a room for somebody at a hotel ☐ *If they're only staying for two nights, I suggest that you book them in at the Palm Beach.*

⑦⑤ boot out (of) *Informal*
make somebody leave a house, job, club, etc, often because of bad behaviour or bad work ☐ *Now that they've decided to build a shopping centre, nearly a hundred local people are going to be booted out of their homes.*

⑤ bottle up
hold back or refuse to give expression to a strong feeling, especially sorrow or anger ☐ *If only she would allow herself to cry, instead of bottling everything up!*

① bottom out
reach the lowest point of a slope, descent or scale ☐ *Sales bottomed out between June and August at approximately forty-five per cent of the January figure.* ☐ *Inflation has at last bottomed out.*

① bounce back
recover quickly from a defeat or setback ☐ *Not many players could bounce back into the first team after such a serious leg injury.*

⑥① bow down (to)
yield or show a respectful attitude to somebody or something; often used in the negative
☐ *They won't bow down to you just because you're rich, you know.*

① bow out
resign or retire, especially from an important position ☐ *After twelve years of faithful service, he has decided to bow out as chairman of the commitee.*

② bow to
accept and act in accordance with a wish, decision, judgement, etc
□ *After some hesitation, she* bowed to *the will of the majority.*

⑤ bowl over
overwhelm or take control of somebody's feelings or impress somebody greatly □ *She was completely* bowled over *by his good looks.* □ *The news of the air disaster* bowled over *the entire population.*

⑤ box in
1 limit the movement of somebody or something □ *The American is running on the outside of the track after being cleverly* boxed in *by his opponents earlier in the race.*
2 build an enclosure around an object in order to hide it from view □ *The bathroom would look much nicer if the pipes were* boxed in.

① branch off
leave a road, path, etc, and go onto a different, usually smaller one
□ *Remember to* branch off *at the next junction, unless you want to go straight on to London.*

⑥① branch out (into)
start or expand something, especially a business □ *He should have stayed with his father's company instead of* branching out *on his own.* □ *Several clothing manufacturers have* branched out into *sportswear in recent years.*

⑥① break away (from)
1 leave or escape from somebody
□ *One of the prisoners* broke away *from the police escort and jumped out of the train.*
2 end an association or political dependence □ *At least three members*

have decided to break away from *the party on account of the change in leadership.*
□ *It was exactly a hundred years ago today that the island* broke away from *colonial rule.*

① break down ¹
1 suddenly develop a fault and stop working, especially of machines □ *If the car* breaks down *just once more, I'm going to get a new one.*
N □ *The technicians are responsible for maintenance and* breakdowns.
2 be overcome by great emotion □ *Both parents* broke down *and wept when the doctor said that the child would be blind.*
3 fail and come to a halt □ *The talks have again* broken down *over the issue of pay.*
N □ *Friends of the couple feel very sad about the* breakdown *of their marriage.*
4 collapse or fail, especially of somebody's mental health
N □ *After the second* breakdown, *he spent six months in a private nursing home.*

⑤① break down ²
1 overcome or suppress something; be overcome or defeated □ *Gifts of food and clothing soon* broke down *the hostility and suspicion with which we were greeted.* □ *Local opposition to the scheme has* broken down *under government pressure.*
2 separate something into different parts or categories □ *Since the bill was unusually high, I asked the waiter to* break *it* down.
N □ *Without a* breakdown *of these figures, they are meaningless.*
3 change the chemical composition of something or experience a chemical change □ *Fats are* broken down *in the body before they can be digested.*

⑤ break in
1 help somebody get used to a new

job ❑ *During the first two weeks we'll be breaking you in with some very simple drawings.*
2 tame a horse so that it can be ridden ❑ *Never buy a horse that hasn't been properly broken in.*
3 make new clothes or equipment less stiff by wear or use ❑ *The boots won't hurt so much once you've broken them in.*

⑥① break in (on/ upon)
interrupt a conversation, meeting, etc ❑ *She kept breaking in with the most ridiculous questions.* ❑ *The operator broke in on our conversation to ask me if I wanted to pay for more time.*

②① break in/ into
force your way into a room or building, often with a criminal purpose ❑ *Thieves broke in last night and stole jewellery valued at thousands of pounds.*
N ❑ *There has been an increasing number of break-ins in the area recently.*

② break into 1
start using an amount of money, supply of food, etc ❑ *So far I've managed not to break into the hundred pounds that my father gave me.* ❑ *If there aren't enough biscuits, we can break into a new packet.*
2 suddenly start to do something, especially sing, laugh, cry, run, etc ❑ *She broke into tears when she heard the news.* ❑ *The rider fell off when the horse unexpectedly broke into a gallop.*

⑤ break off ¹
unexpectedly end or discontinue something, especially a relationship or association ❑ *She threatened to break the engagement off unless he promised to take her on a long honeymoon.* ❑ *Following two days of shooting along their borders, the two countries have broken off diplomatic relations.*

① break off ²
1 stop speaking, suddenly or abruptly ❑ *Feeling the gun in his back, he broke off and slowly raised his hands above his head.*
2 stop work, especially for a short rest or pause ❑ *I suggest that we break off now and meet back here at 3 o'clock when the lorry is supposed to arrive.*

① break out
1 start or arise suddenly, especially of fire, disease or war ❑ *It is believed that the fire broke out in the basement.*
N ❑ *There have been further outbreaks of fighting in the region.*
2 exclaim, especially in anger or impatience ; usually used for reporting speech ❑ *"I refuse to listen to any more of this nonsense!" he broke out, crashing his fist down upon the desk.*

⑥ break out in/ into
1 suddenly develop or become covered with spots, a rash, etc ❑ *One of the baby's legs has broken out in little red spots.*
2 suddenly utter or express something, often in a loud manner ❑ *The audience broke out in peals of laughter when his trousers fell down.*

⑥① break out (of)
escape, especially from a prison ❑ *They planned to break out in the middle of the night, when the guards were asleep.*
N ❑ *Following the improvement of security measures, there have been fewer break-outs.*

⑥ break out of
stop doing something that you do regularly ❑ *He promised to buy her anything she wanted, if only she would break out of the habit of smoking in bed.*

①② break through
force a way through a wall, defence or other

barrier ❐ *After six days of fierce fighting, our troops finally* broke through *the enemy line.* ❐ *The sun keeps trying to* break through.

① break up [1]
1 dissolve or come to an end, especially of a marriage, friendship, partnership, etc ❐ *The relationship began to* break up *when he realised that she didn't really want children.*
N ❐ *We didn't know about the* break-up *of their marriage until you told us.*
2 separate or end a relationship ❐ *Did you hear that John and Sue have* broken up *and that she's now living in Paris?*
3 reach the end of a school term and start a holiday period ❐ *When do you* break up *for your summer holidays?*
4 disperse or depart in different directions, especially after a meeting or other gathering ❐ *The demonstration* broke up *peacefully, so the police were not needed.*

⑤ break up [2]
1 bring a relationship or association to an end, especially without argument or conflict ❐ *After working together for thirty years, they* broke up *the partnership so that George could retire.*
2 cause a crowd to disperse ❐ *The police used tear-gas to* break up *the rioters.*

② break with
cease to have relations or dealings with a person, group, tradition, etc, especially following a disagreement ❐ *He* broke with *his family over their refusal to pay their share of his university fees.*

⑤ bring about
1 cause something to happen ❐ *Nobody knows what* brought about *the change in his political thinking.*
2 reverse the direction of a ship or

other vessel ❐ *Seeing the storm ahead, they* brought *the little fishing boat* about *and set course for the safety of the harbour.*

⑤ bring along/ on
1 help somebody to develop a skill, especially by coaching ❐ *Instead of buying new players, several clubs are attempting to* bring on *their juniors in the hope that one day they will win a place in the first team.*
2 help or encourage the growth of a plant, crop, etc ❐ *A bag or two of fertiliser should* bring *the tomatoes* on *nicely.*

⑦③ bring around/ round (to)
persuade somebody to accept an opinion, belief, etc ❐ *We're sure that she can be* brought round *to adopting the proposal, especially when she learns how little it will cost.*

⑤ bring back
1 cause the memory of something to return ❐ *This song* brings back *the evening we had dinner together, when the waiter upset wine over your new jacket.*
2 restore or reintroduce a rule, law, custom, etc ❐ *The discussion has revealed that most of us are against* bringing back *the death penalty.*

⑥ bring down
1 reduce or persuade somebody to reduce the price of something ❐ *Many shops are having to bring down their prices in order to attract more custom.* ❐ *I tried to* bring *her* down, *but she wouldn't accept less than £10.*
2 cause the defeat of a political body, authority, etc ❐ *Such a disastrous mistake could be enough to* bring *the Government* down *at the next election.*
3 shoot at and hit an aircraft, bird or animal, so that it falls to the ground

① = ●●   ② = ●●○   ③ = ●○●   ④ = ●○●○   ⑤ = ●○● *or* ●●○   ⑥ = ●●●○   ⑦ = ●○●●○

❒ *The plane was* brought down *over northern France just one week before the war ended.* ❒ *He* brought down *the elephant just as it was about to charge.*

4 cause an opponent on a sports field to fall to the ground by a tackle, foul, etc ❒ *The team demanded a penalty when their forward was* brought down *on the edge of the penalty area.*

⑤ **bring forward**

1 advance a meeting to an earlier time; advance a watch, clock or similar instrument ❒ *If you want everybody to come, you'll just have to* bring *the party* forward *a few days.*

❒ *Passengers are reminded to* bring *their watches* forward *before disembarking.*

2 raise a topic for discussion ❒ *It was most surprising that, during the whole meeting, nobody* brought forward *the question of funds.*

3 transfer a figure from one page to the next, or from one period of time to the next ❒ *Don't forget to* bring forward *the £30 from July.*

⑥ **bring in**

1 earn or yield money ❒ *In her new job she* brings in *an extra twenty pounds a month.* ❒ *The six hours a week that I work* bring in *enough to pay the gas and electricity bills.*

2 employ somebody, especially a specialist, for a particular purpose ❒ *A consultant has been* brought in *to advise on suitable areas for company expansion.*

3 introduce something, especially a new law or fashion ❒ *The Government has* brought in *several reforms aimed at improving conditions for old people.*

4 take a criminal or suspected criminal to a police-station ❒ *The police have* brought *the two suspects* in *for questioning.*

5 gather a harvest ❒ *Most farmers managed to* bring in *their crops during the dry spell.*

⑦ **bring in on**

involve somebody in a plan, discussion, etc ❒ *They refuse to* bring *him* in on *the project because he's too unreliable.*

⑤ **bring off**

win or accomplish something in spite of great difficulty or strong opposition ❒ *Nobody dreamt that, with half their players sick, the team could* bring off *such an amazing victory.*

⑤ **bring on**

1 be the cause of something, especially illness or physical discomfort ❒ *The first cigarette she smokes each morning always* brings on *a fit of coughing.*

2 see **bring along/ on**

④ **bring on / upon**

cause trouble, worry, etc, especially for yourself ❒ *She has* brought *all these problems* on *herself by marrying the wrong man.*

⑤ **bring out**

1 reveal, express or show something clearly ❒ *It is impossible to* bring out *the full meaning of the poem in a translation.* ❒ *The sunlight* brought out *the gold in her hair.*

2 publish a book, magazine, etc; release a new product to the public ❒ *Have you tried the chocolate-flavoured toothpaste that has just been* brought out!

3 cause something to emerge, especially a human quality or characteristic ❒ *She believes that money* brings out *the worst in some people, especially their greed.*

4 cause a group of workers to go on strike ❒ *The new union leader is quite capable* of bringing out *the entire work force.*

5 help somebody become less shy ❒ *We tried to* bring *her* out *by sending her to a drama school, but she's still very quiet and nervous.*

6 cause a blossom or flower to open ⊓ *The long hot spell has brought the roses out.*

7 introduce your daughter to society as a debutante ⊓ *Caroline's parents are bringing her out this summer.*

⑦ **bring out in**
cause spots or marks to appear on a body ⊓ *I mustn't eat bananas. They bring me out in a rash.*

⑦⑤ **bring over (to)**
persuade somebody to change their loyalty ⊓ *As long as the salary is attractive, I'm sure he can be brought over to our side.*

⑦③ **bring round (to)**
    see bring around / round (to)

③ **bring round**
cause somebody to revive or regain consciousness ⊓ *It was such a hard punch that it needed a cold sponge to bring him round.*

⑦ **bring round to**
lead a conversation or discussion to a particular topic ⊓ *No matter what we start talking about, she always manages to bring the conversation round to her family problems.*

③④ **bring through**
lead somebody safely through a crisis or ordeal ⊓ *He was brought through the operation by an experienced team of surgeons, working round the clock.*

③ **bring to** ¹   *see* bring round/to

④ **bring to** ²
cause something, especially a bill or calculation, to reach a particular amount ⊓ *Five times eleven, less twenty per cent discount, brings the total to £44 exactly.*

⑤ **bring together**
introduce or reconcile people or parties ⊓ *The more they talk about divorce, the more her father tries to bring them together again.*

⑤ **bring up**
1 provide a home, care and education for a child until it becomes an adult ⊓ *Sally spent most of her childhood with her grandparents, who brought her up in a little village by the sea.*
N ⊓ *The poor girl has had a very sad upbringing.*
2 teach a child over many years to do or believe something; usually followed by a *to*-infinitive ⊓ *We were brought up to respect the elderly.*
3 raise a point or topic during a conversation or discussion ⊓ *Several matters of interest were brought up during the course of the interview.*
4 vomit ⊓ *For a whole week he couldn't eat anything without bringing it up again.*
5 make somebody appear at a court of law for trial ⊓ *His younger brother has been brought up before the magistrate on a charge of disturbing the peace.*

⑦ **bring up against**
make somebody realise or confront something, especially something unpleasant ⊓ *Having spent the last of their money, they were suddenly brought up against the reality of their situation.*

④ **bring upon** *see* bring on/upon

⑦ **bring up to**
1 increase a figure to a particular sum ⊓ *Your uncle's five pounds brings the amount we've been given up to £42.50.*
2 cause somebody or something to reach a particular standard ⊓ *With a good service, the efficiency of the engine can be brought up to that of a new one.*

①= ●● ②= ●●○ ③= ●○● ④= ●○●○ ⑤= ●○● *or* ●●○ ⑥= ●●●○ ⑦= ●○●●○

② **bristle with**
1 display strong emotion, especially anger or hatred ❐ *The mere mention of his name would make her bristle with rage.*
2 display a great number or quantity of something ❐ *The letter simply bristled with the most awful spelling mistakes.*

③ **brown off** *Informal*
bore or annoy somebody ❐ *Addressing envelopes all day is enough to brown anybody off.* ❐ *What really browns me off is the way she wakes the whole household in the middle of the night.*

⑤ **brush aside**
1 dismiss or disregard something, especially a comment, suggestion, etc ❐ *The chairman tended to brush aside any objections he didn't agree with.*
2 remove something, especially a barrier or obstacle, very easily ❐ *The advancing flood waters brushed houses and cars aside like matchsticks.*

⑤ **brush off**
end a conversation or relationship, especially in an abrupt way
❐ *She brushed us off with the excuse that she had another appointment.*
❐ *How can you just brush me off like this after all the years we've been together?*
N ❐ *Henry is afraid to invite the new typist to dinner, in case he gets the brush-off.*

①② **brush past**
move past somebody or something, touching them lightly ❐ *When they brushed past each other in the corridor, he noticed that she was wearing a new perfume.*

② **brush up**
improve or regain a skill or area of knowledge by practice or revision
❐ *You'll need to brush up your German if you get the job in Austria.*

① **buck up** ¹ *Informal*
1 become more cheerful or lively; often used in the imperative ❐ *Buck up! You're making me feel miserable too.*
2 hurry; often used in or with the force of the imperative ❐ *Richard! If you don't buck up, we're going to miss the start of the film.*

⑤ **buck up** ²
make somebody more cheerful or energetic ❐ *I'm sure that the news of the new baby will buck your father up a bit.*

① **bucket down** *Informal*
fall in great quantity, especially of rain ❐ *It's been bucketing down all morning.*

⑥① **buckle down (to)**
begin to apply yourself diligently to a task ❐ *You're going to fail the exam unless you buckle down and do some serious work.*

⑤ **build in**
1 construct something, especially a cupboard, so that it is fixed to or forms a part of a structure ❐ *The wardrobe in the front bedroom has been built in.*
2 include a statement in a written agreement as a necessary part of it ❐ *The new owner wants to build in a clause which will prevent the public from using the footpath.*

② **build on / upon**
use something as a basis for further effort ❐ *The sales figures are pretty miserable, I suppose, but at least they give us something to build on.*

① **build up** ¹
increase in size, strength or intensity ❐ *Several jams have been building up on roads out of London due to holiday traffic.*

N ☐ *Many people are worried about the build-up of tension in the Middle East.*

⑤ **build up** ²
1 develop or increase something gradually ☐ *It took him twenty years to build up the business.* ☐ *A good reputation cannot be built up overnight.*
2 develop or cover an area with buildings, roads, etc ☐ *Most of the city centre had already been built up by the time my father arrived here in the 1960s.*

③ **build up** ³
1 improve somebody's physical condition ☐ *After six weeks in hospital he needs building up.* ☐ *With just one month to go, they've started to build him up for the fight.*
2 develop the image or reputation of somebody or something, often by excessive praise ☐ *He's been built up by the media as one of the heroes of our time.*
N ☐ *After the big build-up we've given her, I hope she doesn't disappoint everybody.*

② **build upon**
see **build on/upon**

① **bum around** *Informal*
spend your time lazily and aimlessly; often used in a derogatory way ☐ *It's about time you stopped bumming around and started to look for a job.*

② **bump into**
meet somebody by chance ☐ *Guess who I bumped into in the market today?*

⑤ **bump off** *Informal*
kill or murder somebody; often used in a light-hearted way ☐ *People say that the old doctor had managed to bump off half his patients by the time he finally decided to retire.*

⑤ **bump up**
increase an amount ☐ *Don't let him know that you like the car, or he'll bump the price up.*

⑤ **bung up**
block a narrow opening, especially in a pipe or tube, often by accident ☐ *You'll bung the sink up if you pour that hot fat down it.*

⑤ **buoy up**
1 make somebody more cheerful; encourage somebody ☐ *It was the thought of one day finishing the book that buoyed him up during the long lonely hours he spent at his desk.*
2 stop a price, value, etc, from falling ☐ *The country's increasing share of the oil market has been buoying up its currency overseas.*

⑤ **burn down**
a building burns down when it is destroyed by fire ☐ *The protesters attempted to burn down the bank.*

③ **burn out**
1 exhaust or over-exert yourself ☐ *By the end of the third set, the older player had obviously burnt himself out.*
2 ruin your health, especially by neglect or maltreatment ☐ *The actress burnt herself out on pills and alcohol.*

② **burn with**
experience emotion very strongly ☐ *She was burning with the desire to have children.* ☐ *If he only wants to see her once a fortnight, I'd hardly say that he's burning with passion.*

⑥① **burst in (on/ upon)**
1 interrupt somebody speaking ☐ *'And who's going to pay for it?' she*

burst in, right in the middle of his opening remarks.
2 disturb somebody by entering suddenly and unexpectedly ❐ *It's very rude to burst in on somebody without knocking! You should know better at your age.*

①② burst in/ into
enter somewhere in a great hurry
❐ *Breathless, the little girl burst into the bedroom, grabbed her doll, and rushed out again.*

② burst into
1 do something suddenly, especially laugh, cry, sing, etc
❐ *As the final curtain fell, the audience burst into loud applause.*
2 develop buds, leaves or flowers
❐ *You know that spring has arrived when you see the trees bursting into blossom.*

① burst out
1 utter something suddenly and with emotion usually used for reporting speech ❐ *'I just wish that all of you would leave me alone!' he burst out.*
N ❐ *His sudden outburst was very much out of character.*
2 suddenly sing, laugh or cry; followed by *-ing* ❐ *She burst out laughing at the expression on his face.*

⑥① burst out (of)
leave or escape from a building, room, yard, etc, especially using force
❐ *Eventually the wall collapsed, and the men burst out of the prison.*

⑥① butt in (on)
interfere or interrupt a conversation often used as part of an apology
❐ *Excuse me for butting in, but there's a telephone call for you, Mr Harrison.*

⑤ butter up   *Informal*
be nice to somebody, especially with the intention of gaining a favour
❐ *She spent the evening buttering up the professor in the hope that he would give her a good reference.*

③ buy in
buy a large quantity of something as a reserve or stock
❐ *She's buying in all the sugar she can, in case there's another shortage.*

⑤ buy off
bribe somebody not to do something
❐ *They know that I could give their names to the police, so now they're trying to buy me off.*

⑤ buy out ¹
buy all of somebody's share or interest in a business ❐ *Buying him out is going to be difficult as long as his profits keep rising.*

③ buy out ²
obtain the release of somebody from the army, navy, etc, by paying a sum of money ❐ *He hates the army but he can't afford to buy himself out.*

① buzz off   *Informal*
leave: often used in the imperative
❐ *Just buzz off and stop annoying me, will you?*

---

① = ●● ② = ●●○ ③ = ●○● ④ = ●○○● ⑤ = ●○● *or* ●●○ ⑥ = ●●●● ⑦ = ●○○●●

C, c

⑤ call away

cause somebody to leave their home, office, etc ☐ *Her husband is always being called away on business.*

⑥① call by (at)

visit or stop somewhere for a short time, especially on your way to somewhere else ☐ *If I have enough time, I'll call by and see you tonight on the way home.*

② call for

1 come or go somewhere, especially to somebody's home, to collect somebody or something ☐ *The train leaves at half-past ten, so she's calling for me at a quarter to.*
2 require or deserve somebody or something ☐ *These wonderful results call for a celebration.* ☐ *The job calls for a man who can accept responsibility.* ☐ *That unkind remark certainly wasn't called for.*

⑤ call in

1 ask a doctor, builder, expert, etc, to come to your home or office ☐ *If you think that the repair is going to be a difficult job, we'll just have to call in a builder.*
2 request or order somebody to return something ☐ *All library books are being called in this week for the annual inspection.*

⑥① call in (at)

visit or stop somewhere for a short time, especially on your way to somewhere else ☐ *If I remember, I'll call in at the chemist's on my way back to collect your pills.*

⑥① call in (on)

pay somebody a short casual visit, especially when this does not require a long journey ☐ *It's only ten o'-clock. Why don't we call in on John instead of going straight home?*

⑤ call off

1 abandon or cancel something ☐ *The strike which was planned to begin on Tuesday has been called off.* ☐ *After six days the search for the missing climbers was called off.*
2 give an order for somebody or something to stop a search or attack ☐ *Call your dog off! I'm the new gardener.*

② call on

visit somebody ☐ *I always try to call on friends when they're ill.*

② call on / upon

1 invite or request somebody to do something, especially to speak to a group of people ☐ *If I were you, I'd make a few notes just in case you are called upon to make a speech.*
2 ask somebody for help, support, etc ☐ *Parents are being called upon to help raise funds for the new swimming pool.*

⑤ call out

1 summon somebody, especially to help in an emergency ☐ *Don't call out the fire brigade unless the smoke gets worse.*
2 order workers to go on strike ☐ *Steel workers stopped work today after being called out by their union leaders.*

① call over / round

pay a short visit to somebody's home, office, etc ☐ *She said she would call round at about half-past three to collect the children.*

① = ●● ② = ●●○ ③ = ●○● ④ = ●○●○ ⑤ = ●○● *or* ●●○ ⑥ = ●●●○ ⑦ = ●○●●○

⑤ **call up**
1 telephone somebody ❑ *I can give you his number if you want to* call *him* up.
2 order somebody to join the army, navy, etc ❑ *Her husband was* called up *right at the beginning of the war, and was away for six years.*

② **call upon** see **call on/upon**

⑤① **calm down**
become or cause somebody to become quiet, relaxed, etc, especially after being excited or worried ❑ *If you don't* calm down, *you're going to have a heart attack.*

② **care for**
1 like somebody or something; often used in the negative ❑ *I certainly don't* care for *the way he treats his wife.*
2 like to have something; usually used to make an offer ❑ *Would you* care for *a cigar?*
3 nurse or be responsible for somebody ❑ *Who's* caring for *the children since his wife went away?*

⑤ **carry away**
inspire somebody; cause somebody to be overcome with emotion or excitement; usually used in the passive ❑ *She refused to let herself be* carried away *by his good looks.*

⑦③ **carry back (to)**
cause somebody to remember something which happened much earlier ❑ *The old photograph* carried *her* back *to the days before the war.*

⑤ **carry forward/ over**
transfer a figure from one page to the next, or from one period of time to the next ❑ *Don't forget the £30 to be* carried forward *from July.*

② **carry off** [1]
win something, especially in a competition ❑ *She's playing so well this year that people expect her to* carry off *all the big prizes again.*

⑤ **carry off** [2]
1 perform a role successfully, especially of an actor or actress
❑ *Considering that he had never played the part of an old man before, he* carried *it* off *remarkably well.*
2 manage or handle a difficult situation successfully ❑ *She postponed the press conference several times, afraid that she would never be able to* carry *it* off.

① **carry on** [1]
1 continue to do something ❑ *Despite all the noise, the girl* carried on *reading.* ❑ *Just* carry on *with your work as if I wasn't here.* ❑ *Most of these machines will* carry on *without an operator.*
2 continue to live or survive ❑ *The poor man doesn't really want to* carry on *since his wife died.*
3 *Informal* keep complaining or making a fuss; often used in a derogatory way ❑ *That woman is always* carrying on *about the price of food.*
N ❑ *I've never heard such a* carry-on *about nothing!*
4 *Informal* have a sexual relationship; often used in a derogatory way ❑ *It seems that they'd been* carrying on *for at least six months before his wife found out.*

② **carry on** [2]
1 cause a conversation, discussion, etc, to continue ❑ *Some of the students were able to* carry on *fairly long conversations in English after just ten lessons.*
2 cause something to continue to happen or exist, especially a business or tradition ❑ *Despite the fire,*

① = ●●   ② = ●●○   ③ = ●○●   ④ = ●○●○   ⑤ = ●○● *or* ●●○   ⑥ = ●●●○   ⑦ = ●○●●○

we're *carrying on* business as usual. ❑ *If you want to* carry on *the family name, you'll have to have a son.*

② carry out
1 execute an order, plan, duty, etc; fulfil a threat or promise ❑ *Unless you* carry out *his instructions, you'll soon be looking for a new job.* ❑ *The workers are worried that the owner will* carry out *his threat to close the factory.*
2 do or conduct an experiment, operation, study, etc ❑ *Doctors are* carrying out *tests to discover the nature of the new disease.*

⑤ carry over
1 postpone something to a later time ❑ *Other business will be* carried over *to the next meeting.*
2 see **carry forward / over**

③④ carry through
1 enable somebody to endure a period of difficulty or suffering ❑ *What carried him through the long years of imprisonment was the hope that he would one day return to his wife and family.*
2 continue to work at something until it is completed ❑ *The building programme was the idea of the previous government, but it was the present one that* carried *it* through.

⑤ carve up *Informal*
1 divide something into parts or shares ❑ *How are you going to* carve up *the winnings? Half each?*
2 beat somebody easily in a competition, race, etc ❑ *He always thought that he was good at chess until he was* carved up *by a beginner.*
3 inflict injuries on somebody with a knife ❑ *Unless you want one of the gang to* carve *you* up, *you'd better keep quiet about the robbery.*

⑥① cash in (on) *Informal*
benefit or make a profit for yourself from something. ❑ *Dozens of news photographers* cashed in *on the tragedy with their pictures of the young widows.* ❑ *Whenever I have a good idea, he always wants to* cash in.

⑥① cast about/around/round (for)
try to find or acquire something, especially by looking in different places ❑ *The boss has been* casting about for *suggestions as to how business might be improved next year.*

⑤ cast aside
reject, abandon or get rid of somebody or something ❑ *Cast all your* cares aside. ❑ *She refused to be* cast aside *for another woman.*

① cast off ¹
untie the rope which stops a boat or ship from moving
❑ *Once everybody's on board, we'll* cast off.

⑤ cast off ²
1 stop wearing something ❑ *It's time you* cast off *that old suit and bought yourself a new one.*
N ❑ *She's too proud to wear other people's* cast-offs.
2 reject, abandon or get rid of somebody or something ❑ *Her mother was rather annoyed with her for* casting off *such a nice young man.*
N ❑ *Tomorrow you'll be just another one of his* cast-offs.

①② cast off ³
finish a piece of knitting by removing the last row of stitches from the needle to make a finished edge
❑ *I'm almost ready to* cast off, *and then I can sew the jumper together.*

---

① = ●●   ② = ●●○   ③ = ●○●   ④ = ●○●○   ⑤ = ●○● *or* ●●○   ⑥ = ●●●○   ⑦ = ●○●●○

①②　cast on

begin a piece of knitting by making the first row of stitches

❏ *It tells you to* cast on *fifty-eight stitches for a thirty-six-inch chest.*

⑤　cast out　reject or dismiss somebody or something　❏ *The immigrants were* cast out *by the rest of the community.*

N　❏ *Homeless, friendless and without a job, he began to feel more and more like an* outcast *from society.*

⑥①　cast round (for)

see cast about/around/round (for)

①　catch on

1 understand something　❏ *Some children take much longer to* catch on, *and it's these slow learners that I feel sorry for.* ❏ *I kept looking at my watch and yawning, but she didn't* catch on.

2 become popular or fashionable

❏ *We thought that the idea of making clothes from old newspapers was a good one, but it didn't* catch on.

③　catch out

1 cause somebody to make a mistake or be unable to give a correct answer; discover somebody doing something wrong　❏ *There was one question in the examination paper that* caught *everybody* out.

2 reveal somebody's guilt, lies, etc

❏ *It was the blood on his jacket that* caught *him* out.

⑥①　catch up (on)

1 bring yourself up to date with news, gossip, etc　❏ *He loves to* catch up on *the news after a trip abroad.*

2 reduce the amount that one is behind in something, especially by making an extra effort　❏ *Why not try and go to bed a bit earlier tonight, and* catch up on *some of the sleep you've lost?*

③①⑥　catch up (with)

1 reach, find or draw level with somebody you are following, chasing or in competition with　❏ *The traffic wasn't so bad when I left, so I drove fast and* caught *the others* up *quickly.*

2 reach a level that others have already reached by making an extra effort　❏ *If you miss too many lessons, you'll never be able to* catch up.

⑥　catch up on

have an effect on somebody's health, work, behaviour, etc; especially a damaging effect　❏ *Don't be surprised if all these cigarettes you are smoking* catch up on *you one day.*

②　cater for

1 provide somebody or something with what is wanted or liked　❏ *Only two of the newspapers* cater for *people who are interested in golf.*

❏ *It's impossible to* cater for *all tastes.*

2 be prepared for something　❏ *We knew that the husband and wife were coming to look at the house, but we hadn't* catered for *them bringing a dozen relatives, too.*

②　cater to

provide what is required to satisfy a particular appetite or demand ❏ *Films that* cater to *the desire for violence on the screen seem to be as popular as ever.*

①　cave in

1 collapse, especially of a roof

❏ *Luckily, most of the men were able to get out of the tunnel before it* caved in.

N　❏ *Wives of the trapped miners wept uncontrollably when they heard about the* cave-in.

2 collapse, fail or be ruined　❏ *His business suddenly* caved in *when a competitor opened a new supermarket just across the street.*

⑤ **chalk up**

add something to a list or score , especially a success ❒ *The boys chalked up a fine victory on Saturday with a win against strong opposition.*

② **chance on / upon**

meet somebody by chance ❒ *The two couples just happened to chance upon each other while on holiday in France.*

① **change down**

change to a lower gear in a vehicle ❒ *You'll have to change down to get up the next hill.*

① **change over / round**

exchange places, activities, roles, etc ❒ *Tell me if you get tired of driving and we'll change over.*
N ❒ *Both sides played much better after the change-over at half time.*

① **change up**

change to a higher gear in a vehicle ❒ *Change up as soon as you can if you want to save petrol.*

② **chase after**

pay a lot of attention to a member of the opposite sex in order to win the person's love, admiration, etc; usually used in a derogatory way ❒ *She's been chasing after him for years, but with little success.*

⑤ **chase up**

1 search for something, especially information ❒ *If you know the name of the author, I can easily chase up the title for you.*
2 urge somebody to do something quickly ❒ *If they haven't paid the bill by the end of the month, we'll have to start chasing them up.*

⑤ **chat up**   *Informal*

talk to somebody in a way that is intended to win their friendship or gain an advantage
❒ *I wouldn't try chatting her up if I were you. She's married to a former world heavy weight champion!* ❒ *She chatted up the producer in the hope of getting a part in his next film.*

⑥① **check in (at)**

1 register, your name, address, etc, especially at the reception desk of a hotel ❒ *You go and check in while I pay the taxi driver.*
2 report your arrival at an airline desk before the departure of your flight ❒ *What time do we have to check in?*
N ❒ *Somebody had lost his ticket, so there was a long queue at the check-in.*

①⑥ **check out / out of**

pay the bill and return the room key before leaving a hotel ❒ *We'll need at least an hour to check out and get to the airport.*
N ❒ *We'd like to remind our guests that check-out is no later than twelve o'clock.*

⑤ **check off**

put a mark against a name or item on a list, especially to show that the person or item is present, correct, etc ❒ *A polite young lady came round checking off the guests one by one.*

①⑤ **cheer up**

become or cause somebody to become happier; often used in the imperative ❒ *Cheer up, John! It can't be as bad as all that.*

⑤ **cheese off**   *Informal*

bore and depress somebody ❒ *Hearing the same joke three times in one evening is*

① = ●●   ② = ●●○   ③ = ●○●   ④ = ●○●○   ⑤ = ●○● *or* ●●○   ⑥ = ●●●○   ⑦ = ●○●●○

enough to cheese *anybody* off. ❑ *I'm really* cheesed off *with this bad weather.*

⑤ chew over *Informal*
consider something carefully, especially before reaching a decision ❑ *It's an interesting suggestion, but we need a bit longer to* chew *it* over.

①⑥ chicken out/ out of *Informal*
withdraw from something because of anxiety or fear; usually used in a derogatory way ❑ *Having seen how far it was to swim to the other side of the lake, he* chickened out.

⑥① chime in (with)
interrupt a conversation or discussion ❑ *'And about time too, if you ask me!' a voice at the back* chimed in.

①⑥② chip in (with)
1 interrupt, especially to contribute ideas, facts, etc, to a discussion ❑ *I'd like to remind you all that you are free to* chip in *at any time.*
2 give money to a collection, especially to buy a gift for a colleague ❑ *If we're going to give Henry something special for his retirement, each member of staff will have to* chip in *at least 5 pounds.*

⑦ chisel out of *Informal*
get something from somebody, especially money, by cheating or deceiving them ❑ *Surely she wasn't stupid enough to let him* chisel *her* out of *her savings, was she?* ❑ *He's not going to* chisel *another penny* out *of me.*

⑤ choke back
prevent yourself from expressing anger or sadness ❑ *She tried her best to* choke back *the tears, but the sight of his thin white hand on the sheet was too much for her.*

① chop about *Informal*
keep changing your plans, opinions, etc ❑ *I wish they'd stop* chopping about *and decide whether they want to sell the house or not.*

⑤ chuck in/ up *Informal*
resign from a job; abandon a course, etc ❑ *He stayed with the firm for just six weeks and then* chucked *it* in.

⑦⑤ chuck out (of) *Informal*
1 dismiss or expel somebody from a company, school, club, etc, especially because of bad work or behaviour ❑ *They* chuck *you* out *if you fail your first-year exams more than once.*
2 make a person leave a club, bar, restaurant, etc, especially by using physical force ❑ *The last time he tried dancing on the table, they* chucked *him* out.

⑥ chum up with
become friendly with somebody ❑ *He was lonely for several weeks until he* chummed up with *one of the other new boys.*

⑤ churn out
produce something quickly or in great quantities, like a machine ❑ *Some of these journalists* churn out *stories faster than people can read them!*

① clam up
become silent or refuse to talk about something ❑ *As soon as I mentioned his research, he immediately* clammed up.

⑥① clamp down (on)
make an effort to restrict or prevent something, especially criminal or undesirable behaviour ❑ *Her husband's firm is beginning to* clamp down on *time-wasting.*

---

① = ●● ② = ●●○ ③ = ●○● ④ = ●○●○ ⑤ = ●○● *or* ●●○ ⑥ = ●●●○ ⑦ = ●○●●○

⑦⑤ clean out (of) *Informal*
1 take all somebody's money, especially by winning or stealing it ☐ *Of course they cleaned you out: they're professional gamblers.*
2 take all the money or an entire stock of something from a bank, shop, etc, especially by stealing it ☐ *Another jeweller's was cleaned out of all its stock on Saturday night.*

① clear off *Informal*
go away; often used in a derogatory way ☐ *She cleared off after lunch without even saying goodbye.* ☐ *Clear off or I'll call the police!*

①⑥③⑦ clear out (of)
leave somewhere, especially quickly, or cause somebody or something to do this ☐ *We all cleared out as soon as we heard the alarm.*

① clear up ¹
become fine, especially of weather ☐ *They're lucky that the weather has cleared up in time for the tennis match.*

⑤① clear up ²
disappear or cause something to disappear, especially a problem, mystery or disagreement ☐ *All it needed was a little explanation to clear up the misunderstanding.*

⑥① climb down (over)
stop pursuing a claim, argument, etc, especially while admitting your weakness or mistake ☐ *There is little possibility of the newspaper's owner climbing down once he has threatened to sell it.*
N ☐ *They must have hated having to admit that they were wrong. What a climb-down!*

① clock in/ on
record your time of arrival at work, especially by using a machine made for this purpose ☐ *What time do you have to clock in in the morning?*

① clock out/ off
record the time of your departure from work, especially by using a machine made for this purpose ☐ *Don't forget to remind the new girl to clock out before she goes home.*

①⑤ close down ¹
stop operating, or cause something to stop operating
☐ *The factory closes down for two weeks in August.* ☐ *We're losing so much money that I think we'll have to close the business down.*

① close down ²
stop broadcasting for the day ☐ *They normally play the National Anthem before closing down.*
N ☐ *Close-down is at midnight after the late news summary.*

① close in
become shorter, especially of days ☐ *As the days gradually closed in, we began to stay at home more in the evenings.*

⑥① close in (on/upon)
approach or surround somebody or something, especially in a threatening way ☐ *The police quietly closed in on the house where the escaped prisoners were hiding.*

① club together
combine to do something, especially to share the cost of something ☐ *Let's club together to buy them something they really need, like a washing machine.*

---

⑤ cock up *Informal*

spoil something or do something badly;usually used in a derogatory way ❐ *He really wanted the job, but was so nervous that he cocked up the interview.* **N** ❐ *She's made a complete cock-up of the translation.*

① come about

happen or occur ❐ *I just don't understand how it came about that you weren't informed.*

② come across ¹

find something or meet somebody by chance ❐ *If you come across any records by French singers in that pile, would you keep them for me?*

②① come across ²

1 be communicated effectively ❐ *It doesn't matter how good your ideas may be if they don't come across clearly in the book.*
2 make an impression, especially at a first meeting ❐ *If you want to be given the job, it's vital that you come across well when you meet the directors.*

⑥ come across with *Informal*

provide something, especially money, on demand or request ❐ *You can rely on John to come across with the cash whenever you need it.*

② come after

pursue somebody, often in a threatening way ❐ *You'll have the police coming after you if you start taking things that don't belong to you.*

① come along / on

1 improve or progress, especially in connection with work, growth or health ❐ *How's your piano-playing com-ing along these days?* ❐ *The vegetables are coming on nicely, thanks to all the rain we've been having.* ❐ *The doctors are pleased with the way he's been coming along since the operation.*
2 hurry, make more effort; often used in the imperative ❐ *Come on! We're going to be late again.* ❐ *Come along, Mary! You can do better than that.*

① come apart

1 fall or break into pieces ❐ *He says that the cup came apart in his hands, but I think he must have dropped it.*
2 be separated into parts or be opened ❐ *How does the watch come apart when it needs a new battery?*

① come around/ round

1 happen or arrive, especially in the case of a yearly event ❐ *Birthdays come round all too quickly once you're past thirty.*
2 stop being angry, annoyed, etc, and return to your normal mood ❐ *It usually takes about an hour for him to come round after an argument.*

② come at

attack somebody ❐ *I keep having this nightmare about a madman coming at me with a knife.*

⑥① come away (from)

become detached from something, especially unexpectedly ❐ *I reached down to open the door, but the handle came away in my hand.*

① come back

1 become popular or fashionable again ❐ *I never thought I'd see high heels come back again.*
N ❐ *The pop group failed to make the come-back that they'd been hoping for.*

---

① = ●● ② = ●●○ ③ = ●○● ④ = ●○●○ ⑤ = ●○● *or* ●●○ ⑥ = ●●●○ ⑦ = ●○●●○

2 be remembered or recalled ❐ *For weeks I couldn't remember her name, and then suddenly it came back to me.*

3 be reintroduced or restored ❐ *I wonder how many of us would like to see the death penalty come back?*

⑥ **come back at**
reply to something somebody has said, especially critically ❐ *Those of you who don't like my suggestion will have the chance to come back at me later on.*

⑥ **come back to (on)**
talk again to somebody on a particular matter ❐ *I can't answer your question immediately, I'm afraid. Can I come back to you on that in half an hour?* ❐ *I'll need to come back to you later with the name of our representative.*

② **come before**
1 be of more importance than something else ❐ *The child's education comes before summer holidays abroad.*
2 be brought in front of a court or committee for consideration ❐ *The accused came before the judge.* ❐ *The plan will come before next week's council meeting.*

② **come between**
interfere with a relationship or cause two people or animals to separate ❐ *She didn't accept her daughter's choice of husband, and for a long time tried to come between them.*

② **come by**
obtain or receive something ❐ *How did you come by all that dirt on your sleeve?* ❐ *Good jobs were hard to come by in those days.*

① **come down¹**
1 be reduced, especially of prices ❐ *Did you know that sugar's coming down next week?*

2 collapse or be demolished ❐ *The town council has said that all these lovely old buildings have got to come down by the end of the year.* ❐ *Of all the tents I've erected, only one has ever come down.*
3 be passed from one generation to the next ❐ *The writing desk must be antique by now if it has come down through all those generations.*
4 be hit by gunfire, etc, and fall to the ground, especially of aircraft ❐ *The aeroplane came down over France.*
5 lose your wealth or status ❐ *Since he left the company, he's really come down in the world.*
N ❐ *She was a top pop star once, so playing in night-clubs must be quite a come-down.*

② **come down²**
reach a decision about who or what to support ❐ *After several hours of discussion, the union leaders came down in favour of a return to work.* ❐ *The court came down on the side of the defendant.*

⑥ **come down on/ upon**
1 scold or criticise somebody ❐ *The headmaster came down heavily on them for not wearing their uniforms to school.*
2 demand money from somebody ❐ *What will you do if the tax people suddenly come down on you?*

⑥ **come down to**
1 amount to something, especially of a question, argument, etc ❐ *The whole issue comes down to whether we are prepared to fight for our freedom or not.*
2 be forced to lower your standards ❐ *Since her husband lost his job, they've come down to accepting any work the pair of them can get.*
N ❐ *I can't believe he's gone bankrupt. What a come-down!*

---

① = ●● ② = ●●○ ③ = ●○● ④ = ●○●○ ⑤ = ●○● *or* ●●○ ⑥ = ●●●○ ⑦ = ●○●●○

⑥ come down with
catch or develop an illness ☐ *Her younger daughter has* come down with *measles.*

① come forward
1 present yourself, especially to provide information ☐ *The police would like anybody who saw the accident to* come forward.
2 give or offer something, especially money, in response to a public request ☐ *Several members of the public have* come forward *with large sums in answer to the appeal.*

② come from
1 originate from somewhere ☐ *Where do you* come from? ☐ *You can tell he* comes from *Scotland by listening to his accent.*
2 have a particular family background ☐ *She's a pleasant girl and* comes from *a good family.*

① come in
1 arrive ☐ *I hope the train* comes in *on time.*
2 be received, especially of a communication ☐ *A lot of letters have* come in *asking us to repeat the programme.* ☐ *News has just* come in *of a shooting in the centre of London.*
3 be introduced, especially of a new law or fashion ☐ *The law on wearing seat belts* came in *in 1983.* ☐ *Long hair* came in *with the Beatles.*
4 become available in the shops, especially of fresh foods ☐ *She waits for the strawberries to* come in *before she starts her jam-making.*
5 finish a race ☐ *Poor old Henry! His horse always* comes in *last.*
6 be earned or received by a family, community, etc, especially of money ☐ *There's a bit more* coming in *now that his wife has found herself a part-time job.*

7 gain power or be elected ☐ *How many of its promises has the government kept since it* came in *three years ago?*
8 take part; have a role or serve a purpose ☐ *It sounds like an interesting project, but I'd like to know where I* come in?
9 approach and cover the shore, of the sea or tide ☐ *Why don't we stay on the beach until the tide* comes in, *and then go for a drive?*
10 take a turn in a game, especially of a batsman ☐ *The last player to* come in *was hit by the first ball he received, and had to retire hurt.*

⑥ come in for
receive or attract something, especially criticism ☐ *Some of the violent scenes in the film* came in *for angry comments from the mothers in the audience.*

⑥ come in on
take part in a project, scheme, etc ☐ *I'm very honoured that you've invited me to* come in *on such an interesting project.*

⑥ come in with
become the business partner of somebody or share the cost of something with somebody ☐ *I'm looking for somebody with sales experience and a bit of spare cash to* come in *with me.*

② come into
receive or inherit something ☐ *If I* came into *a fortune, I'd spend it all on travel.*

② come of
1 result from something ☐ *I'm afraid that nothing will* come of *your application, because you don't have the right qualifications.*
2 happen to somebody; usually used in a question ☐ *Do you know what* came of *that young man you used to play tennis with at university?*

---

① = ●●   ② = ●●○   ③ = ●○●   ④ = ●○○●   ⑤ = ●○● *or* ●●○   ⑥ = ●●●○   ⑦ = ●○●●○

① come off ¹

1 succeed, especially of a plan, business deal, etc ◻ *The attempt to shoot the President would almost certainly have come off, if it hadn't been for one of his bodyguards.*
2 happen or take place ◻ *They argue so much these days that it will be a miracle if the wedding ever comes off.*
3 cease to be shown or performed, especially of a film, play, etc ◻ *The show you've been wanting to see comes off at the end of the month.*

② come off ²

emerge from a situation, especially a conflict, with a level of failure or success ◻ *The other boxer was stronger and had a longer reach, so everybody knew who was going to come off worse.*

①② come off ³

1 become detached from something ◻ *The last time I bought a cheap shirt, all the buttons came off in the wash.* ◻ *The mirror comes off the wall very easily, if you just undo those screws.*
2 be removable from something, especially by cleaning or erasing ◻ *If you spill glue on the carpet, it will never come off.*
3 fall from something ◻ *He wants to paint the house himself, but is worried about coming off the ladder.*
4 leave a motorway ◻ *Remember that you come off just after the second service station.*
5 stop taking a medicine ◻ *I didn't know that you'd come off these pills.*

① come on

1 see **come along / on**
2 begin; develop ◻ *If you keep sneezing, perhaps you have a cold coming on.* ◻ *His work is coming on well.*

3 stop worrying, crying, etc; used only in the imperative ◻ *Come on, Ann! Dry your eyes!*
4 appear on stage, at a sports ground, etc, in order to perform ◻ *After each act a comedian came on and told a few jokes.* ◻ *The crowd cheered as the teams came on again after half-time.*
5 be shown at the cinema, on TV, etc ◻ *What time does the news come on?*
6 fall, especially of rain ◻ *The rain came on before they could get to any shelter.*

② come on / upon

meet or find somebody or something by chance ◻ *I came upon the necklace in a tiny little shop on the outskirts of Paris. I was looking for a ring at the time.*

① come out

1 appear, especially of the sun, moon, etc ◻ *On holiday he likes to sip a cold drink on his balcony, and watch the stars come out.*
2 bloom or flower ◻ *It's been too cold recently for the blossom to come out.*
3 be published or produced, and become available to the public ◻ *His new novel comes out in the autumn.* ◻ *Why don't you wait for the new model to come out?*
4 become known or public, especially of a secret, truth, set of facts, etc ◻ *Eventually it came out that not one word of his story to the police was true.*
5 go on strike ◻ *I see that the railwaymen are coming out again.*
6 be announced, released or broadcast ◻ *The news has just come out that there is to be another royal wedding in the autumn.*
7 produce a clear picture; used of camera film ◻ *She was very disappointed that her holiday photographs didn't come out.*

① = ●●   ② = ●●○   ③ = ●○●   ④ = ●○○●   ⑤ = ●○● *or* ●●○   ⑥ = ●●●○   ⑦ = ●○○●○

8 produce an answer, especially of a calculation, problem, etc ❑ *I spent at least an hour adding, dividing, and subtracting, and then the whole thing came out wrong!*

9 emerge or become evident, especially of a human quality or characteristic
❑ *You'll often find that a person's courage comes out in a crisis.*

10 be conveyed or shown
❑ *The artist's true feelings about women don't come out in this painting.* ❑ *You always come out well in photographs.*

⑥ come out against
declare your opposition to something, especially by criticising it
❑ *Our advisers came out against the plan, saying that it would be too costly.*

⑥ come out at
have as a final cost or result ❑ *With the fitting costs, the carpet comes out at ten pounds a square metre.*

⑥ come out in
develop spots, marks, etc, on your skin, especially as a sign of illness
❑ *If the child has come out in a rash, you'd better call the doctor.*

⑥① come out (of)
be removable from something, especially by cleaning
❑ *I'm worried that these ink stains won't come out of the tablecloth.*

⑥ come out with
say something, especially something that causes surprise or shock ❑ *You just can't imagine the hurtful things she came out with when we said we were going to live abroad.*

① come over [1]
travel from another country, especially to visit somebody ❑ *Our American friends are coming over in July for three weeks.*

② come over [2]
1 take hold of somebody, especially of an unpleasant feeling ❑ *A sudden wave of sickness came over me, and I had to rush out of the room.*
❑ *I really don't know what came over me. I'm not usually aggressive.*
2 experience a feeling of sickness, dizziness, etc; ❑ *At the top of the stairs she suddenly came over very faint, and had to sit down.*

⑥① come over/ round (to)
1 pay somebody a short visit, especially for pleasure ❑ *We've got a few friends coming over on Saturday night and we thought you might like to come round as well.*
2 change your belief, opinion, loyalty, etc, and agree with or join the side of somebody ❑ *With just a little more persuasion, I'm sure she'll come round to our way of thinking.*

① come round
see **come around / round**

① come round / to
regain consciousness ❑ *The driver of the car didn't come round until two days after the accident.*

①② come through [1]
survive a serious illness, operation or dangerous situation ❑ *He became so weak from loss of blood that at one time we started to think that he wouldn't come through.*

---

① = ●●   ② = ●●○   ③ = ●○●   ④ = ●○●○   ⑤ = ●○● *or* ●●○   ⑥ = ●●●○   ⑦ = ●○●●○

① **come through** ²
reach or arrive somewhere, especially of a message, telephone call, etc
☐ *Have your instructions come through from London yet?*

② **come to** ¹
1 make a total ☐ *How much does the bill come to?*
2 concern, involve or be a matter of something; always preceded by it ☐ *When it comes to cameras, you really can't beat the Japanese.*
3 enter somebody's mind, especially of a thought, idea, etc ☐ *While I was sitting there working, it suddenly came to me that what I was doing was a complete waste of time.*

① **come to** ²
    see **come round / to**

① **come together**
form a relationship with somebody ☐ *David and I would never have come together if it hadn't been for your introduction.*

② **come under**
1 belong in a particular category or under a particular heading ☐ *What does 'language testing' come under? 'Language' or 'testing'?*
2 be controlled or managed by somebody or something ☐ *All these schools come under the regional education authority.*
3 become the target or victim of something ☐ *The report came under heavy criticism.*

① **come up**
1 happen or arise, especially unexpectedly ☐ *I'll see you tonight at seven, unless something important comes up and*
I have to work late. ☐ *Let me know if any interesting jobs come up while I'm away.*
2 be mentioned, discussed or considered ☐ *Your name came up several times during the meeting, so they obviously haven't forgotten your application for the job.*
3 be selected, especially of a lottery ticket ☐ *She's convinced that this is going to be the lucky week when her number comes up.*
4 become clean, bright, etc, especially as a result of being polished ☐ *Look how well these silver spoons have come up. Just like new!*
5 be vomited ☐ *Everything she eats comes up again five minutes later. We'd better get the doctor.*
6 appear above the horizon ☐ *The coldest moment of the day is just before the sun comes up.*

⑥ **come up against**
encounter a problem, obstacle, etc ☐ *We were making fairly good progress until we suddenly came up against a lack of funds.*

⑥ **come up to**
reach a particular standard ☐ *This new book doesn't come up to his previous writing.*

⑥ **come up with**
discover, invent or provide something ☐ *Is it true that the professor has come up with a way of getting chickens to lay hard-boiled eggs?* ☐ *She's always coming up with interesting suggestions.*

② **come upon** *see* **come on/upon**

② **conjure up**
1 cause somebody to imagine or form a mental picture of something

---
① = ●●   ② = ●●○   ③ = ●○●   ④ = ●○●○   ⑤ = ●○● *or* ●●○   ⑥ = ●●●○   ⑦ = ●○●●○

❏ *The holiday brochure* conjured up *a very false impression of the hotel.*
2 cause something to be remembered ❏ *This music* conjures up *the time we spent together in Hong Kong.*

① **conk out** *Informal*
stop functioning, especially of a mechanism; die ❏ *The last time I flew in this plane, one of the engines* conked out.

⑤ **cook up**
invent an excuse, story, etc ❏ *It's amazing how she's always able to* cook up *a reason for being late.*

①⑤ **cool down**
become, or cause somebody to become, calmer ❏ *He* cooled down *as soon as I offered to pay for the damage.*

① **cool off**
1 become less excited or angry ❏ *After exchanging so many insults, they're going to take a long time to* cool off.
2 become less enthusiastic ❏ *Her new boyfriend soon* cooled off *when he discovered that she wore false teeth.*

⑥① **cotton on (to)** *Informal*
understand the point of something or how to do something ❏ *He'd never been shown how to fish before, but he soon* cottoned on.

①⑤ **cough up** *Informal*
provide or hand over, especially money or information ❏ *How are we going to get our deposit back if they refuse to* cough up?

② **count against**
cause people to judge or regard somebody unsympathetically ❏ *His years in prison* counted against *him when he tried to get a job.*

⑤ **count in**
include somebody or something, especially when doing a calculation ❏ *There's a coach trip to London on Tuesday. Can we* count you in?

② **count on/upon**
1 rely or trust somebody to do something ❏ *You can always* count on *John to be there on time.*
2 expect or anticipate something; usually used in the negative ❏ *We certainly hadn't* counted on *the house falling down two weeks after we moved in!*

⑤ **count out**
1 exclude or disregard somebody or something ❏ *If there aren't enough seats for all of us to go, you can* count me out.
2 declare that a boxer has lost a fight when he fails to get up from the ground within ten seconds ❏ *The former champion was* counted out *at the end of the seventh round.*

⑤① **cover up**
prevent something from becoming known or being noticed ❏ *Her parents tried to* cover up *the scandal, but somehow the story got into the newspapers.*
N ❏ *It was such a clever* cover-up *that the truth wasn't discovered until twenty years later.*

⑥ **cover up for**
prevent something from becoming known in order to protect somebody ❏ *Naturally his wife will try to* cover up for *him, so we can't believe everything she says.*

⑥① **crack down (on)**
become more strict with somebody ❏ *The police are really beginning to* crack down on *drivers who park their cars just where they like.*

① crack up *Informal*
become mentally or emotionally ill
❒ *Stop talking to yourself, or people will think you're cracking up!*

⑤ cream off
choose and take the best
❒ *The students with the highest marks are being creamed off and sent to overseas universities.*

① crop up
occur or appear, especially unexpectedly ❒ *We should be finished by September, as long as no more difficulties crop up.*

⑤④ cross off
remove something from a list by drawing a line through it ❒ *When you said that you didn't want to go on the trip after all, I crossed your name off.*

⑤ cross out
draw a line through something, especially to show a mistake, cancellation, etc ❒ *If you've made a spelling mistake, I suggest that you cross the word out and write it again.*

① cry off
withdraw from an arrangement; usually used in a derogatory way
❒ *I do get annoyed with people who accept an invitation and then cry off at the last minute.*

⑥① cry out (for)
be in urgent need of something
❒ *The whole house is crying out for a good coat of paint.*

①② cut across
cross an area in order to shorten your journey ❒ *The gardener used to hate it when we cut across his beautiful lawn.*

①⑥⑤ cut back (on)
reduce something especially because of economic circumstances ❒ *In these difficult times, even the universities have had to cut back on their staff.*
N ❒ *The government is planning several major cutbacks in national spending over the next twelve months.*

①⑥⑤ cut down (on)
reduce something, especially to save money or promote health ❒ *He has managed to cut down his cigarettes to ten a day.* ❒ *She'd rather stay fat than have to cut down on chocolate.*

⑥① cut in (on)
move suddenly in front of a person or moving vehicle ❒ *If I hadn't braked when he cut in, there would have been an accident.* ❒ *That stupid fool suddenly cut in on me.*

⑥① cut in (with)
interrupt a conversation ❒ *We got more and more annoyed with her for the way she kept cutting in with silly comments.*

⑤ cut off [1]
1 disconnect somebody who is having a telephone conversation, usually by accident
❒ *No sooner had she answered than we were suddenly cut off.*
2 cause somebody or something to be isolated or separated ❒ *The sea comes in very quickly along this stretch of the beach, and can easily cut you off if you're not careful.* ❒ *She feels very cut off in that village in the middle of nowhere.*
3 disconnect a supply of gas, electricity, water, etc ❒ *The telephone company have cut us off for not paying our last bill.*

---

① = ●● ② = ●●○ ③ = ●○● ④ = ●○●○ ⑤ = ●○● *or* ●●○ ⑥ = ●●●○ ⑦ = ●○●●○

4 disinherit somebody ❑ *His father has cut him off without a penny for marrying without his permission.*

② **cut off** ²
block the route or passage of somebody or something to prevent escape ❑ *We cut off their retreat by destroying the bridge.*

⑤ **cut out** ¹
1 stop eating or drinking a particular food or drink; discontinue a habit ❑ *The doctor told me that if I didn't start cutting out potatoes, I'd soon look like one.* ❑ *Cut out the smoking and you'll live for another ten years.*
2 delete or exclude something ❑ *The story reads much better with some of the long descriptive passages cut out.*
3 stop doing something; often used in the imperative ❑ *Either cut out the talking or leave the examination hall.* ❑ *Cut it out, will you!*

① **cut out** ²
1 fail to function, especially of an engine ❑ *Each time I stop at the traffic lights, the car cuts out.*
2 stop automatically ❑ *As soon as the water reaches the temperature you want, the boiler cuts out.*

D, d

⑤ **damp down**
cause a fire to burn less quickly ❑ *She usually damps the fire down before going to bed.*

⑤ **dash off**
produce something very quickly ❑ *Could you dash off these letters before lunch?*

⑥ **date back to**
be known to have existed since a certain time in the past ❑ *The university dates back to the seventeenth century.*

② **dawn on/ upon**
be realised by somebody ❑ *It suddenly dawned on me that she didn't want to go.* ❑ *The extent of the damage slowly dawned on them.*

② **deal in**
buy and sell certain goods regularly to earn money ❑ *His company deals in tobacco.*

② **deal with**
1 be concerned with something ❑ *Her new book deals with the subject of childbirth.*
2 be responsible for handling somebody or something, especially an enquiry, problem, complaint, etc ❑ *She's never had to deal with an emergency before.*
3 do business with a person or company ❑ *We only deal with firms that are well known.*

④ **debar from** *Formal*
prevent somebody from doing something, usually by law ❑ *Foreigners are debarred from buying property here.*

⑦③ deck out (in)

dress somebody in or decorate something with something bright or attractive ☐ *Her father has decked himself out in a new suit for the wedding.*

④ deck with

decorate a place or thing with something, especially for a celebration ☐ *The whole of the city centre had been decked with flags and banners to welcome the team home.*

② delight in

receive pleasure from doing something ☐ *Some students think that their teachers delight in finding mistakes.*

⑦⑤ deliver over / up (to)

pass or surrender somebody or something, especially to somebody in authority ☐ *The two suspects were delivered over to the police for questioning.* ☐ *After the battle the last of the enemy soldiers delivered themselves up.*

② depend on / upon

1 rely or be dependent on somebody or something ☐ *You can depend on John. He never misses a game.* ☐ *All the major banks can be depended upon nowadays.*
2 be influenced or determined by something ☐ *Where we go for our holiday depends upon how much money we have to spend.*
3 expect confidently that something will happen ☐ *The farmers are beginning to say that we can depend upon a very good harvest this year.*

② derive from

come from or get something from a source ☐ *A lot of English words derive from Latin.* ☐ *She derives a great deal of pleasure from writing stories for children.*

② descend on/ upon

1 visit somewhere or somebody unexpectedly, especially in large numbers ☐ *Every summer thousands of holidaymakers descend on the town.* ☐ *The whole family descended on me last Christmas.*
2 attack somebody or something in large numbers ☐ *Most of the crew were killed when five enemy aircraft suddenly descended upon the ship.*

② descend to

do something which reduces your status, dignity, etc ☐ *He's proud and won't descend to accepting charity.* ☐ *People say that he even descended to robbing his own family.*

② detract from

reduce the quality, value, attractiveness, etc, of something ☐ *The thought of having to return to work detracted from the pleasure of their holiday.*

① die away

become weaker or fainter until no longer heard, felt, etc ☐ *The sound of their footsteps eventually died away in the distance.*

① die down

become less violent or intense ☐ *All the passengers will be seasick if this storm doesn't die down.* ☐ *Wait until all the fuss has died down.* ☐ *The applause gradually died down.*

② die for

need or want something very much ☐ *I'm dying for a cigarette.*

② die of / with

have an intense feeling of something, especially curiosity, hunger or thirst ☐ *Is dinner nearly ready? I'm absolutely dying of hunger.*

---

① = ●●   ② = ●●○   ③ = ●○●   ④ = ●○○○   ⑤ = ●○● *or* ●●○   ⑥ = ●●●○   ⑦ = ●○●●○

① die out

gradually cease to exist or be practised, especially in the case of a race, species, tradition, etc ❑ *Is the elephant really in danger of dying out?* ❑ *That old custom died out a long time ago.*

① dig in ¹

begin to do something with a great deal of energy, especially to eat ❑ *Come on! Dig in before the food goes cold.* ❑ *The job won't take long if we all dig in.*

①③ dig in ²

1 dig a hole or trench in the ground for protection against enemy fire ❑ *Our soldiers have landed and are now digging themselves in.*
2 establish a secure position for yourself ❑ *The more the boss tries to get rid of her, the more she digs in.*

⑦⑤ dig out (of)

find or obtain something, especially information, by searching ❑ *He's gone to the library to dig out a few facts and figures for the report.* ❑ *The headmaster finally dug the truth out of the boy; he'd stolen the watch.*

⑤ dig up

reveal or discover something that has been secret or hidden for a long time ❑ *He's worried about what the police might dig up if they start asking too many questions.*

① dine in

have dinner at home ❑ *I'd better see what there is to eat if we're dining in tonight.*

① dine out

have dinner at a restaurant ❑ *Tom prefers to dine out because then he avoids the washing-up.*

① dip in

take a share of something that is offered ❑ *An enormous tin of biscuits was passed round and everybody except Helen dipped in.*

② dip into

1 read or glance at something in a casual way ❑ *I've dipped into the report but haven't had time to read it properly yet.*
2 make a brief or casual study of a subject ❑ *He enjoys dipping into branches of science that he knows nothing about.*
3 use part of a stock or supply of something, especially money ❑ *If we're having a holiday abroad this year, we'll have to dip into our savings.*

② disagree with

have a bad effect on your health or physical comfort, especially of food and weather ❑ *He used to love onions until they started to disagree with him.*

⑤ dish out

1 serve food, especially to a group ❑ *Shall I dish out the potatoes, or do you want to help yourselves?*
2 *Informal* distribute or hand out something ❑ *Don't dish out the question papers until all the students are in their seats.*
3 *Informal* give or inflict something, especially advice, criticism, punishment, etc, in a careless way ❑ *She's always eager to dish out the blame when something goes wrong.* ❑ *The manager doesn't seem to be happy unless he's dishing out orders to somebody.*

①⑤ dish up ¹

put cooked food onto plates ready for people to eat ❑ *I'm not going to dish up until you're all ready to sit down at the table.*

① = ●●　② = ●●○　③ = ●○●　④ = ●○●○　⑤ = ●○● *or* ●●○　⑥ = ●●●○　⑦ = ●○●●○

⑤ **dish up** [2]
present something, especially information, opinions, etc, in a lazy, boring or repetitive way ❑ *Every night you get the same old rubbish dished up on the television.*

② **dispense with**
1 get rid of something or somebody ❑ *We won't ever make a profit unless we dispense with some of the staff.*
2 make something unnecessary ❑ *I'm not convinced that buying a sunlamp would dispense with the need for a holiday.*

② **dispose of**
1 remove, sell or get rid of something ❑ *Before buying a new piano, we'd better dispose of the old one.*
2 remove a complaint, problem, etc, by finding an answer or explanation for it ❑ *Disposing of these objections isn't going to be easy.*

① **dive in**
do something without hesitation, especially eat ❑ *Dive in, everybody, before the ice cream melts!*

④ **divest of**
1 take something, especially clothing, away from somebody ❑ *At the end of the ceremony, they were glad to divest themselves of the heavy robes.*
2 take a power, right, title, etc, away from somebody ❑ *The prisoners who tried to escape were divested of all their privileges.*

② **do as/ for**
be able to be used as something ❑ *These empty beer cans will do as ashtrays.*

⑥ **do away with**
1 discontinue, abolish or get rid of something, especially a law, institution, etc ❑ *Slavery was done away with a long time ago.*
2 kill somebody or yourself ❑ *When his wife left him, the poor fellow did away with himself.*

③ **do down**
speak about somebody in an unkind way ❑ *It's unforgivable that you should do your own children down.*

② **do for**   see **do as / for**

⑤ **do in**   *Informal*
murder somebody ❑ *She threatened to do him in if she caught him stealing from her purse again.* ❑ *I wonder how many more of us are going to be done in before the police catch him?*

⑤ **do out**
1 clean or tidy something, especially a room or cupboard ❑ *I've got to do out the bedroom before I go shopping.*
2 decorate a room ❑ *It won't take more than two days to do out the kitchen if we're only going to paint it.*

⑦ **do out of**
deprive or cheat somebody of something ❑ *Don't let them do you out of our travelling expenses.* ❑ *He's been done out of the opportunity of a week in Paris.*

③ **do over**   *Informal*
attack and beat somebody in a planned attack, especially of a gang ❑ *He had to spend a week in hospital after being done over for talking to the police.*

⑤ **do up** [1]
1 repair, modernise or decorate something ❑ *The house is very cheap because it needs doing up.* ❑ *You should have seen the state of the place before it was done up.*

---

① = ●● ② = ●●○ ③ = ●○● ④ = ●○○● ⑤ = ●○● *or* ●●○ ⑥ = ●●●○ ⑦ = ●○●●○

2 fasten something, especially something which has to be buttoned, knotted or zipped ☐ *Not many children of his age can* do up *a shoe-lace without help.*
3 make a parcel of something ☐ *I can't* do *the books* up *without any string.*

① do up ²

be able to be fastened together
☐ *None of your trousers will* do up *if you continue to eat so much.*

③ do up ³

make yourself look particularly attractive ☐ *She* did *herself* up *for the office party.*

② do with

1 need or want something; used after *can* or *could* ☐ *I could* do with *something to eat. How about you?* ☐ *We can always* do with *a bit more help.*
2 tolerate something which annoys or irritates; used in the negative and with *can* or *could* ☐ *I just can't* do with *all this noise when I'm trying to concentrate.*

② do without ¹

be better or happier without something; used after *can* or *could* ☐ *We could* do without *his interference all the time.* ☐ *I could have* done without *her arriving just as I was about to start work.*

①② do without ²

manage without something ☐ *On holiday he prefers to* do without *a watch.* ☐ *You simply can't* do without *a phone if you're in business.*

⑤ dole out

distribute something, especially in a routine way ☐ *Their government has started* doling out *food coupons again.*

③ doll up   *Informal*

use a lot of cosmetics or dress yourself in unusually elaborate or colourful clothes; often used in a derogatory way ☐ *Isn't she a bit too old for* dolling *herself* up *like that?*

① doss down   *Informal*

find yourself somewhere free or cheap to lie down and sleep, especially a floor or a public place ☐ *It's surprising how many homeless people* doss down *on railway platforms at night.*

② dote on/ upon

have exaggerated love or affection for somebody ☐ *I've never seen parents* dote on *a child as much as they do.*

① double back

return along the same route, especially in a hurry ☐ *If you've forgotten your wallet, you'd better* double back *and get it.*

①③ double up ¹

bend or cause somebody to bend at the waist, especially because of laughter or pain ☐ *The whole audience* doubled up *at some of the jokes.* ☐ *The blow to his stomach* doubled *him* up.

① double up ²

share a flat, room, etc, with somebody ☐ *Would you mind* doubling up *just for one night?*

① doze off

fall asleep unintentionally ☐ *You must have* dozed off *while you were watching television.*

①② drag behind

be unable to stay level with somebody or something ☐ *You know when*

---

① = ●●   ② = ●●○   ③ = ●○●   ④ = ●○○●   ⑤ = ●○● *or* ●●○   ⑥ = ●●●○   ⑦ = ●○●●○

the child is getting tired by the way he starts *dragging behind*. ❑ *Her results were quite good last term, but this term she's dragging behind the others.*

⑤ drag down
cause somebody or something to deteriorate, especially in health, behaviour or rank ❑ *I warned you that she would drag you down if you married her!* ❑ *To open another betting shop would really drag down the whole area.*

⑤④ drag in / into
1 introduce a topic into a conversation, discussion, etc, especially one which is not directly relevant ❑ *Why do you have to drag in the question of money all the time?*
2 cause or force somebody to become involved in an argument, activity, etc ❑ *Don't try dragging me into your family rows.*

① drag on
continue, especially with the effect of making people bored, impatient or unhappy ❑ *How much longer is this ridiculous meeting going to drag on!*

⑤ drag out
cause something to continue for longer than usual or necessary, especially with the effect of making people bored or irritated ❑ *He dragged the speech out so much that we almost fell asleep.*

⑥ drag up **1** *Informal*
fail to bring up a child properly ❑ *It's obvious from the way he talks to you that he's been dragged up.*
2 cause something, especially something unpleasant or embarrassing, to be remembered or talked about ❑ *I'm worried about what her lawyer might be able to drag up.*

① draw in
grow dark progressively earlier, especially of days during autumn ❑ *You won't be able to play tennis in the evening once the days start drawing in.*

①② draw in/ into ¹
slow down and stop at a platform or at the side of the road ❑ *Carriage doors began to open as the train drew in.* ❑ *The car in front of us drew into a petrol station.*

⑤④ draw in / into ²
attract or persuade somebody to enter or join something ❑ *The football club isn't drawing in as big a crowd as it used to do.* ❑ *I refuse to be drawn into other people's arguments.*

① draw on
approach, especially of a time, season, etc ❑ *It's important that we feed the birds now that winter is drawing on.*

② draw on / upon
make use of something ❑ *He doesn't want to draw upon his savings if he can possibly avoid it.* ❑ *You can draw on my advice as much as you like, as long as you pay me for it!*

③ draw out ¹
make somebody feel less shy ❑ *He still feels very awkward in company, although we've done all we can to draw him out.*

① draw out ²
stay light for longer, especially of days or evenings ❑ *As soon as the evenings begin to draw out, we have our dinner in the garden.*

⑥① draw out (of) [1]

move away from a station or from the side of the road ☐ *A whistle sounded and the train drew out of the station.* ☐ *Always look in the mirror before you draw out.*

⑦⑤ draw out (of) [2]

1 extract a secret, confession, piece of information, etc, from somebody ☐ *Hope you managed to draw all the details we need out of him.*
2 take money from an account ☐ *I'll need to draw out some more money if we've got to buy petrol too.*

① draw up [1]

arrive at a place and stop, especially of a driver or vehicle ☐ *A black car drew up in front of the gates.*

⑤ draw up [2]

1 compose and write down something in a formal way, especially an agreement, contract, list, etc
☐ *The contract has been drawn up, but it hasn't been signed yet.*
2 move something near or next to a particular place ☐ *She drew a chair up and sat down right in front of my desk.*

② draw upon see draw on/upon

② dream of   *Informal*

consider the possibility of something; used in the negative and with *would* or *should* ☐ *I wouldn't dream of smoking inside a church.*

⑤ dream up

invent or imagine something
☐ *He's always dreaming up new ways of making a fortune.*

①⑤ dress up [1]

1 dress somebody or yourself in smart clothes ☐ *Do we have to dress up for tonight's dinner party?*

2 dress somebody or yourself in the clothes of another person or well-known character, usually for fun
☐ *The children love to see him dressed up as Father Christmas.*

⑤ dress up [2]

make something seem more attractive or acceptable, especially by making small additions to it ☐ *I like the story that you've written, but now you need to dress it up a bit with a few details.*

⑤ drink in

watch, listen to or experience something with great enjoyment or interest
☐ *The audience sat right to the end of the show, drinking in every word their hero sang.*

② drive at

suggest, mean or try to express something; used after *what*
☐ *What exactly are you driving at?*

⑤/④ drive in/ into

cause something to be learnt, understood or remembered, especially by using a lot of repetition
☐ *The point I'm trying to drive in is that you won't pass the examination unless you start doing some work.*

① drop back

1 reduce speed in order to move behind somebody or something ☐ *The American runner has decided to drop back and let somebody else take the lead.*
2 fail to maintain speed and be left behind ☐ *The car that had been in second position dropped back with engine trouble.*

①② drop behind

be overtaken or left behind by somebody or something ☐ *Our team dropped behind in the league when a third of the players went on holiday.* ☐ *In terms of annual production, the country has dropped behind the rest of Europe.*

---

① = ●● ② = ●●○ ③ = ●○● ④ = ●○●○ ⑤ = ●○● *or* ●●○ ⑥ = ●●●○ ⑦ = ●○●●○

⑥① drop by/ in (on)

pay somebody a short casual visit, especially when this does not require a long journey ❑ *I thought I'd drop in to see if you needed any shopping.* ❑ *Since we're going almost past her house, why don't we drop in on Mary?*

③ drop in/ off

bring or take something to somebody's house, place of work, etc, and leave it there ❑ *If you still need the book, I could drop it in tonight.*

① drop off ¹

fall asleep unintentionally ❑ *The film was so boring that Sharon kept dropping off.*

⑤ drop off ²

let somebody out of a vehicle or deliver something ❑ *I wonder if you could drop me off at the bank?* ❑ *Can you drop off my coat at the dry cleaner's on your way?*

① drop out

leave a college, university, etc, before the end of a course
❑ *Students who discover that they don't like engineering soon drop out.*
N ❑ *Quite a few teenagers become drop-outs at college.*

⑥① drop out (of)

cease to belong to or take part in something ❑ *Several countries dropped out of the competition for political reasons.* ❑ *3 members have dropped out already since the club's new manager arrived.*

① drop round

pay a short casual visit, especially when this does not require a long journey
❑ *Can I drop round to see you later?*

⑤/④ drum in / into

cause something to be learnt or remembered, especially by using a lot of effort and repetition
❑ *I've tried drumming in the fact that we can't afford another holiday, but she won't listen.*

⑤ drum up

obtain interest in a cause by publicity ❑ *We've managed to drum up a lot more support for the plan.*

① dry up   1

be completely used, exhausted or finished
❑ *If the funds dry up, we'll have to ask for a loan.*
2 be unable to continue speaking, especially in public
❑ *The poor man had only just started his speech when he suddenly became very nervous and dried up.*
3 *Informal* stop talking; usually used in the imperative in anger or irritation
❑ *If you can only make stupid comments, just dry up!*

⑥① duck out (of)

avoid doing or being involved in something
❑ *Her little boy always tries to duck out of going to see the dentist.*

② dwell on/ upon

spend a long time thinking, talking or writing about something
❑ *Why do news programmes dwell on death and violence all the time?*

E, e

① ease off/ up

become slower, less intense or less violent ❐ *It was an hour before her headache began to ease off.* ❐ *I'm not going out until this rain eases up a bit.*

⑥① ease off/ up (on)

use something with less force or in less quantity ❐ *He eased off on the accelerator the minute he saw the police car.* ❐ *Ease up on the shampoo, will you! I want to wash my hair too.*

⑤ eat away

reduce, remove or destroy something, especially of moving water, fire or acid ❐ *The river is eating the bank away in several places.*

① eat in

have a meal at home
❐ *Of course I don't mind eating in again, as long as you do the cooking.*

② eat into

1 attack and destroy or make a hole in something, especially of chemical action ❐ *Can you see where the rust has begun eating into the bottom of the driver's door?*
2 use part of a reserve of money, stocks, etc ❐ *The money they spent on the washing machine ate into their holiday savings.*

① eat out

have a meal at a restaurant instead of at home ❐ *They're always complaining that they can't afford to eat out nowadays.*

② eat up

consume something, especially fuel or money, quickly or in great quanti-

ties ❐ *It's true it's a comfortable car, but it eats up the petrol.*

⑦ ⑤ edge out (of)

cause somebody to resign or be removed from a job or position of authority ❐ *The other directors have been trying to edge him out ever since he lost our best customer.* ❐ *The previous government was edged out of office by just a handful of votes.*

⑦ ⑤ egg on (to)   *Informal*

encourage or urge somebody to do something ❐ *Her mother kept egging her on to enter the song contest.*

② eke out

1 cause a small amount of something to be sufficient, either by using it carefully or by adding something to it ❐ *In those days we had to eke out my husband's small salary to feed the whole family, his parents as well.*
❐ *If necessary, you could always eke out the meal with a little rice.*
2 struggle to earn or produce enough to live ❐ *In the south of the country it's much harder to eke out a living from the land. The soil is so poor and there is little rain.*

② embark on/ upon

begin a new project, pastime, occupation, etc ❐ *At your age I would think very carefully before embarking upon a career in journalism.*

② end up

1 conclude a series of actions, processes, etc, in a certain state, place or condition ❐ *Did you know that Andrew has ended up working for his father after all?* ❐ *After doing the shopping and then seeing a film, we ended up at Alan's for coffee.* ❐ *Most of the white liquid running out of these trees ends up as rubber tyres.*

2 do something or be somewhere as a result of a previous action ❐ *If you don't watch the road more carefully, you'll* end up *having an accident.*

② **enlarge on / upon**
expand or explain something in more detail ❐ *The speaker proceeded to* enlarge upon *his initial statement.*

② **enquire/ inquire after**
ask for news or information, especially about somebody's health or activities ❐ *Of course he still remembers you. In fact, he* enquired after *you the last time I saw him.*

② **enquire/ inquire into**
seek information by asking questions, especially about something mysterious or unpleasant ❐ *The police are now* enquiring into *the events which led up to his disappearance.*

②④ **enter for**
register or enrol somebody for a competition ❐ *They've* entered *me* for *the beauty contest, but I'm sure I won't win.*

② **enter into**
1 take part or become involved in a conversation, discussion, written agreement, etc ❐ *The Prime Minister refuses to* enter into *further negotiations with the railwaymen until they have all returned to work.*
2 begin to report or discuss something at length or in detail ❐ *Before we could stop her, she had* entered into *a long and boring account of how the deputy mayor's wife had invited her to tea.* ❐ *There won't be enough time at today's meeting to* enter into *the question of overseas aid.*

3 be included in a discussion, plan, calculation, etc; usually used in the negative ❐ *The fact that the office already has a good accountant simply didn't* enter into *the decision.*

② **enter on/ upon** *Formal*
begin something, especially a new stage of your life or work ❐ *Next month the President will* enter upon *his second term of office, knowing that there is much work to be done.*

① **even out¹**
become level or steady, especially of ground, prices, etc ❐ *At the end of the first year the repayments* even out *at thirty pounds a month.*

⑤ **even out ²**
1 make a surface flat
❐ *Naturally, you'll have to* even out *the ground before planting anything.*
2 make two or more things equal
❐ *Unless the company* evens out *the rates of pay, those on a low wage are going to complain.*

⑤ **even up**
make two or more things equal
❐ *Let me pay for the meal this time, just to* even *things* up *a bit.* ❐ *The visitors* evened up *the score with an unexpected goal two minutes before half-time.*

⑤ **explain away**
remove or dismiss an objection, criticism, piece of evidence, etc, by giving a reasonable explanation
❐ *Professor Jones, how do you* explain away *the fact that nine times out often your theory simply doesn't work?*
❐ *At the police station he tried to* explain *the gold watches* away *by saying that they were birthday presents from his rich uncles.*

---

① = ●●   ② = ●●○   ③ = ●○●   ④ = ●○●○   ⑤ = ●○● *or* ●●○   ⑥ = ●●●○   ⑦ = ●○●●○

F, f

⑥ face up to
accept or confront something, especially responsibility, danger or an unpleasant fact ☐ *He faced up to the fact that he would never walk again with remarkable bravery.*

③ fag out *Informal*
tire or exhaust somebody ☐ *Swimming is good fun, but it can really fag you out if you're not fit.* ☐ *After a hard day's work, I'm utterly fagged out!*

① fall about
laugh uncontrollably
☐ *The whole class fell about when they saw what the teacher had drawn on the blackboard.*

① fall apart
break into pieces, fail or disintegrate
☐ *Cheap clothes tend to fall apart when you wash them.* ☐ *Both his business and his marriage were falling apart during those years.*

⑥① fall away (to)
1 slope downwards towards somewhere ☐ *Just beyond the trees the ground falls away sharply, so we use it for grazing.*
2 drop to a lower level ☐ *The number of people who go to the cinema is steadily falling away these days.*

① fall back
move back or retreat, especially in a war or battle ☐ *So many of the troops were getting killed that they had to fall back.*

⑥ fall back on/ upon
use or go to a reliable source of help, especially after other sources have been tried unsuccessfully ☐ *If we run out of cash, we can always fall back on our savings in the bank.* ☐ *It's wonderful to have a friend like John to fall back on.*

①② fall behind
be overtaken or left behind by somebody or something, especially by a competitor ☐ *A long illness caused him to fall behind the rest of the class.* ☐ *Why have all these industrial countries fallen behind Japan?*

⑥① fall behind (with)
fail to do or complete something by a particular time ☐ *She's very worried about falling behind with the rent.*

① fall down
fail or be unsatisfactory ☐ *The plan falls down by relying too much on the co-operation of the work force.* ☐ *Her test results were very good, but she fell down at the interview.*

② fall for
1 be strongly attracted to or charmed by somebody or something ☐ *She fell for his good looks.*
2 be easily deceived by a story, argument, suggestion, etc ☐ *You didn't fall for or his story about being a prince, did you?* ☐ *If you tell him that it will make him a lot of money, he's bound to fall for the idea.*

⑥ fall in with
1 become friendly or associate with somebody, especially after a chance meeting ☐ *On holiday she fell in with another visitor staying at the same hotel.*
2 accept or agree to something, especially a plan, proposal, etc ☐ *She*

said that she would *fall in with* our
arrangements for the outing.

② fall into

have a particular number of divisions
❏ *The book falls into three sections.*
❏ *How many categories do English nouns
fall into?*

① fall off

1 become less or fewer
❏ *The product was selling well in the first
three months of the year, but since April
sales have fallen off.* ❏ *Attendances tend
to fall off during the cold weather.*
2 become worse ❏ *The food was very
good when the restaurant first opened, but
recently it's been falling off.*

② fall on

be on a particular day of the week,
especially of an anniversary, public
holiday, etc ❏ *Your birthday falls on a
Tuesday this year.*

② fall on / upon

1 attack somebody or something
❏ *The children fell upon the trapped animal with sticks.*
2 seize something eagerly, especially
food ❏ *After five days without supplies,
they fell on the food that the rescue team
had brought.*
3 become the responsibility of
somebody ❏ *I know that somebody
has to pay for these things, but why does it
always fall on the parents?* ❏ *Meeting visitors at the airport usually falls upon a
member of staff.*

① fall out   cease to be involved or
active in an organisation, project,
etc ❏ *Two members of the original team
fell out when they realised how long the
project would take.*

⑥① fall out (with)

quarrel and cease to be friendly with
somebody ❏ *The young couple next
door seem to have fallen out with each
other. She never speaks to him.*

① fall through

fail or be discontinued ❏ *The whole
scheme fell through because there weren't
enough funds.*

① fall to

begin to do something, especially
with energy and enthusiasm
❏ *When we realised that she had nobody
to help her, we all fell to.*

② fall under

be classified as something ❏ *Do our
fares to work every day fall under travelling expenses?* ❏ *The advertisement fell
under the heading of 'Property for Sale'.*

② fall upon   see   fall on/upon

① fan out

spread out in the shape of a fan
while going forwards, especially of a
search party, group of soldiers, etc
❏ *The team of police and volunteers
fanned out across the hillside in their hunt
for the murder weapon.*

⑤ farm out

pass something for which you are
responsible to somebody else, especially a piece of work or the care of a
child ❏ *If you don't have enough men and
machines to complete the order in time,
you'll just have to farm some of it out.*
❏ *She's thinking about farming out the
youngest boy so that she can go to work.*

② fasten on / onto / upon

1 accept or adopt an idea, proposal,

etc ❐ *The local people took a long time to* *fasten onto* *the idea of forming queues.*
2 seize a particular point or remark, especially to use in a debate or conflict ❐ *His lawyer was quick to* *fasten* *upon this piece of new evidence.*

② **feel for**
have sympathy for somebody ❐ *I really* *feel for* *all the parents whose children were in the crash.*

⑤ **feel out**
discover somebody's attitude or opinion in a careful and tactful manner ❐ *I suggest that you* *feel out* *the Prime Minister to make sure that you have his support, before you make a public statement.*

⑥ **feel up to**
1 feel well or energetic enough to do something ❐ *Do you* *feel up* *to going out tonight, or are you too tired?*
2 feel capable of doing something, especially because of having the necessary skill, experience, etc
❐ *You'd better resign if you* *don't feel up to* *the job.*

②③ **fend off**
protect yourself, somebody or something from a blow, insult, accusation or attack by turning it aside ❐ *He managed to* *fend off* *most of the blows with his arms.* ❐ *She's very skilled at* *fending off* *difficult questions.*

⑤ **ferret out**
find or reveal something by searching for it in a busy and determined way ❐ *The librarian sometimes offers to* *ferret out* *the information you need.*

① **fight back** [1]
recover, especially with a struggle
❐ *It's amazing how she has* *fought back*

since the operation. ❐ *He was almost bankrupt just a year ago, but look how he has* *fought back.*

⑤ **fight back** [2]
struggle to control a strong emotion
❐ *It became increasingly difficult for her to* *fight back* *the tears.*

②③ **fight off**
struggle to overcome an attack, criticism, illness, etc ❐ *He's been* *fighting off* *a cold for the last three days.* ❐ *She bravely tried to* *fight off* *her depression.*

② **figure on**
expect or forecast something, often used in the negative ❐ *We certainly didn't* *figure on* *the new computer being so popular.*

⑤ **figure out**
1 calculate or produce the answer to something ❐ *It was a very complicated question, but she eventually* *figured it out.*
2 understand somebody or something; often used in the negative
❐ *I just couldn't* *figure out* *how she could be in two places at the same time.*
❐ *It took me ten years of married life to* *figure him out.*

⑤ **fill in**
1 complete a form with the information required ❐ *It took only five minutes to* *fill in* *the questionnaire.*
2 write the details that are required
❐ *If you* *fill in* *your name and address on this card, I'll send it to you as soon as the book is returned.*

⑥① **fill in (for)**
do the work or take the place of a person during their absence
❐ *We need somebody to* *fill in for Alan* *while he's on holiday.*

⑦③ **fill in (on)**
give somebody information about something, especially recent developments ☐ *Could you fill John in on what was said at yesterday's meeting?*

① **fill out** ¹
become fatter ☐ *Her face has filled out a lot since we saw her in hospital.*

⑤ **fill out** ²
give something more detail, content, body, etc ☐ *Having finalised the structure of the report, they proceeded to fill it out.* ☐ *It's a good book, except that one or two of the characters need filling out.*

①② **find out** ¹
learn or discover something, especially by making enquiries ☐ *We were about to buy the house until we found out that it was next door to a pub.* ☐ *See if you can find out her name and address.*

③ **find out** ²
discover somebody is guilty of a dishonest or criminal act ☐ *He'd been stealing from the company for several years before they found him out.*

⑤ **finish off** *Informal*
1 kill somebody or something, especially a person or animal that is injured or wounded ☐ *He was in such pain that he asked the doctors to finish him off.*
2 completely exhaust somebody ☐ *The row we had last night just finished me off.*

② **finish with**
1 end a relationship ☐ *Is it true that she's finished with her new boyfriend already?*

2 no longer require or need to use something or somebody ☐ *Have you finished with my dictionary yet?*
3 finish scolding, criticising or punishing somebody ☐ *By the time I've finished with them, they'll wish they hadn't tried to cheat me.*

① **fire away**
begin to do something, especially to ask questions; often used in the imperative ☐ *I don't have very long to answer your questions, so fire away!*

② **fish for**
try to obtain something, especially information or compliments, in an indirect or cunning way ☐ *When she tells you how awful she looks, she's only fishing for compliments.* ☐ *It became quite obvious that he was fishing for an invitation.*

⑦⑤ **fish out (of)**
bring something from a place, especially after searching ☐ *I know that there is a copy of report somewhere in the building. I'll try to fish it out for you.* ☐ *The child suddenly fished a mouse out of his pocket.*

⑥① **fit in (with)**
be in agreement or harmony with somebody or something ☐ *He's never had to work in a busy office before, so I hope he fits in.* ☐ *How does this decision to buy a big house fit in with what you were saying about avoiding responsibilities?* ☐ *Do you think that the green carpet fits in with the yellow walls?*

⑤/④ **fit in / into**
1 have, find or make enough space for somebody or something ☐ *It's a big car but, even so, I can't fit you all in.* ☐ *You can't fit a piano into that little room!*

---

① = ●● ② = ●●○ ③ = ●○● ④ = ●○●○ ⑤ = ●○● *or* ●●○ ⑥ = ●●●○ ⑦ = ●○●●○

2 have or make time for something, especially to see, treat or examine somebody □ *Mrs Smith has broken a front tooth, and she wonders if you can fit her in this afternoon.* □ *I can't fit more that three interviews into one hour!*

⑦⑤ fit out /up (with)
provide somebody or something with necessary equipment, clothes, etc □ *The kitchen has been fitted out with new cupboards and shelves.* □ *We just can't afford to fit him out with a new uniform.* **N** □ *Is that a new outfit she's wearing?*

⑦⑤ fit up (with)
supply somebody with a piece of equipment □ *Where can I go to be fitted up with a new pair of glasses?*

② fix on decide on a date, time etc
□ *Have you fixed on a date for the wedding yet?*

⑦⑤ fix up (with)
supply or provide somebody with something they want, especially by making the necessary arrangements □ *If you need work in London, I know somebody who can fix you up.* □ *He asked me if I could fix him up with a girlfriend.*

① fizzle out
end in a disappointing way □ *Their relationship got worse and worse and eventually just fizzled out.*
□ *Nobody is interested in his new project after the last one fizzled out.*

⑤ flag down
stop a moving vehicle by waving your arm or a flag
□ *We tried flagging down at least a dozen taxis, but not one of them stopped.*

① flake out *Informal*
faint or collapse □ *I'm going to flake out if I don't get some fresh air soon.*

① flare up
suddenly become angry, fierce or violent, especially of a fire, temper, battle, etc □ *The fighting in the Middle East flared up again over the weekend with heavy losses on both sides.* □ *You can't speak to him about anything these days without him flaring up.* **N** □ *The government is deciding what to do about the recent flare-up of violence in our cities.*

③ flash about/ around
display something, especially to gain admiration; usually used in a derogatory way □ *I hate the way he's always flashing his money about.*

⑥① flash back (to)
return to an earlier point in time, especially during a film, story, etc □ *Just before she died, we flashed back to the beginning of the film, to the time when she was a child.* **N** □ *The whole story was arranged as a series of flashbacks.*

⑤ flesh out
give something more content, body or support □ *The government's second defence document, due out this weekend, will flesh out its case for independence.*

② flick through
look at a book, magazine, newspaper, etc, while quickly turning the pages □ *He flicked through the paper looking for the sports page.*

② flinch from
try to avoid something painful or unpleasant □ *She flinched from telling her husband that she'd smashed their new car up.*

---

① = ●●   ② = ●●○   ③ = ●○●   ④ = ●○●○   ⑤ = ●○● *or* ●●○   ⑥ = ●●●○   ⑦ = ●○●●○

①② flood in/ into

arrive somewhere in great quantities, especially of letters, telephone calls, complaints, etc ❐ *Applications flooded into the office in response to the advertisement.*

⑤ flood out

force somebody to leave their home, place of work, etc, because of floods ❐ *All of the families in the valley were flooded out when the river broke its banks.*

⑦⑥ flush out (of)

force somebody, especially a criminal, to leave or emerge from a hiding place ❐ *Police flushed the four men out of the bank with the help of smoke bombs.* ❐ *One of the men in this photograph is a spy, and it's your job to flush him out.*

② fly at

suddenly attack somebody, either physically or verbally ❐ *I've never seen her fly at him like that before. She must have been very annoyed.*

⑦③ fob off (with)

get somebody to buy, accept or believe something, especially faulty goods, an excuse, a lie, etc ❐ *The salesman tried to fob the old lady off with a packet that was half empty.* ❐ *She refused to be fobbed off with such an absurd explanation.*

⑦ fob off on / onto

get rid of something worthless by selling it ❐ *That shop will try to fob any old rubbish off onto you.*

⑦④ foist (off) on / onto

get somebody to buy, accept or take responsibility for something, especially something damaged, inferior or unpleasant ❐ *She's always trying to foist her unwanted furniture off onto people.*

① fold up

1 bend with pain or laughter ❐ *The goalkeeper folded up when a knee hit him in the stomach.*
2 collapse or fail, especially of a business, project or a person's spirits ❐ *The company folded up when people stopped buying plastic furniture.* ❐ *He completely folded up when his wife left him after twenty years of marriage.*

⑦③ follow through (to)

continue to develop or work on something, especially until it is finished, put into operation, etc
❐ *If you follow the argument through to its logical conclusion, you'll discover that it is absolute nonsense.*
❐ *Once you've started on a project, you should follow it through.*

⑤ follow up

1 investigate something, especially a rumour, story, new piece of information, etc
❐ *The police are now following up new evidence in connection with the case.*
2 pursue, develop or exploit something ❐ *The boss seems to like the idea, so I think you should follow it up.* ❐ *The series of programmes was so successful that it is surprising nobody has followed it up.*
N ❐ *His new book is a follow-up to the last one.*

④ force on / upon

press or compel somebody to accept or buy something
❐ *She didn't really want the money, but her uncle forced it upon her.* ❐ *Don't let the sales assistant force the perfume on you if you don't like it.*

---

① = ●● ② = ●●○ ③ = ●○● ④ = ●○●○ ⑤ = ●○● *or* ●●○ ⑥ = ●●●○ ⑦ = ●○●●○

①⑥② ⑥ **fork out (for)**   *Informal*
pay for something, especially unwillingly ☐ *Do you realise how much I have to*
fork out for a television licence nowadays?

⑤ **foul up**   *Informal*
spoil or ruin something ☐ *Unless you do*
well in the exam, you'll foul up your chances
of getting into university. ☐ *He blames his*
mother for fouling up his marriage.

① **freak out**   *Informal*
behave in an excited, detached or
uncontrolled way ☐ *The girls at the*
front of the crowd freaked out when the
film star held out his hand. ☐ *He enjoys*
freaking out on the dance floor from time
to time.

①③ **freshen up**
have a wash and comb your hair,
etc, especially when feeling tired
and dirty after a journey
☐ *Would you like me to show you the*
bathroom so that you can freshen up be-
fore we eat? ☐ *I'd love a quick shower to*
freshen myself up.

⑦⑤ **fritter away (on)**
spend your time or money on something in a wasteful way
☐ *She frittered away all the money he*
earned on new dresses.

① **frost over**
become covered with frost
☐ *How will you see out of the windscreen*
if it frosts over?

② **frown at / on / upon**
disapprove of something
☐ *A lot of people still frown upon the idea*
of ending a sentence with a preposition.

G, g

①② **gad about/ around**
keep moving from place to place,
especially for fun or pleasure; often
used in a derogatory way ☐ *Our son*
is never at home for more than five minutes
these days. He's always gadding about on
his new motorbike.

② **gain on / upon**
move faster than somebody or
something you are following, chasing, or in competition with, etc
☐ *I couldn't go any faster, even though the*
car behind was gaining on us.
☐ *Many Japanese industries are continu-*
ing to gain upon the rest of the world.

⑤ **gamble away**
lose something, especially money,
by betting, speculation, etc
☐ *His father left him a fortune, but he*
gambled it all away.

② **gamble on**
rely upon something happening;
often used in the negative
☐ *He may accept the invitation, but I*
wouldn't gamble on it.

⑥ ① **gang up (on / against)**
unite in opposition to somebody or
something ☐ *The head of the depart-*
ment is worried that some of his senior
staff are ganging up against him.

④ **gear to**
organize or adapt something so that
it suits a particular purpose ☐ *He*
thinks that university courses should be
more geared to the needs of society.

① = ●●   ② = ●●○   ③ = ●○●   ④ = ●○●○   ⑤ = ●○● *or* ●●○   ⑥ = ●●●○   ⑦ = ●○●●○

①⑤ gear up

prepare somebody or something for an important event ❑ *The major political parties have begun to* gear *themselves* up *for an autumn election.*

①⑥③⑦ gen up (on)

learn or give somebody all the facts about something ❑ *None of us will know how to use the new machine unless you* gen *us* up on *how it works.*

①② get about/ around/ round

1 travel or visit many places ❑ *I suppose that you* get around *quite a lot in your job.*
2 walk or move about after an illness, in old age, etc ❑ *It wasn't until six weeks after the operation that she started to* get about *again.* ❑ *Even at ninety-four she still* gets around.
3 spread or circulate somewhere, especially of news, gossip, etc ❑ *It's surprising how fast the news* got about. ❑ *News* got round *the college quickly.*

①⑥③⑦ get across (to)

communicate with somebody ❑ *It took him a whole hour to* get *the message* across to *the audience.* ❑ *I just can't* get across to *him nowadays. We seem to speak completely different languages.*

① get ahead

progress or succeed ❑ *He told his daughter to choose a career in which there were good opportunities for* getting ahead.

⑥① get ahead (of)

progress or advance more than somebody else, especially by working hard ❑ *By spending every evening in the library, he managed to* get ahead of *the rest of his class.*

① get along

continue on your way after stopping to speak to somebody; usually used to close a conversation ❑ *I must be* getting along *now, I'm afraid. I'm meeting my husband in ten minutes.*

⑥① get along/ on (with)

1 be on friendly terms with somebody ❑ *Apart from the occasional quarrel, we* get along *very well.* ❑ *How's John* getting on with *his new girlfriend?*
2 progress or advance with something ❑ *She was* getting on *wonderfully until they moved her to a new school.* ❑ *How are you* getting on with *the French lessons?*

⑥① get along (without)

continue to live or work, especially in spite of a difficulty, setback or tragedy ❑ *Since he died, she's been learning how to* get along without *him.*

①② get around
see **get about/around/round**

② get around / round

1 to persuade somebody by using flattery
❑ *She's going to see if she can* get round *her boss to give her the afternoon off.*
2 overcome or avoid a problem, obstacle, etc ❑ *There must be some way of* getting round *our money difficulties.*

⑥ get around / round to

manage to find enough time for something, especially after a long delay ❑ *So you finally* got round to *answering my letter!*

② get at

1 reach or gain access to somebody or something ❑ *The cat climbed to the*

top of the tree, and none of us could get at it. ☐ *He's a very busy man, and extremely hard to get at, even on the telephone.*
☐ *After two hours in the library, she finally got at the information she wanted.*

2 suggest or insinuate something
☐ *If I had known what she was getting at, I would have complained to the chairman.*
☐ *What are you getting at?*

3 criticise somebody, especially repeatedly ☐ *He's always getting at me for smoking in the kitchen.*

4 influence or persuade somebody, especially with a bribe or threat
☐ *The witness had obviously been got at. He refused to tell the jury what he had seen.*

① **get away**
1 leave or escape ☐ *It was impossible to get away from the meeting.* ☐ *The thief got away by running into a busy store.*
N ☐ *The bank robbers made a quick getaway.*
2 go on a trip, holiday, etc ☐ *We'd love to get away for a few days, but we're just too busy.*

⑥ **get away with**
1 escape punishment for something
☐ *I wonder how many criminals actually get away with the crimes they commit?*
2 succeed in doing something, especially against expectation; ☐ *We knew he was applying for an extra week's leave, but we never thought he'd get away with it.*
3 receive only a light punishment
☐ *He got away with a fine.*

① **get back**
1 return to the place that you left, especially your home or country
☐ *He leaves school at four o'clock and gets back here by five.* ☐ *I thought you were still in Indonesia. When did you get back?*
2 return to a previously held office or position ☐ *The team will have to*

play much better if they want to get back into the first division.
3 move away, especially when ordered ☐ *The police told the crowd to get back to give the firemen more room.*

⑥ **get back at**
retaliate or take revenge on somebody ☐ *She has promised that she will get back at him for the things he said about her poems.*

⑥ **get back to**
1 return to something ☐ *I wonder if we could get back to the original question of cost.*
2 return to somebody in order to communicate or discuss something
☐ *I'll get straight back to head office and inform them of your decision.*

⑥ ① **get behind (with)**
fail to do or complete something by a particular time ☐ *Try not to get behind with your reading during the first term.*
☐ *If you get too far behind, you'll never be able to pass the exam.*

①② **get by** ¹
pass through or along somewhere, especially with difficulty ☐ *The boxes had been left right in the doorway, so that it was impossible to get by.*

① **get by** ²
manage to do or pass something; just manage to be approved or accepted ☐ *I don't care if I don't do well in the exam. I just want to get by, that's all.*
☐ *Do you think I'll get by without a tie, or will they stop me from entering?*

⑥ ① **get by (on/ with)**
manage to live, survive or continue in spite of difficulty or hardship

□ *How does she* get by on *such a small salary? It's amazing.* □ *We've just enough money to* get by *till pay day.*

① get down ¹

leave the table after a meal, especially of children □ *Can I* get down *now, Mummy?*

⑤ get down ²

1 record a talk, announcement, etc, in writing □ *Why don't you just listen to the lecture instead of trying to* get *every word* down?
2 swallow something, especially with difficulty □ *The meat was so tough that I simply couldn't* get *it* down.

③ get down ³

make somebody feel depressed □ *All this rain every day is really* getting *me* down.

⑥ get down to

start to concentrate on something, especially a job or task □ *It's about time you* got down to *some serious work. The exams are next month.*

⑤ get in ¹

1 ask a doctor, builder, electrician, etc, to come to your home or office □ *We'll have to* get *the doctor* in *if she gets any worse.*
2 buy, collect or harvest something □ *She always* gets *her shopping* in *on Tuesday.* □ *The manager wants me to* get *all the rents* in *before the end of the month.* □ *We want to* get *the hay* in *before the weekend.*
3 manage to do or say something, especially in difficult circumstances □ *I was hoping that I might* get in *an hour's reading before they all arrive.* □ *She talks so much that you can't* get *a word* in.

① get in ²

benefit from being among the first people to do something □ *The shirts are so cheap that they'll all be sold unless you* get in *quickly.*

⑥⑦ get in on

take or cause somebody to take part in something □ *If it means a free holiday, everybody will want to* get in on *it.*

①② get in/ into ¹

1 arrive home; arrive, especially of a train, plane, passenger, etc □ *She usually* gets in *from work at about six o'-clock.* □ *Her flight was delayed and eventually* got into *Gatwick three hours late.*
2 be elected or admitted to a committee, the government, etc □ *The opposition has very little chance* of getting in *at the next election in October.*

①③/②④ get in/ into ²

be admitted or cause somebody to be admitted to a school, college, hospital, etc □ *With such poor examination results, she's very lucky to* get in. □ *We want to* get *him* into *a private hospital.*

②④ get into ¹

1 fasten a piece of clothing after putting it on □ *He'd eaten so much that he couldn't* get into *his trousers.*
2 develop or cause somebody to develop a feeling, mood, habit, etc □ *She suddenly* got into *a temper when I told her that the baby was crying.* □ *Whatever* got you into *the habit of eating with just a fork?*
3 learn or teach somebody how to do something □ *The job is a bit difficult at first, but you'll soon* get into *it.*
4 become or cause somebody to become involved in something, especially an unpleasant situation

---

① = ●●   ② = ●●○   ③ = ●○●   ④ = ●○●○   ⑤ = ●○● *or* ●●○   ⑥ = ●●●○   ⑦ = ●○●●○

☐ *He spent more than he was earning, and soon* got into *debt.*
☐ *Don't expect me to help you if your behaviour* gets you into *trouble.*
5 become or cause somebody to become interested in something
☐ *I found the first chapter a bit slow, but I've really* got into *the book now.*

② get into ²
1 take control of somebody or something's behaviour ☐ *I don't know what* got into *me yesterday! I'm sorry!*
2 interfere or play with something
☐ *Our baby* gets into *everything these days.*

⑥ get in with
become friendly with somebody, especially because you want to help them ☐ *She hopes that by* getting in with *the professor, she'll be given more time for her research.*

① get off ¹
1 leave; start a journey
☐ *We had planned to* get off *early and arrive before lunch.*
2 escape from an accident, especially without serious injury ☐ *You're lucky to* get off *with just a few bruises. The other driver broke his leg!*

①② get off ²
be released from work
☐ *What time do you* get off *tonight?*

①③ get off ³
1 escape or save somebody from punishment ☐ *A good lawyer should be able to* get you off *with just a warning.*
2 be sent, posted, cabled, etc; send something or somebody ☐ *Make sure that these letters* get off *today, will you?*
☐ *I have to* get *the children* off *to school before I can go back to bed.*

②④ get off ⁴
stop or cause somebody to stop discussing or talking about a particular subject ☐ *Let's* get off *the question of who is to blame for these low figures, and think about how we can improve them.*
☐ *It's not easy to* get *a cat-lover* off *the subject of cats.*

⑥⑦ get off with   *Informal*
have or cause somebody to have a sexual relationship with somebody
☐ *If she didn't already have a boyfriend, I might try to* get off with *her.*

① get on
1 become late or have little time left
☐ *Since the time is* getting on, *perhaps we should leave discussion of this new problem until tomorrow's meeting.*
2 become old ☐ *She's* getting on *a bit. She must be at least sixty.*
3 be successful in life or in a career
☐ *Most parents want their children to* get on.
4 manage, fare or perform, especially in a new or difficult situation
☐ *How did you* get on *when your husband's boss came to dinner?* ☐ *I'm afraid that I didn't* get on *very well in the exam.*

⑥① get on (with)
1 see get along/on (with)
2 continue after an interruption or pause ☐ *As soon as the rain stopped, we* got on with *our game of tennis.*
⑥ get on at
criticise, nag or urge somebody to do something ☐ *For the last 6 months she's been* getting on at *me to paint the house.*

⑥ get on for
be almost a certain age, time, price, amount, etc ☐ *It was* getting on for *midnight by the time she arrived.*
☐ *She must be* getting on for *thirty.*

---

① = ●●   ② = ●●○   ③ = ●○●   ④ = ●○●○   ⑤ = ●○● *or* ●●○   ⑥ = ●●●○   ⑦ = ●○●●○

⑥ **get on to**
1 contact somebody
❐ *When the shop refused to refund my money, I got on to my lawyer straightaway.*
2 detect or discover a criminal or criminal activities ❐ *He'd managed to cheat four old ladies of their savings by the time the police got on to him.*
3 proceed to a new topic, activity, etc ❐ *Let us now get on to the main point of today's meeting: the election of a new chairman.*

① **get out** **1**
1 become known, especially of secret information ❐ *Nobody would fly in the aircraft after the news of the design fault got out.*

2 leave your home or office for a while and go somewhere for pleasure ❐ *We like to get out at the weekend and enjoy some fresh air.*

⑤ **get out** **2**
manage to say something, especially with difficulty ❐ *He was so nervous about having to read aloud, that he could hardly get the words out.*

③ **get out** **3**
1 publish or produce something for inspection ❐ *The publishers hope to get the new edition out before Christmas.* ❐ *How long will it take you to get the figures out?*
2 find the answer to a problem, calculation, etc ❐ *It looked like an easy calculation, but it took the child a whole hour to get it out.*

⑦③ **get out (of)**
1 cause somebody to leave or abandon a room, building, job, etc ❐ *You can't get a tenant out if the accommodation is unfurnished.*

2 borrow something from a library
❐ *I wonder if you would get a book out for me if you're going to the library.*

⑥ **get out of** **1**
avoid doing something ❐ *He's always trying to get out of making decisions.*

⑦ **get out of** **2**
1 gain or derive pleasure, profit, satisfaction, etc, from something
❐ *It's a fairly elementary course, so advanced learners won't get much out of it.*
❐ *All we got out of the holiday was an empty bank account!*
2 obtain or extract something from somebody, especially by force of strong persuasion ❐ *Somehow we have to get the information out of him.*
❐ *You could always use blackmail to get the money out of her.*

⑥⑦ **get out of** **3**
abandon or cause somebody to abandon a habit ❐ *I can't get out of the habit of waking up at six o'clock.*
❐ *You'll have to get her out of biting her nails. They look awful.*

② **get over**
1 recover from an illness, shock, bad experience, etc ❐ *It took him six months to get over the heart attack.*
❐ *I don't think she'll **ever** get over the death of her father.* ❐ *It took him a long time to get over Cathy, but he eventually found a new girlfriend.*
2 overcome or deal successfully with a problem, difficulty, etc ❐ *It will be a miracle if the country manages to get over its present financial difficulties.*
3 continue to be surprised or shocked at something; used in the negative ❐ *I just can't get over the way she married again only six weeks after her first husband died.*

① = ●● ② = ●●○ ③ = ●○● ④ = ●○○● ⑤ = ●○● *or* ●●○ ⑥ = ●●●○ ⑦ = ●○○●○

4 cease to be worried or troubled by something ☐ *Do you think that she'll ever get over her shyness?*

⑦③ **get over (to)**
make yourself or something understood by somebody ☐ *If you try to get too many points over in the lecture, you'll only confuse the students.*

③ **get over (with)**
do or finish doing something unpleasant so that you don't have to worry about it any more ☐ *We have to pay the bill at some time, so why not pay it now and get it over with?* ☐ *She'll be happier once she's got her exams over.*

② **get round** [1]
see **get around/round**

①② **get round** [2]
see **get about/around/round**

⑥ **get round to**
see **get around/round to**

①②③④ **get through** [1]
1 pass or be responsible for somebody passing a test, examination, etc ☐ *Just over half the students who took the exam got through.* ☐ *I'm very grateful to John for getting me through my driving test.*
2 be approved or cause something to be approved by a group of officials ☐ *We were pleased to get our application through the committee.*

② **get through** [2]
1 spend or consume something; use something until it is no longer usable ☐ *When he's hungry, he can get through a three-course meal in less than twenty minutes!* ☐ *I wonder how many pairs of shoes you get through in a year.*

2 manage to do or complete something ☐ *How long will it take you to get through the whole book?*

①⑥③⑦ **get through (to)**
1 contact a person by telephone; connect somebody with the person they are telephoning
☐ *I've been ringing all morning, but I can't get through.* ☐ *The operator will get you through if you ask her.* ☐ *What's the number you're trying to get through to!*
2 reach or cause something to reach somebody, especially after a difficult journey ☐ *Not enough food is getting through to the earthquake victims.*
3 make somebody understand something; communicate with somebody ☐ *I can't get through to my son nowadays. He seems to be living in a different world.* ☐ *You'll have to get it through to her that she will fail the examination unless her work improves.*

⑥⑦ **get through to**
reach or cause somebody to reach a particular stage in a competition
☐ *The team did very well to get through to the final round.*

⑥ **get through with**
1 finish a task ☐ *Once I get through with the housework, I'll be free for the afternoon.*
2 finish scolding or attacking somebody ☐ *He'll wish he hadn't tried to cheat me when I get through with him!*

① **get together**
meet informally for a discussion or pleasure ☐ *It's an interesting idea. Why don't we get together and discuss it further?*
N ☐ *Are you going to the Spanish Society's get-together on Tuesday?*

---

①③ get up [1]
rise or cause somebody to rise out of bed, especially in the morning
❒ *I usually get up a bit later on holiday.*

① get up [2]
develop or increase in strength, especially of a wind or storm
❒ *In Singapore you know that it's going to rain if the wind suddenly gets up.*

③ get up [3]
make yourself look unusually smart or attractive, especially for a party, wedding, interview, etc ❒ *She spent hours getting herself up for the dinner party.*
N ❒ *That's an outrageous get-up you're wearing, Sarah!*

⑤ get up [4]
organise something, especially a party, petition, group activity, etc
❒ *We're getting up a coach trip to Scotland and thought you might like to join us.*

⑥ get up to
1 do or get involved in something, especially something naughty or mischievous ❒ *Don't think I don't know what you're getting up to behind that armchair!* ❒ *The things these children get up to!*
2 reach a particular place or standard
❒ *I only got up to the third page, I'm afraid. Your writing is so hard to read.*

⑤ ginger up
make somebody or something more lively or interesting
❒ *The courtesy campaign needs gingering up a bit. People seem to have forgotten it.*

⑤ give away
1 betray somebody or reveal a secret
❒ *He said that unless I shared the money*
with him, he would give me away to the police. ❒ *She assured me that they had enough money, but the holes in her shoes gave her away.* ❒ *I promised never to give her secret away.*
N ❒ *The answer to the question was very obvious. It was a real give-away.*
2 lose or fail to make use of something
❒ *When he lost the fight, he gave away his last chance of regaining the world title.*
3 formally present a bride to her husband at their wedding ceremony
❒ *It's usually the bride's father who gives her away.*

⑦⑤ give in (to) [1]
pass or submit something to somebody, especially something you have written ❒ *Don't forget to give in your homework before you leave the classroom.*

⑥① give in (to) [2]
yield or surrender to somebody or something ❒ *Although the smaller child was obviously losing the fight he refused to give in.* ❒ *I was forced to give in to the opinion of the majority.*

② give off
emit or release something into the air, especially a smell, gas, heat, etc
❒ *That old gas fire doesn't give off much heat. I'm freezing.* ❒ *The market was full of dried fish, giving off the worst smell that you can imagine.*

⑤ give out [1]
1 distribute something ❒ *It shouldn't take more than five minutes to give out the question papers and answer books.*
2 announce or broadcast something
❒ *This morning the headmaster gave out that the school is going to have a new science laboratory.* ❒ *It was given out on the news that there are to be heavier penalties for dangerous driving.*

① give out ²

1 cease to function, especially because of a fault ☐ *You can imagine how concerned I became when I saw one of the plane's engines give out.*

2 come to an end, especially of a supply that has been consumed, used or spent;☐ *The expedition had very few problems, except for the time when the water gave out.*

① give over   *Informal*

stop doing something; usually used in the imperative to express annoyance or irritation. ☐ *Give over, you lot! How can I work when you're so noisy?*

⑦ give over to

1 resign yourself to live in a certain way ☐ *By his early twenties he had given himself over to a life of crime.*

2 transfer the care of a child to somebody ☐ *She was forced to give the girl over to foster parents.*

② give up ¹

1 stop doing something, especially something habitual ☐ *I wish I could give up smoking.* ☐ *She's given up playing tennis since she finished with John.*

2 abandon an attempt, pursuit or other activity, especially as a sign of defeat ☐ *Yorkshire police today gave up their search for the missing Leeds girl.* ☐ *I gave up trying to play the violin when I listened to one of my recordings.*

⑤ give up ²

1 leave or resign from a job, course, profession, etc ☐ *His doctor has advised him to give the job up and find something less strenuous.* ☐ *Why did you decide to give up medicine, Dr Green?*

2 let somebody have something that is yours ☐ *He gave up his seat to* the old lady. ☐ *They were told that unless they gave up their guns, they would all be killed.* ☐ *He's had to give up his house in order to pay his debts.*

3 present a wanted person, especially yourself, to the police, army, etc ☐ *He was frightened of what they would do to him if he gave himself up.*

4 end a relationship with somebody, especially a boyfriend or girlfriend ☐ *She gave up her last boyfriend because he used to drive too fast.*

5 devote time to something ☐ *I'm certainly not prepared to give up all my weekends to cleaning the house.*

6 renounce or abandon an idea, belief, principle, etc ☐ *She said that she wouldn't marry him unless he gave up his religion.*

③ give up ³

1 stop expecting somebody to arrive ☐ *We'd just given her up when the doorbell rang.*

2 stop expecting somebody to recover from an illness, operation, misfortune, etc ☐ *The expression on the doctor's face told her that he had given her husband up.*

① give up ⁴

acknowledge defeat or stop trying ☐ *Will you tell me the answer if I give up?* ☐ *Some of the players had given up and stopped running.*

①② glance off

strike something lightly and be deflected ☐ *Fortunately the stone glanced off the windscreen without shattering it.*

② glance over/ through

look very briefly at a magazine, report, letter, etc ☐ *I won't even have time to glance through the manuscript until next week, I'm afraid.*

① = ●●   ② = ●●○   ③ = ●○●   ④ = ●○●○   ⑤ = ●○● *or* ●●○   ⑥ = ●●●○   ⑦ = ●○●●○

② glory in

obtain great pleasure from something
□ *I hate the way she seems to glory in other people's misfortunes.* □ *We left both parents still glorying in the birth of their baby boy.*

② gloss over

try to hide or ignore a fault, mistake, criticism, etc □ *We are tired of the management's habit of glossing over our complaints instead of giving them proper attention.*

② go about

1 approach or start work on a job, problem, etc □ *It's an easy job if you go about it the right way.* □ *How do you go about getting a passport these days?*
2 perform or keep busy with a task or activity □ *You could see that the illness had affected him from the way he now went about his exercises.*

① go about/ around/ round

circulate or be passed from person to person □ *There's a rumour going about that the price of petrol is going to double by September.* □ *Apparently there's a lot of illness going around at the moment.*

① go about /around /round (with)

spend time regularly with somebody, especially for pleasure □ *How do you like your daughter going around with the son of a millionaire?*

② go after

pursue or try to get somebody or something □ *I went after her to stop her from posting the letter, but it was too late.* □ *She's decided to go after a job she saw in yesterday's newspaper.*

② go against

1 be or act in opposition to something □ *Working on a Sunday would go against his principles.* □ *She went against her parents' expressed wishes by marrying him.* □ *What will happen to him if the court's decision goes against him?*
2 reduce or weaken something, especially a person's chances of doing something □ *This new injury will certainly go against his chances of winning the championship.*

① go ahead

1 permit or encourage somebody to do something □ *Go ahead and buy it if you really like it.*
N □ *They won't start building until they get the go-ahead.*
2 proceed or progress □ *The work on the new airport is going ahead as planned, and so far there have been no major setbacks.*

① go along

proceed or continue to do something □ *The job will be easier if you clean up as you go along.*

⑥ ① go along (with)

accompany somebody □ *They want me to go along with them to see the manager.*

⑥ go along with

be or act in agreement with somebody or something □ *I knew that she would never go along with sending the child to a boarding school.*
□ *There are several points in the report that I can't go along with, I'm afraid.*

① go around

see **go about/around/round**

⑥ ① go around (with)

see **go about/around/round (with)**

② go at
1 attack someone or something fiercely ❐ *The two women went at each other like wild cats.*
2 do something with great energy or effort ❐ *With only an afternoon to complete the job, they really went at it.*

①⑥② go back (to)
be known to have existed since a certain time in the past ❐ *The custom goes back to my great-grandfather's generation.*

⑥ go back on
fail to keep a promise or change your mind about something you said before ❐ *He never goes back on his word.* ❐ *You seem to be going back on what you said earlier about the importance of discipline.*

⑥ go back to
resume an old habit, especially a bad one ❐ *It's a pity he's gone back to smoking again.*

① go by ¹
pass or elapse, especially of time or an opportunity ❐ *Several years went by before they met again, this time in Poland.* ❐ *You'd be silly to let this chance of improving your qualifications go by.*

② go by ²
1 form a judgement on the basis of something ❐ *Going by the way she speaks, she must have had a good education.*
2 be guided by something ❐ *Don't go by my watch. It's slow.*

① go down
1 sink to the bottom of the sea, especially of a ship ❐ *The ship went down so quickly that it is surprising that anyone survived.*
2 disappear beneath the horizon ❐ *It's surprising how cold it gets when the sun goes down.*
3 be swallowed or digested, especially of food ❐ *Most meals go down more easily with a glass of wine.*
4 be reduced, especially of prices, etc ❐ *If the society could attract more members, the fees might go down.*
5 fall to the ground ❐ *She tripped over the carpet and went down with a crash.*
6 decrease in size, level, pressure, etc ❐ *I'm glad that your temperature has gone down.* ❐ *One of my tyres keeps going down.*
7 decrease in value or quality ❐ *The value of the property went down the day they started to build a factory opposite it.* ❐ *The service in this restaurant has gone down a lot since it opened last year.*
8 become less violent ❐ *You'd better hold onto your hat until the wind goes down a bit.*

⑥ ① go down (in)
1 be recorded in writing ❐ *Every word I said went down in the officer's notebook.* ❐ *He'll go down in history as one of the cleverest men ever to enter Parliament.*
2 fail an examination paper ❐ *She passed physics but went down in chemistry.*

①⑥② go down (with)
be received or well received by somebody ❐ *Your joke about unemployment didn't go down with the Prime Minister, I'm afraid.* ❐ *I thought that his speech went down very well.* ❐ *The idea of shorter working hours went down badly with the boss.*

⑥ go down to
1 be defeated by someone, especially in a sports competition ❐ *I wouldn't mind going down to a good team, but losing to that lot is disgraceful!*

2 reach as far as a certain date or period in history ❐ *This book only goes down to the eighteenth century.*

⑥ go down with
become ill with something ❐ *Their youngest child has gone down with measles.*

② go for
1 go to fetch or get somebody or something ❐ *He's just this minute gone for a newspaper.*
2 attack somebody either physically or verbally ❐ *The dog went for me as I opened the gate.* ❐ *She'll go for you if she thinks you're criticising her.*
3 be sold for a certain amount of money ❐ *The flat went for over £60,000 eventually, although it took a long time to find a buyer.*
4 be attracted by somebody or something ❐ *She tends to go for tall men with beards.*
5 be applicable to somebody or something ❐ *You'll be in trouble if you don't get to school on time, Jenkins! And that goes for the rest of you, too!*
6 aim to get, win, or do something ❐ *The team are so confident this year that they are going for the championship and have said so.*

① go in
1 be hidden by cloud, of the sun, moon, etc ❐ *It's colder now that the sun has gone in.*
2 be understood or remembered ❐ *I keep telling him what he should do, but none of it seems to go in.*

⑥ go in for
1 enter an examination, competition, etc ❐ *Her teacher recommended her to go in for the Lower Cambridge Examination.*
2 make something your career, hobby, sport, etc ❐ *I don't know why he chose to go in for architecture.*
3 do something regularly for enjoyment ❐ *Our neighbours go in for large dinner parties, but we don't.*

② go into
1 examine, consider or investigate something carefully ❐ *The report should be gone into very thoroughly before you reach a decision.* ❐ *We still need to go into the question of cost.*
2 make a career of something ❐ *They want their son to go into medicine.* ❐ *He decided to go into the navy.*
3 enter a particular mental or physical condition ❐ *When we saw the egg run down his face, we all went into shrieks of laughter.* ❐ *The doctors are worried that she may go into a coma.*
4 divide a number mathematically ❐ *How many times does 6 go into 72?*

① go off ¹
1 explode, be fired or make a loud noise ❐ *Another car bomb went off today in London, killing six people.* ❐ *I nearly fell out of bed when the alarm went off this morning.*
2 go bad, especially of food and drink ❐ *This milk smells a bit strange. It must have gone off in the heat.*
3 deteriorate or become worse in quality ❐ *Local craftsmanship has gone off a lot since tourists started coming here.*
4 cease to operate or be available ❐ *The lights go off at midnight and come on again at eight.* ❐ *What's happened? The water has suddenly gone off!*
5 become less intense or no longer felt ❐ *Has your headache gone off yet?*
6 fall asleep ❐ *I can't hear the baby any more. He must have gone off.*

---

① = ●●   ② = ●●○   ③ = ●○●   ④ = ●○○●   ⑤ = ●○● *or* ●●○   ⑥ = ●●●○   ⑦ = ●○○●○

② **go off** [2]

stop liking somebody or something

❑ *I went off motor racing the day I saw a driver get killed.*

②① **go off** [3]

happen in a particular way

❑ *The rehearsal went off very well.*

⑥ **go off with**

1 leave your home, husband, parents, etc, to be with or marry somebody

❑ *She went off with her friend's husband.*

2 take something without permission and leave with it ❑ *Our first gardener went off with just about all of Henry's tools.*

① **go on** [1]

1 happen or take place ❑ *It sounds as if there was an argument going on upstairs.*

N ❑ *Did you hear about the strange go-ings-on up at the farm last night? They think they've got a ghost.*

2 be in operation, especially of lights, heating, etc ❑ *A lot of drivers would like the lights on the motorway to go on much earlier.*

3 pass, especially of time ❑ *She became more relaxed as the evening went on.*

4 behave, especially in an unusual or outrageous way ❑ *If they keep going on like that, they'll be asked to leave the restaurant.*

5 continue along a route or road, etc, ahead of the other people you are travelling with ❑ *You two go on, and we'll catch you up after we've had a little rest.*

6 continue speaking, especially after a pause ❑ *If there are no objections, I'll go on.* ❑ *'The next item on the agenda,' he went on, 'is housing.'*

7 continue, especially for an excessive length of time ❑ *How much longer is this ridiculous play going to go on?*

② **go on** [2]

1 continue doing something; usually followed by *-ing* ❑ *You can't go on working all night without a rest.*

2 proceed to do, say or become something ❑ *Although they only just managed to qualify, they went on to win the competition.*

3 be spent on something ❑ *Most of his salary goes on food for the family.*

4 be guided or influenced by something ❑ *The jury shouldn't go on the evidence of a known criminal.*

⑥ ① **go on (about)**

talk a lot about something, especially in a boring way ❑ *I'm tired of the way she's always going on about cat diseases.* ❑ *That awful woman does go on!*

⑥ ① **go on (at)**

keep complaining in an angry way about something ❑ *She's always going on at me about the money I spend on cigarettes.*

⑥ ① **go on (with)**

resume or continue doing something

❑ *If we don't finish the painting today, we can always go on with it tomorrow.*

⑥ **go on for**

be almost a certain age, time, price, etc ❑ *It's going on for ten o'clock. It's time we left.*

⑥ **go on to**

change to a new system or scale

❑ *The company has gone on to a three-day week.* ❑ *It's many years since we went on to the metric system.*

① **go out**

1 stop burning or giving light ❑ *He put some more wood on the fire to stop it going out.* ❑ *The lights on the island always go out at midnight.*

---

① = ●●   ② = ●●○   ③ = ●○●   ④ = ●○●○   ⑤ = ●○● *or* ●●○   ⑥ = ●●●○   ⑦ = ●○●○○

2 leave your home and go somewhere, especially for entertainment ❐ *His wife complains that they never go out.*

3 become obsolete or unfashionable ❐ *That type of design went out five or six years ago.*

4 be sent, announced or broadcast ❐ *Have all the invitations gone out?* ❐ *The first programme in the new series goes out on Thursday.*

5 be eliminated from a competition by being beaten ❐ *The London team went out in the first round last night, losing 2-0 to Ipswich.*

6 reach a lower level, especially of the sea or tide ❐ *Once the tide goes out, the children can go and play on the beach.*

7 begin a strike ❐ *The men at the car factory are going out from tomorrow.*

⑥ ① **go out (to)**
go overseas or emigrate to another country ❐ *She's going out to Australia to see her daughter.*

⑥ ① **go out (with)**
be regularly in the company of a boyfriend or girlfriend ❐ *Jim went out with Rachel for only six weeks.*

② **go over**
1 examine or check something ❐ *I went over the figures three times, but always reached the same total.*

2 repeat something, especially an explanation, details, etc ❐ *Could you go over what you have said, for the sake of the people who have just arrived?*

3 search somebody or something ❐ *They spent thirty minutes going over me at the customs, but forgot to look under my hat.*

4 inspect a property when deciding whether to buy it ❐ *After going over the house very carefully, I realised that it would require a lot of repair work.*

5 clean, service or repair something ❐ *I need somebody reliable to go over the car.*

N ❐ *She gave the room a good going-over.*

6 review or rehearse something ❐ *The gang went over the robbery a dozen times, until each member knew exactly what he had to do.*

7 be received by somebody ❐ *Considering the bad news it contained, his speech went over surprisingly well.*

⑥ **go over to**
change your allegiance or preference to something else ❐ *Why don't you go over to margarine? It's cheaper than butter and better for you.* ❐ *After all these years, he's suddenly gone over to the Worker's Party.*

①② **go round** ¹
be sufficient for everybody ❐ *Is the cake big enough to go round?*

① **go round** ²
see go about/around/round

⑥ ① **go round (with)**
see go about/ around/ round (with)

① **go through** ¹
1 be officially approved or accepted ❐ *We were rather relieved to hear that the application had gone through.*

2 be successfully completed ❐ *Why didn't the deal go through? I thought they were ready to sign.*

② **go through** ²
1 use, spend or consume something ❐ *You'll soon go through your savings if you start gambling.*

2 search or examine something, especially to find something that may have been hidden ❐ *I must look guilty. They always stop me at the customs and go through my bags.*

---

① = ●● ② = ●●○ ③ = ●○● ④ = ●○○● ⑤ = ●○● *or* ●●○ ⑥ = ●●●○ ⑦ = ●○●●○

3 suffer or endure something ◻ *The poor girl has gone through a lot of pain in the last twelve months.*
4 review or discuss something
◻ *Shall we quickly go through the major points again?*
5 rehearse something
◻ *Let's go through that scene again.*

⑥ **go through to**
reach a particular stage in a competition ◻ *I'm sure our team will go through to the next round.*

⑥ **go through with**
finish doing something you have already started, or do something that you have planned or promised to do
◻ *Once all the arrangements had been made, he felt that he had to go through with the marriage.*

② **go to**
be given or awarded to somebody or something ◻ *The first prize goes to Jennifer Smith.* ◻ *All her money went to charity after her death.*

① **go together**
1 be regularly in the company of somebody, especially a boyfriend or girlfriend ◻ *How long have Peter and Mary been going together?*
2 be a suitable combination ◻ *Do you really think ice cream and onions go together?*
3 be commonly found together
◻ *People say that money and happiness don't always go together.*

① **go under**
1 sink, dive or be drawn beneath the surface of ◻ *Those who had been rescued watched their ship go under.*

2 fail or collapse, especially of a business ◻ *We're bound to go under unless we can widen our range of products.*

⑥ ① **go under (to)**
be defeated or overcome by somebody or something ◻ *A lot of small businesses went under when supermarkets were introduced.*

① **go up 1**
rise or increase, especially of prices
◻ *I see that the price of petrol has gone up again.*
2 be built ◻ *Another new factory is going up where we live.*
3 be destroyed by an explosion or by fire ◻ *If you had lit a match, the whole kitchen could have gone up.*

② **go with**
1 be included as part of something
◻ *Do the carpets and curtains go with the house?*
2 match or suit something ◻ *Does this blue hat go with my coat?*
3 be regularly in the company of somebody, especially a boyfriend or girlfriend ◻ *I didn't know that John was going with your sister.*

①② **go without**
not have or manage without something ◻ *He often goes without his dinner so that he can get more work done.* ◻ *If you don't want your fish and chips, you'll have to go without.*

④ **goad into**
provoke somebody to do something by harassing them. ◻ *He didn't really want to apply for the job. His mother goaded him into it.*

① = ●●　② = ●●○　③ = ●○●　④ = ●○○●　⑤ = ●○● *or* ●●○　⑥ = ●●●●　⑦ = ●○●●○

③ **goad on**
incite or entice somebody, especially to do something mischievous, illegal, etc ❐ *He would never have stolen the car if he hadn't been goaded on.*

⑥ ① **grind away (at)**
work laboriously at something
❐ *You're not still grinding away at that essay, are you?*

⑤ **grind down** ¹
gradually destroy the vitality or resistance of somebody ❐ *All this work is going to grind you down if you don't get somebody to help you.*

① **grind down** ²
slow down gradually and come to a halt ❐ *Everything grinds down towards the end of term.*

① **grind on**
move forwards relentlessly ❐ *The enemy tanks ground on through the night.*

② **grow on**
become more attractive or appealing to somebody ❐ *I didn't like this piece of music at first, but it's slowly growing on me.*

⑥ **grow out of**
become too old or too big for something; especially of children ❐ *She's grown out of all the clothes she wore last summer.* ❐ *Most kids are afraid of the dark, but they grow out of it sooner or later.*

① **grow up**
1 get older; become an adult ❐ *He's beginning to look more like his father as he grows up.*
N ❐ *Andrew prefers the company of grown-ups to children.*

2 behave, think or talk sensibly ❐ *I wish you would grow up and stop acting like a child!*

3 arise or originate, of customs, traditions, etc ❐ *The custom is believed to have grown up in India.*

② **guard against**
take precautions to avoid something
❐ *We must always try to guard against bringing innocent people to trial.*

⑤ **gun down**
shoot somebody, especially in a cowardly way ❐ *The group's latest victim was gunned down as he was getting into his car.*

② **gun for**
seek to attack or take revenge on somebody ❐ *He's bound to be gunning for you after the awful things you wrote about his last book.*

H, h

⑥ ① hammer away (at)

1 work hard at a task or on a problem ⬚ *Just keep hammering away and you'll soon have the answer.*

2 attack somebody with questions, criticism, arguments, etc ⬚ *Our lawyer hammered away at the witness for at least an hour, but she wouldn't change a single detail.*

3 to force a fact, idea, opinion, etc, upon somebody by constantly repeating it ⬚ *I hammered away at the point all night but nobody took any notice.*

⑤ hammer in

teach somebody something by emphasising it or repeating it many times ⬚ *The message I'm trying to hammer in is that you'll never lose weight if you keep eating so many biscuits.*

⑤ hammer out

1 remove or tackle a problem, difficulty, etc, through serious discussion ⬚ *Sooner or later we shall have to sit down and start hammering out the objections that have been raised.*

2 produce a solution, policy, agreement, etc, as a result of concentrated or serious discussion ⬚ *The point of the meeting is to hammer out ways of saving the college from closure.*

⑦ ⑤ hand back (to)

1 return or restore something to somebody, especially to its owner ⬚ *The islands were handed back just two years after the war.*

2 return a radio or television audience, etc, to a previous speaker or presenter ⬚ *Well, that's all we have time for today from the Chelsea Flower Show. I'll now hand you back to Peter Barker in the studio.*

⑤ hand down / on

pass something from one person or generation to a younger one ⬚ *Why throw away the baby's clothes when you can hand them down? ⬚ Their religious customs have been handed down since time began.*

⑤ hand in

present or submit something, especially something written, completed or no longer required

⬚ *Don't forget to hand in your answer sheets before you leave. ⬚ Why has he handed in his resignation if he doesn't feel responsible?*

⑦ ⑤ hand on (to)

1 pass something, especially something that you have no further use for, to somebody ⬚ *Once you've read the book, perhaps you would like to hand it on to Richard.*

2 see **hand down/ on**

⑤ hand out

1 distribute something, especially printed sheets of paper ⬚ *At the beginning he would always hand out an outline of the lecture.*

N ⬚ *Some of the handouts were unreadable.*

2 give food, clothing, money, etc, to people in need ⬚ *The government has been handing out free milk to families on a low income.*

N ⬚ *He's much too proud to accept handouts from the government.*

3 offer, give or allocate criticism, work, punishment, etc ⬚ *That man is always handing out unwanted advice.*

① = ●● ② = ●●○ ③ = ●○● ④ = ●○●○ ⑤ = ●○● *or* ●●○ ⑥ = ●●●○ ⑦ = ●○●●○

⑤ hand over [1]
give or pass something or somebody to another person ☐ *She refused to hand over the car keys until he promised to wear his safety belt.* ☐ *The thief was handed over to the police.*

⑤① hand over [2]
transfer power, control, responsibility, etc ☐ *He wants to handover all his responsibilities and retire as soon as we can find a replacement.*
N ☐ *The outgoing president has suggested July as a suitable month for the hand-over.*

①② hang about / around
wait or spend time somewhere, especially doing nothing ☐ *The last guests hung about till the early hours of the morning.* ☐ *Since he lost his job, he just hangs around the house all day.*

⑥ ① hang back (from)
be slow or reluctant to do something, especially because of shyness, fear, etc ☐ *It's only her modesty that's making her hang back from showing you her examination results.*

① hang on   1 *Informal*
remain, stop or wait ☐ *Why don't you hang on here while I go and fetch the others.* ☐ *Hang on! Isn't the restaurant closed on a Sunday?*
2 continue to do something ☐ *Despite his head injury, the goalkeeper was able to hang on until the end of the match.*

② hang on / upon
depend upon or be conditional upon something ☐ *We want to move as soon as we can, but everything hangs on whether we can sell our flat.*

⑥ hang on to
keep or retain something, especially instead of selling it or giving it away ☐ *If I were you, I'd hang on to that old chair. It might be valuable.*

① hang out   *Informal*
live or spend a lot of time in a place ☐ *Until he found a job, he spent most of the day hanging out in coffee bars.*
N ☐ *If he's not at home, he'll be at his favourite hang-out.*

⑥ ① hang out (for)
resist, especially by refusing to return to work, in the hope of obtaining something ☐ *The steel workers are still hanging out for more money.*

① hang together
1 remain united or in support of one another ☐ *Unless the party hangs together, we're going to lose the next election.*
2 be consistent, especially of two or more statements ☐ *Although some of the observations are very interesting, the whole thing doesn't really hang together as a book.*

⑥ ① hang up (on)
abruptly end a telephone conversation with someone by replacing the receiver ☐ *As soon as I said that I wouldn't be home until late, she hung up on me.*

② hang upon
    see hang on/upon

② hanker after / for
have a strong wish, urge or yearning for something
☐ *She's been hankering after a trip to the States for the last six years.*

① = ●●   ② = ●●○   ③ = ●○●   ④ = ●○●○   ⑤ = ●○● *or* ●●○   ⑥ = ●●●○   ⑦ = ●○●●○

② happen on/ upon

find or meet somebody or something by chance ☐ *If you should happen upon her address, perhaps you would let me have it.*

⑥ ① hark back (to)

recall or refer to something said or done earlier ☐ *His grandfather loved to hark back to the good old days, when cigarettes were cheap.*
☐ *Harking back to your first question, it is my firm belief that the safety of the drug has still to be demonstrated.*

⑥ ① harp on (about)

mention or criticise something repeatedly, usually with the effect of annoying somebody ☐ *My mother is always harping on about my hair being untidy.*

③ have around/in/over/round

invite somebody to your home for a drink, meal, social visit, etc ☐ *Since it's John's birthday on Friday, we thought we'd have a few friends round for the evening.*

⑤ have back ¹

have something returned to your possession ☐ *He's had your camera for nearly six weeks now. Don't you think it's about time you had it back?*

③ have back ²

allow a marriage partner, boyfriend, etc, to return to you after a period of desertion ☐ *Surely she won't have him back after all the suffering he has caused her?*

③ have in   1

have or arrange to have a doctor, builder, etc, at your home

☐ *We've had the painters in all week, but they don't seem to have done very much.*
2 see **have around/ in/over/round**.

③ have on ¹

1 have an engagement, appointment, meeting, etc; often used in the negative or as part of a question ☐ *How about a drink tonight, or do you have something on?*
2 *Informal* try to make a person believe something untrue or fantastic, usually for fun ☐ *He told me that the quickest way to learn a language was to eat the pages of a dictionary. Do you think he was having me on?*

⑤ have on ²

be wearing something ☐ *Naturally, he had his best suit on for his daughter's wedding.* ☐ *His wife had on one of the most ridiculous hats you've ever seen!*

④ have on ³

1 have evidence against or information about somebody; usually used in the negative or as part of a question ☐ *How can we send them to prison if we don't have anything on them?*
2 be inferior or superior to something
☐ *All these modern clothes have nothing on the old styles, in my opinion.*

③ have out

have something removed or extracted by a surgeon or dentist
☐ *Both children have had their tonsils out.* ☐ *Poor old Tom is having two teeth out this afternoon.*

⑦ ③ have out (with)

discuss with somebody something which has been causing disagreement or bad feeling, especially in a direct and often angry way ❑ *If you think that he's been paying you too little, why don't you* have it out *with him?*

③ have over / round
see have around/in/over/round

⑦ ③ have up (for)
bring somebody to court for an offence ❑ *That's the second time he's been* had up for *drunken driving.*

② head for
1 go in the direction of somewhere or something ❑ *The last time we saw them, they were* heading for *the swimming pool.*
2 act in a way likely to cause disaster, ruin, defeat, etc; often used as part of a warning ❑ *If you refuse to listen to what the doctor tells you, you're* heading for *trouble.*

⑤ head off
1 cause a person or animal to change direction by getting in front of them ❑ *We managed to* head off *half the herd, but the rest continued straight into the river and drowned.*
2 prevent or avoid something unpleasant ❑ *She was very good at* heading off *embarrassing questions.*

② hear from
receive a letter, telephone call, etc, from somebody ❑ *I haven't* heard from *Andrew for weeks. I hope he's all right.*

② hear of
1 become aware of the existence of somebody or something ❑ *Have you ever* heard of *a little town called Pingy Pongy?*
2 receive news or reports of something ❑ *Every day we* heard of *more lives being lost by both sides in the war.*

3 allow something to happen or be suggested; usually used in the negative as part of a strong refusal ❑ *'Won't you let me pay for the meal this time?' 'Certainly not! I wouldn't* hear of *it!'*

③ hear out
listen to the whole of an apology, suggestion, statement, etc ❑ *The judge insisted upon* hearing *the witness* out.

⑦ help off with
assist somebody to remove something they are wearing ❑ *I* helped *him* off with *his boots and then made a cup of tea.*

⑦ help on with
assist somebody to put on clothes, shoes, etc ❑ *Let me* help you on with *your jacket.*

⑤① help out
assist somebody to overcome a problem or difficult situation ❑ *The neighbours were good enough to* help us out *by watering the plants while we were away.* ❑ *She's always willing to* help out *in an emergency.*

④ help to
serve somebody or yourself with food ❑ *Can I* help anybody to *more potatoes?*

⑤ hem in
restrict the movement or freedom of somebody or something ❑ *She felt that marriage was* hemming *her* in.

② hinge on/ upon
depend or be conditional upon something ❑ *The outcome of the debate* hinges upon *which way the chairman decides to vote.*

② hit on / upon

have a new idea or discover something suddenly and unexpectedly ❏ *While making a list of his students' mistakes, he hit upon the idea of bringing them all together in a book.*

⑥ ① hit out (at/against)

criticise somebody or something in a wild or violent manner ❏ *The speaker hit out at the Government for its handling of the crisis.*

⑤ hive off   *Informal*

transfer part of a task, operation, firm, etc ❏ *The government wants to hive off parts of the nationalised industries to make different companies.*

④ hold against

consider something, especially a past crime, misdeed, etc, as being to somebody's discredit ❏ *I know that you spent a year in prison, but I won't hold it against you as long as you behave yourself while you are working for me.*

⑤ hold back

1 refuse or be slow to provide something that is wanted by somebody ❏ *I don't understand why he is holding back the examination results, especially since the students keep asking for them.*
2 prevent or hinder the progress of somebody or something ❏ *Her lack of qualifications is almost certain to hold her back sooner or later.*

⑥ ① hold back (from)

be slow or reluctant to do something, especially because of shyness, fear, etc ❏ *Two of the horses immediately came over to us, but the third held back, more cautious than his compan-*

ions. ❏ *I held back from answering the letter for as long as I could.*

⑤ hold down

1 prevent a price, figure, level, etc, from rising ❏ *I won't be able to hold down my expenses once I have to start using the car.*
2 force somebody to live with reduced freedom ❏ *The faces of the men and women showed that they had been held down by a dictatorship for long enough.*

⑥ ① hold forth (on)

speak on a subject at length or in public; often used in a derogatory way ❏ *If that ridiculous woman starts holding forth on the dangers of stamp collecting, I'm going home.*

⑤ hold in

repress the expression of an emotion ❏ *She did her best to hide her excitement, but eventually she just couldn't hold it in.*

① hold off [1]

1 not arrive, fall or occur, especially of bad weather ❏ *You were lucky that the rain held off for your tennis match.*
2 refrain from doing something, especially attacking ❏ *Our men held off for the length of the cease-fire.*

⑤ hold off [2]

resist an attack or advance ❏ *She always carries a big stick for holding off dogs.*

① hold on

1 wait or stop; often used in the imperative ❏ *If you hold on a minute, I'll come with you.* ❏ *Hold on! I'd like some of that apple-pie too, you know!*

2 survive, especially in a difficult or dangerous situation ❐ *We won't be able to* hold on *for much longer without fresh supplies of food and medicine.*

⑥ **hold on to**

keep or retain something, especially instead of selling or returning it ❐ *Do you mind if I* hold on to *the book you lent me for another week or so?*

① **hold out**

1 continue to resist
❐ *With just a handful of weapons, we never thought we'd be able to* hold out *for so long.*

2 last or be sufficient ❐ *I'm worried about the water* holding out *during the trip. Do you think that we have enough?*

⑥ ① **hold out (for)**

wait, especially in the hope of a better offer ❐ *What will you do if the owners decide to* hold out for *a better price?*

⑥ ① **hold out (on)**

refuse to offer or provide something somebody needs, especially information ❐ *I swear I'm not* holding out on *you. If I knew where she was, I'd tell you.*

⑤ **hold over**

postpone something, especially a discussion ❐ *In view of the time, the matter of rent increases was* held over *until the next meeting.*

④ **hold to** ¹

make somebody keep their promise
❐ *He said he would do anything for her if she married him, and she's certainly* holding *him* to *it.*

② **hold to** ²

persist in holding an opinion, principle, belief, etc ❐ *I've always* held to *the*

belief that the more people have, the more they want.

⑤ **hold up**

1 obstruct or stop the progress of somebody or something ❐ *Whenever there is an accident on this stretch of the motorway, the traffic is* held up *for hours.*

N ❐ *Without any* hold-ups, *the whole job shouldn't take more than an hour.*

2 seize money or valuables from a bank, post office, security van, etc, by the use of guns ❐ *Four armed men today* held up *a post office in the city centre and escaped with stamps and postal orders to the value of £6000.*

N ❐ *If there's one more* hold-up *at the bank, I'm going to start keeping my money under the bed.*

② **hold with**

approve or be in favour of a principle, fashion, habit, etc; usually used in the negative ❐ *She doesn't* hold with *the present trend in ladies' swimwear. She thinks it vulgar.*

⑥ **home in on**

detect and move towards something, especially a target
❐ *Once one of these new missiles* homes in on *you, you can say goodbye.* ❐ *I don't know how the sales manager finds all these new markets for us to* home in on.

① **horse about/around** *Informal*

play or have fun in a wild or noisy way, especially of young adults ❐ *Will you people stop* horsing around *just for one minute? I'm trying to make a phone call!*

① **hot up** *Informal*

become faster, greater or more in-

---

tense

☐ *Whenever I hear talk of the nuclear arms race* hotting up, *I simply have to stop listening.*

② **hunger after / for**
have a great longing or desire for something

☐ *The child* hungered after *love and affection.*

⑥ **hunt out**
find something by searching

☐ *I'm not sure where I put my old stamp album, but if I manage to* hunt *it* out, *you can have it.*

⑤ **hush up**
prevent something from becoming publicly known or discovered

☐ *I don't care who is to blame. Unless we can* hush *the whole shameful business* up, *we're all finished.*

I, i

①⑤ ice up
become or cause something to become covered with or full of ice ☐ *During the winter months I often cover the windscreen with a newspaper to stop it icing up.*

① idle about/ around
spend time in a lazy way, especially doing no work
☐ *She hates to see people idling around, especially when the shop is full of customers.*

⑤ idle away
spend an amount of time in a lazy, relaxed or wasteful way ☐ *He loves to idle away an hour or two down by the river, ideally with a fishing rod in his hands.*

⑤ ink in
cover or trace something with ink ☐ *Once the drawing was to his satisfaction, he carefully began to ink it in.*

② inquire after / into
see **enquire/ inquire after, enquire/ inquire into**

③ invite around/ over/ round
ask somebody to your home for a drink, meal, social visit, etc ☐ *Why don't we invite your sister over for dinner tomorrow?*

③ invite in
ask somebody to enter your house, room, etc, especially for a short social visit and without any previous arrangement ☐ *She was obviously expecting me to invite her in, but I was too busy.*

③ invite out
ask somebody to meet or accompany you somewhere, especially for entertainment ☐ *The Bakers have invited us out for a meal tonight.*

③ invite over/ round
see **invite around/over/round**

⑤ iron out
solve a problem or remove a difficulty by means of discussion and action ☐ *It's time we ironed out the causes of the disagreement once and for all.*

② itch for
feel an urgent need or desire for something to happen ☐ *She talked so much that within five minutes we were both itching for her to leave.*

---

① = ●● ② = ●●○ ③ = ●○● ④ = ●○●○ ⑤ = ●○● *or* ●●○ ⑥ = ●●●○ ⑦ = ●○●●○

J, j

⑤ jack in   *Informal*

1 resign from a job or abandon a course, project, etc
❐ *If you think that philosophy would be more interesting, why don't you* jack in *history and ask for a transfer?*

2 abandon or give up a bad habit
❐ *I didn't know that you had* jacked in *smoking cigarettes.*

3 stop doing something temporarily
❐ *After six hours of trying to mend the radio, they decided to* jack *it* in *for the night.*

⑤ jack up   *Informal*

raise or increase a price, figure, salary, etc ❐ *In some countries you find that the prices are suddenly* jacked up *if the traders realise that you are a stranger.*

⑤ jam in

block the passage of a vehicle ❐ *That stupid lorry driver has gone and* jammed *us* in.

⑤ jam on

cause something to operate forcibly or suddenly, especially the brakes of a moving vehicle ❐ *Although he* jammed on *his brakes, he still couldn't avoid hitting the dog.*

⑤ jazz up   *Informal*

1 rewrite or play a piece of music in a style associated with jazz ❐ *I don't care if they want to* jazz up *Bach, but I wish they would leave Beethoven alone.*

2 make somebody or something more lively, colourful, exciting, etc
❐ *If you're going to be a pop star, we'll have to* jazz *you* up *a bit. How about some pink trousers?*

② jockey for

1 move about in order to gain an advantageous position, often by pushing or obstructing your competitors ❐ *One of the Canadian runners fell, as the group* jockeyed for *the inside lane.*

2 manoeuvre politically in order to win favour, promotion, etc ❐ *It's amusing to watch members* jockeying for *the Prime Minister's attention prior to a Cabinet reshuffle.*

① jog along / on

continue in a routine way, with little excitement or progress ❐ *He's been* jogging along *in the same job for over twenty years now.*

① join up

become a member of one of the armed forces ❐ *She tried to stop him from* joining up, *since one of her sons had already been killed.*

② juggle with

alter or revise a set of figures, accounts, statistics, etc, especially with the intention of deceiving somebody ❐ *He hoped that by* juggling with *the receipts, he would disguise the size of the firm's profits.*

② jump at

accept an offer, invitation, opportunity, etc, eagerly and without hesitation ❐ *If somebody asked me to go to America,* I'd jump at *the chance.*

② jump on

criticise something or somebody sharply and excitedly ❐ *If the boss is in one of his bad moods, he'll* jump on *you for the slightest thing.* ❐ *Her driving instructor* jumped on *every little mistake, which made her very nervous.*

---

① = ●●   ② = ●●○   ③ = ●○●   ④ = ●○●○   ⑤ = ●○● *or* ●●○   ⑥ = ●●●○   ⑦ = ●○●●○

K, k

① keel over

1 fall to the ground, especially somebody who is ill □ *Tourists who are not used to the heat sometimes keel over if they stay in the sun too long.*
2 overturn or lean to one side, especially of a boat or ship □ *The vessel keeled over after being hit by enemy fire.*

② keep after

1 continue to chase somebody □ *We kept after the stolen car for twenty minutes.*
2 ask or remind somebody repeatedly to do something □ *You'll have to keep after them if you want the work done. They're so lazy!*

② keep at ¹

continue to make an effort, especially in spite of difficulties or tiredness □ *You'll never improve your piano playing unless you keep at it.*

④ keep at ²

persuade or force somebody to continue working, etc □ *Good teachers know how to keep their pupils at a task without using threats or punishments.*

⑦ ⑤ keep back (from)

1 deliberately withhold information □ *We decided to keep the rest of the bad news back from her until she was feeling stronger.*
2 retain or not return something □ *The owner of the boat kept back half their deposit to pay for the damage they had done.*

⑤ keep down

1 prevent or control the increase or spread of something, especially pests, weeds, etc □ *Singapore has been very successful in keeping down the number of its mosquitoes.*
2 restrict the freedom or advancement of a person, group or society □ *She thinks that women have been kept down by men for long enough.*
3 retain or hold food or drink in the stomach □ *She'll just get weaker if she can't keep her food down.*

② keep from ¹

restrain yourself from doing something; usually used in the negative □ *I liked his suit so much that I just couldn't keep from asking him where he had bought it.*

④ keep from ²

1 prevent somebody from doing something □ *I'm not keeping you from your work, am I?* □ *The new information kept us from making a serious mistake.*
2 deliberately not give information about something to somebody □ *I was so excited that I couldn't keep the good news from her any longer.*

⑤ keep in ¹

1 make somebody, especially a child, stay indoors, in school, etc, often as a punishment □ *His mother kept him in until he had finished his homework.*
2 keep control of an emotion, especially anger □ *As I listened to her, it became harder and harder for me to keep in my indignation.*

①③ keep in ²

continue or cause something to continue to burn □ *The fire kept in all night, so the room was still warm in the morning.*

① = ●● ② = ●●○ ③ = ●○● ④ = ●○○● ⑤ = ●○● *or* ●●○ ⑥ = ●●●○ ⑦ = ●○●●○

⑥ keep in with

continue to receive the friendship, favour, sympathy, etc, of somebody ☐ *If you want him to give you a good reference one day, you should try to keep in with him.*

① keep off ¹

not arrive, fall or occur, especially of bad weather ☐ *Fortunately, the rain kept off for most of our holiday.*

②④ keep off ²

1 avoid or cause somebody to avoid a subject, topic, issue, etc ☐ *He embarrasses the government by refusing to keep off the problem of unemployment.*
2 not eat, drink or take something or cause somebody to do this, especially for reasons of health ☐ *The doctor has advised him to keep off alcohol.*

② keep on ¹

1 continue doing something ☐ *Despite the noise of the workmen outside the window, the students kept on writing.*
2 do something repeatedly or regularly; followed by **-ing** ☐ *She kept on writing me letters during the months I was away.*

① keep on ²

1 continue in the same direction, along the same road, etc
☐ *Turn right at the traffic lights and then keep on until you come to a large petrol station.*
2 persist or continue to try despite difficulties ☐ *Although he failed his driving test five times, he kept on and eventually passed.*

③ keep on ³

continue to wear something ☐ *Do policemen really keep their uniforms on in bed?*

⑤ keep on ⁴

1 continue to employ somebody ☐ *The factory can't afford to keep on more than a hundred men after July.*
2 continue to own or rent a house, flat, etc ☐ *Are you going to keep the flat on if your company sends you abroad?*

⑥ keep on at (about)

mention or complain about something repeatedly, especially in an irritating way ☐ *His mother keeps on at him about the length of his hair.*

⑥⑦ keep out of

avoid or prevent somebody from becoming involved in something, especially a conflict ☐ *He's a very quiet sort of person and usually tries to keep out of arguments.*

②④ keep to

1 not wander or not allow somebody to wander from something, especially when travelling or talking ☐ *You'll get to the station more quickly if you keep to the main road.* ☐ *The meeting has to end at four o'clock, so the chairman must keep speakers to the point.*
2 act or cause somebody to act according to a plan, promise, set of rules, etc ☐ *We'll never finish building the boat unless we keep to the instructions.*
3 stay or cause somebody to stay somewhere, especially in bed or indoors ☐ *Illness has kept him to his bed since December.*

③ keep under

1 continue to have control over something, especially a fire, feeling, disease, etc ☐ *They won't be able to keep the flames under once they reach the paint store.*

---

① = ●●　② = ●●○　③ = ●○●　④ = ●○●○　⑤ = ●○● *or* ●●○　⑥ = ●●●○　⑦ = ●○●●○

2 restrict the freedom or advancement of a person, group or society ❏ *The country's prisons are full of men and women who refuse to be* kept under *by a dictator.*

①⑤ **keep up** ¹
remain or maintain something at a high or normal level
❏ *Her husband has started working overtime to* keep *his wages* up. ❏ *You must eat properly to* keep up *your strength.*

① **keep up** ²
continue without change, especially of weather ❏ *You won't be playing much tennis today if this rain* keeps up.

①② **keep up** ³
continue or maintain something without stopping or relaxing ❏ *How long can our forces* keep up *the attack?* ❏ *The stream of questions* kept up *for over an hour.*

② **keep up** ⁴
continue or maintain a course, relationship, tradition, etc.
❏ *Having arrived in Paris, they wished they had* kept up *their French lessons.* ❏ *The two girls* kept up *their friendship by writing to each other.*

⑤ **keep up** ⁵
maintain a property in good condition ❏ *It was a lovely house, but they couldn't afford to* keep *it* up.
N ❏ *The* upkeep *of the garden involved a lot of hard work.*

③ **keep up** ⁶
prevent somebody from going to bed ❏ *She* kept *me* up *half the night, talking about her problems at work.*

⑥ ① **keep up (with)**
maintain the same level, speed, etc, as somebody or something ❏ *Towards the end of the race his legs suddenly tired and he couldn't* keep up. ❏ *Wages haven't* kept up with *price increases over the last twelve months.*

⑥ **keep up with**
be informed about recent events, developments, research, etc, by making an effort to obtain news or read reports ❏ *When I'm abroad, I like to* keep up with *what's happening back home.* ❏ *It's important that a doctor* keeps up with *all the new drugs.*

③ **key up**
prepare somebody, usually yourself, physically or mentally for an important event ❏ *The players are already starting to* key *themselves* up *for next month's big match.*

①② **kick about / around** *Informal*
1 lie or remain in a place, especially of something unwanted or forgotten
❏ *I wonder whose shirt this is?It's been* kicking about *the changing-room for months.*
2 travel somewhere in a casual way without a plan or schedule ❏ *He spent a whole month just* kicking around *the countryside, enjoying the peacefulness and the fresh air.*
3 be alive and active somewhere
❏ *We never dreamt that old Tom would still be* kicking around *after such a serious operation.*

③ **kick around** *Informal*
1 discuss or consider the possibilities of something in a casual or informal way ❏ *We started* kicking *the idea* around *right back in January, but a decision hasn't been made yet.*

---

2 give somebody a lot of orders, especially to display your authority or power ❏ *The people who work for him tend to be kicked around like slaves.*

① kick off ¹
begin, especially of a football match ❏ *The crowd got more and more impatient as they waited for the players to kick off.* **N** ❏ *The first goal came just two minutes after the kick-off.*

①② kick off ² *Informal*
begin or cause something to begin ❏ *I was surprised when they kicked off the interview by asking me about my girlfriend.* **N** ❏ *For a kick-off, we can't afford a new car, and what's more we don't need one.*

⑦ ⑤ kick out (of) *Informal*
make somebody leave a room, school, job, etc, often on account of bad behaviour or work
❏ *He was kicked out of the club because he was so rude to the manager.*

② kick up
make a lot of noise or fuss ❏ *The children kicked up a terrible noise as soon as the teacher left the room.*

① kip down *Informal*
lie down somewhere to sleep ❏ *Do you mind if I kip down on your floor for the night?*

⑦ ⑤ kit out (with)
equip somebody or something with clothes, personal items, etc ❏ *How much will it cost to kit the children out with new school uniforms?*

③ knock about
hit, punch or beat somebody ❏ *Whenever he gets drunk, he starts knocking his wife about.*

⑥ ① knock about (with) *Informal*
have a friendly or sexual relationship with somebody ❏ *I wonder why John and Sandra have stopped knocking about together?*

①② knock about / around *Informal*
1 travel in a casual way without a plan or schedule ❏ *He spent his summer holidays knocking about India.*
2 be active or seen in a place ❏ *You must know Arthur. He's been knocking around for years.*
3 lie or remain in a place ❏ *How much longer are these shoes going to knock about the bedroom before you put them away?*

⑤ knock back ¹
drink something quickly or in great quantities; often used in a humorous way ❏ *He certainly knows how to knock back the whisky!*

③④ knock back ² *Informal*
cost somebody an amount of money, especially a large amount ❏ *That new dress must have knocked her back a few pounds!*

⑤ knock down
1 make somebody or something fall by hitting them, especially of a driver or moving vehicle ❏ *His wife is in hospital after being knocked down by a taxi.*
2 demolish or remove a building or structure ❏ *They're going to knock all these old houses down to make room for a new block of flats.*
3 reduce or make somebody reduce the price of something; often used with an expression of amount ❏ *We managed to knock the price down to five*

---

① = ●●   ② = ●●○   ③ = ●○●   ④ = ●○●○   ⑤ = ●○● *or* ●●○   ⑥ = ●●●○   ⑦ = ●○●●○

pounds. ❏ *Can't you* knock *him* down *a pound or two?*

①② **knock off** ¹ *Informal*
stop work ❏ *What time do you usually* knock off *for lunch?*

⑤④ **knock off** ² *Informal*
deduct an amount from the price of something ❏ *Since we are regular customers, he's agreed to* knock *a few pounds* off *the bill.*

⑤ **knock off** ³ *Informal*
1 steal something ❏ *Of course the television is cheap. It was* knocked off*!*
2 complete something, especially in a hurried way ❏ *Some writers can* knock off *a book in less than three months.*
3 kill somebody ❏ *People are saying that he* knocked *her* off *for her diamonds.*

⑤ **knock out**
1 cause somebody to become unconscious, especially of a blow, drug, alcoholic drink, etc ❏ *All of his last twelve opponents have been* knocked out *within five rounds.* ❏ *If you can't sleep, your doctor can give you something to* knock *you* out.
N ❏ *People expect that the fight tomorrow night will end in a* knock-out.
2 *Informal* shock or amaze somebody ❏ *We were completely* knocked out *by their generosity.* ❏ *The news of the tragedy really* knocked *us* out.

⑦⑤ **knock out (of)**
eliminate a person or team from a competition by defeating them ❏ *United's supporters were disappointed when their side was* knocked out *in the first round.*

⑤ **knock together/ up**
prepare, make or build something, especially in a hurried or unplanned way ❏ *It won't take me more than five minutes to* knock up *a snack.*

⑤ **knock up** ¹
wake and get somebody out of bed, by ringing their doorbell, etc ❏ *If he's already asleep, we'll just have to* knock *him* up.

③ **knock up** ² *Informal*
make somebody, especially yourself, ill or exhausted, usually by working too hard without enough rest ❏ *If you don't take a holiday soon, you're going to* knock *yourself* up.

① **knock up** ³
practise before the beginning of a tennis match, squash match, etc ❏ *The players were given five minutes to* knock up.
N ❏ *Shall we start straight away, or would you like a* knock-up*?*

⑥① **knuckle down (to)**
start to concentrate seriously on your work ❏ *Now that the holidays are over, it's time to* knuckle down *again.*

⑥① **knuckle under (to)**
submit or learn to obey somebody or something ❏ *Some of the new boys are not used to obeying rules, and take a long time to* knuckle under.

L, l

①② lag behind

move or progress more slowly than somebody or something ❑ *The youngest child soon got tired and began to lag behind.* ❑ *We'll continue to lag behind other companies until we invest in new machinery.*

① land up

finish a journey, career, series of actions, etc, in a particular place or position ❑ *Don't forget to leave the motorway at the next junction, or you'll land up in Scotland.* ❑ *After trying six different jobs, he landed up working for his father.*

④ land with

leave somebody with something they don't want ❑ *That husband of hers always manages to land you with the bill!*

⑤ lap up

take in something eagerly, especially praise or entertainment ❑ *She sat there lapping up the compliments, too stupid to realise that they were mostly insincere.* ❑ *His jokes were really funny the audience simply lapped them up.*

① lark about / around

play or behave in a silly way, especially for fun ❑ *If you boys are going to lark about, you'd better go outside!*

⑥ ① lash out (at)

attack somebody physically or verbally ❑ *The youth lashed out with both fists as the police officers tried to arrest him.* ❑ *In his speech this afternoon the President lashed out at the press for the way they have reported recent events.*

⑥ ① lash out (on)

spend money freely, especially on luxuries ❑ *He's decided to lash out on a trip to the States this summer.*

⑥ ① latch on (to)

1 attach yourself to a person or group, especially in an insistent way ❑ *Don't let the vicar's wife latch on to you at the meeting, or you won't get the chance to meet anybody else.*
2 understand something ❑ *These examination papers suggest that very few of the students have latched on to the theoretical issues.*

② laugh at

1 ridicule or make fun of somebody, especially in an unkind way ❑ *You shouldn't laugh at her just because her English isn't very good.*
2 disregard or underestimate the importance, significance, danger, etc, of something ❑ *The government's threat to withdraw its support is certainly not to be laughed at.*

⑤ laugh off

dismiss a danger, threat, mistake, etc, by making a joke of it ❑ *How do some people manage to laugh off their misfortunes?*

② launch into

start a long speech, story, description, etc, especially in an eager way ❑ *At the first opportunity he launched into one of his long stories about life in the tropics.*

⑥ ① launch out (into / on)

begin a new business, career, etc, especially in a daring way ❐ *What made you decide to launch out into journalism?*

⑤ lay aside / by

save money for a future need ❐ *I'm sure that most parents lay by a few pounds for their daughter's wedding.*

⑤ lay down

1 state or declare a rule, law, condition, etc ❐ *These new rules have been laid down for the safety of the club's members.*

2 put bottles of wine, etc, in a store or cellar to mature ❐ *He admitted that, just after the war, he had laid down a dozen bottles of port, especially for this celebration.*

⑤ lay in

provide yourself with a supply of something ❐ *We usually lay in extra coal in case of emergencies.*

② lay into *Informal*

attack somebody physically or verbally ❐ *He's frightened to stay out late in case his mother lays into him again.*

⑤ lay off ¹

dismiss somebody from work, especially temporarily ❐ *Most of us were laid off until the firm received new orders.* **N** ❐ *The men have only just returned after a six-week lay-off, and now they're being laid off again!*

①② lay off ² *Informal*

1 stop eating, drinking or doing something, especially something that is unpleasant or bad for your health ❐ *The doctor advised me to lay off the cigarettes.*

2 stop worrying, harassing or hurting somebody; often used as an imperative ❐ *Just lay off and leave me alone!* ❐ *She can't lay off the poor child for more than five minutes at a time.*

⑤ lay on

supply or organise something ❐ *As soon as the water and electricity are laid on, they'll be able to start using the house.* ❐ *The firm always lays on a special meal for the staff round about Christmas.*

⑤ lay out

1 arrange things neatly or so that they can be clearly seen ❐ *She laid all her new clothes out on the bed.*

2 spend a lot of money on something ❐ *Do you realise how much I have to lay out on their school fees each year?* **N** ❐ *After the initial outlay, we didn't have anything else to pay.*

3 make somebody unconscious by hitting on the head ❐ *It was the last punch on the chin that really laid him out.*

4 prepare a body for burial ❐ *The bodies of the victims had to be laid out before their relatives were asked to identify them.*

5 plan or design something, especially a building ❐ *The ground floor had been laid out very sensibly.* **N** ❐ *I didn't like the lay-out upstairs.*

⑤ lay up

1 store or save something ❐ *We laid up so much fuel for last winter that we haven't had to buy any since.*

2 cause somebody to stay in bed or indoors ❐ *The flu can lay you up for more than a week if you're really unlucky.*

⑥ ① lead in (with)

begin or introduce a speech, performance, show, etc ❐ *He usually*

leads in with a song and then tells a few jokes.
N ☐ *It was such a long lead-in that the speech seemed very short.*

①② lead off
begin a speech, performance, meeting, etc ☐ *The principal led off by welcoming all the new students.*

③ lead on
encourage somebody to believe or do something, especially in an attempt to fool, deceive, or trick them
☐ *If you have no intention of marrying her, you shouldn't keep leading her on.*

⑥ lead up to
1 happen before something, especially of events ☐ *The Prime Minister has demanded an investigation of the incidents that led up to the riots.*
2 approach a topic, request, confession, etc, in a gradual or indirect way ☐ *I don't know what she's leading up to, but I wish that she would hurry up and say it!*

② leaf through
look at a book, magazine, newspaper, etc, while quickly turning the pages ☐ *I leafed through a couple of photography magazines while waiting to see the dentist.*

① leak out
become known, especially of a secret ☐ *Whatever happens, we must make sure that this information doesn't leak out.*

② lean on
1 depend upon somebody for support ☐ *It was a comfort to know that she could always lean on her daughters if the need arose.*

2 *Informal* put pressure on somebody to do something, especially by the use of threats or violence ☐ *If you pay the gang the thousand pounds, they'll only lean on you for more.*

② leap at
accept an offer, invitation, opportunity, etc, eagerly and without any hesitation ☐ *We leapt at the offer of their car for two weeks.*

⑤ leave in
not remove or delete something ☐ *The editor finally agreed to leave the paragraph in.*

⑤ leave off
stop wearing something ☐ *You'll be able to leave off that jacket when the warmer weather arrives.*

①② leave off ²
cease or stop doing something
☐ *The rain hasn't left off all morning.*
☐ *I left off writing to them, because I never got a reply.* ☐ *Leave off and go and annoy somebody else!*

⑤ leave on
let something remain alight, burning or working ☐ *It's expensive to leave the electric fire on all day.*

⑦ ⑤ leave out (of)
fail to include somebody or something ☐ *The headmaster won't like it if we leave his son out of the team.*

③ leave over
delay or postpone something until a later date ☐ *In view of the time, perhaps the discussion of these final points could be left over until our next meeting.*

---

① = ●● ② = ●●○ ③ = ●○● ④ = ●○●○ ⑤ = ●○● *or* ●●○ ⑥ = ●●●○ ⑦ = ●○●●○

④ leave to
pass a task to somebody ❑ *This letter needs answering. Can I* leave *it* to *you?*

⑦ leave up to
give somebody the responsibility for deciding or choosing something ❑ *At some colleges, the amount of work you do is* left *entirely* up to *you.*

④ lend to
have suitable qualities for a particular treatment or adaptation ❑ *The book really* lends *itself* to *film treatment.*

⑤ let down
1 lengthen a piece of clothing ❑ *That coat would still fit you if you got a tailor to* let *it* down.
2 disappoint somebody, especially by breaking a promise, or by failing to do what is expected ❑ *You can trust John. He'll never* let *you* down.
N ❑ *The 'dream holiday' was a complete* let-down.
3 release the air from a tyre, balloon, etc ❑ *I always* let *my tyres* down *a little bit in the warmer weather.*

⑦ let in for
accept or cause somebody to accept responsibility for something, especially for a lot of work, expense, problems, etc ❑ *Do you realise how much work you are* letting *me* in for!

⑤/④ let in / into
allow somebody or something to enter somewhere ❑ *These big windows* let in *a lot of light.* ❑ *They won't* let *you* into *the shop until nine o'clock exactly.*

⑦ let in on
allow somebody to share a secret or take part in something
❑ *The Ministry of Education has agreed to* let *the headmaster and three senior teachers* in on *the discussions.*

④ let into
1 put something into a groove, recess, opening, etc, in a surface ❑ *In order to save space, the back of the boiler had been* let into *the wall.*
2 see let in/into

⑤ let off ¹
1 cause something to fire or explode ❑ *He shouldn't be allowed to* let *fireworks at his age. He's only three!*
2 release or excuse somebody without punishment ❑ *It was the first time that he had done anything wrong, so they* let *him* off.

⑤/④ let off ²
1 allow a passenger to leave a bus, train, ship, etc ❑ *The conductor won't* let *anybody* off *between stops.*
2 excuse from a task, chore, etc ❑ *You're lucky that they* let *you* off *all that washing-up.*

①⑥② let on (about)
reveal something that somebody wants to be kept a secret ❑ *Don't* let on about *the price of the car.* ❑ *One of the children* let on *that they were trying to sell the house.*

② let out ¹
utter a cry, scream, yell, etc ❑ *She* let out *the most terrible scream I'd ever heard.*

⑤ let out ²
1 make a piece of clothing wider, especially round the waist ❑ *I know a tailor who could* let *the trousers* out *for you.*
2 cause something, especially a se-

cret, to become known ❐ *Somebody must have* let *the information* out *without realising the danger involved.*

3 release or escape from an unpleasant or tedious activity, obligation etc ❐ *If neither of us wants to go to the party, we'll have to find an excuse to* let *us* out.

⑦ ⑤ **let out (of)**
release somebody or something from a prison or confined space ❐ *After six years they* let *him* out *for good behaviour.* ❐ *If the tyres are too hard, just* let *some of the air* out.

① **let up**
relax, diminish or stop ❐ *You'll have a heart attack if you don't* let *up a bit.*
N ❐ *It's been pouring all day, without a single* let-up.

④ **level against/at**
direct a charge or accusation towards somebody ❐ *Are you aware of the allegations that have been* levelled against *you?*

④ **level at**
aim a gun, etc, at somebody or something ❐ *He* levelled *the rifle* at *the animal and fired.*

① **level off / out**
stop climbing and stay at the height that has been reached ❐ *Five minutes after take-off, the aircraft* levelled out *at 30,000 feet.*

② **lie behind**
be the reason or explanation for something ❐ *Do you know what* lies behind *her sudden departure for London?*

① **lie in**
stay in bed late ❐ *It's Sunday tomorrow, so you can* lie in.

N *You can have a good* lie-in *in the morning.*

① **lift off**
leave the ground, especially of a plane or rocket ❐ *The rocket is due to* lift off *at noon on Friday.*
N *We've just witnessed another perfect* lift-off.

② **light on / upon**
discover something, especially by chance ❐ *Tell us how you* lit upon *the idea for your invention.*

① **light up**
1 light a cigarette, pipe, etc ❐ *He usually* lights up *immediately after supper.*
2 switch on or be switched on, especially of street or car lighting ❐ *Drivers who forget to* light up *at night often cause accidents.*
3 suddenly display emotion, especially happiness or excitement ❐ *Her eyes* lit up *when I mentioned a holiday.*

④ **liken to**
compare something with something else ❐ *His big hands are usually* likened to *bunches of bananas.*

① **limber up**
do exercises in order to loosen the muscles, especially in preparation for more strenuous activity ❐ *I like to* limber up *for five minutes before a race.*

①⑤ **line up** ¹
arrange people or things in lines, rows or ranks, or cause them to be arranged in this way ❐ *Every morning the prisoners were* lined up *to be counted.* ❐ *He loves to* line *his toy soldiers* up *into rows.*

④ line up 2

form a queue ❐ *People without tickets had been* lining up *all day outside the theatre.*

⑤ line up 3

organize the visit or gathering of a number of entertainers, sportsmen, etc ❐ *The organisers are* lining up *some of the finest musicians in the country for next autumn's concerts.*

N ❐ *There are two new names in the* line-up *today.*

⑥ ① listen in (on / to)

deliberately listen to a private conversation ❐ *It's rude to* listen in *on other people's telephone calls.*

⑥ ① listen in (to)

listen to a radio broadcast ❐ *People used to* listen in *regularly before the days of television.* ❐ *I always try to* listen in *to the news.*

⑤ live down

cause people to forget or ignore your past behaviour, reputation, etc ❐ *Twenty years later, his family are still trying to* live *the scandal* down.

② live for

have somebody or something as your main or only interest in life ❐ *He says that he has nothing to* live for *since his wife died.* ❐ *Both boys just* live for *football.*

① live in

have your home where you work, study, etc ❐ *It's cheaper for most nurses to* live in.

② live off

1 get somebody to provide you with food, shelter, etc ❐ *Since he lost his job, he's been* living off *his parents.*
2 get enough money or what you need to live by doing a particular job or activity ❐ *I don't know how she manages to* live off *her painting.*

① live on 1

survive or endure ❐ *The composer's work will always* live on.

② live on 2

1 support yourself on a certain income ❐ *How do you manage to* live on *such a small salary?*
2 have something as your only food ❐ *For a whole week we had to* live on *fish and chips.*

① live out

have your home away from where you work, study, etc ❐ *Most of the students prefer to* live out.

② live through

survive or endure something, especially a bad experience ❐ *We never dreamt we'd have to* live through *another war.*

① live together

live as husband and wife, but without being legally married ❐ *How long have they been* living together?

⑥ live up to

reach, match or fulfil a particular standard or expectation
❐ *The hotel didn't* live up to *its great reputation.* ❐ *The child found it hard to* live up to *the school's standards of excellence.*

② live with

1 gradually accept or tolerate something unpleasant ❐ *It was very difficult* *when she first lost her hearing, but she has learnt to* live with *it.*

2 live in the same house, etc, with someone, as husband and wife, but without being legally married ☐ *She* lived with *him for a couple of years before they got married.*

①⑤ liven up

become or cause somebody or something to become more lively or cheerful ☐ *We need some music to* liven *the party* up *a bit.* ☐ *When I suggested a walk, she* livened up.

⑦⑤ load down (with)

place a great weight or burden on somebody or something ☐ *The poor car was completely* loaded down *with all my bags.* ☐ *She's always trying to* load me down *with her problems.*

⑤ lock out

prevent workers from entering their place of work, especially of employers ☐ *The men were* locked out *in response to their refusal to operate the new machines.*

N ☐ *The prospect of a* lock-out *may encourage the workers to agree to our terms.*

⑦⑤ lock up (in)

1 put somebody in prison ☐ *He's been* locked up *for receiving stolen goods.*
2 make an investment in something that cannot easily be changed into cash ☐ *All my money has been* locked up *in property for the last ten years.*

② look after

1 take care of somebody or something ☐ *I'll give you the piano as long as you promise to* look after *it.*
2 be responsible for something, especially paying a bill ☐ *The boys'*

grandfather has kindly offered to look after *their school fees.*

① look (a)round

explore something and try to understand what it is like ☐ *I* looked around *for months before I decided which car to buy.*

② look at

1 examine or inspect something ☐ *If your arm isn't better by tomorrow, I'd get the doctor to* look at *it.*
2 consider something ☐ *If your offer is too low, the people selling the house won't even* look at *it.*

① look back

stop making progress; always used in the negative ☐ *Once he had gained a little self-confidence, he never* looked back.
N ☐ *After his first book was published, there was no* looking back.

⑥① look back (on)

think about the past ☐ Looking back, *it's easy to see where we went wrong.*
☐ *She* looked back *on their relationship with feelings of deep regret.*

⑥ look down on

regard somebody or something as inferior or unworthy
☐ *I'm sure that they* look down on *me because I'm married to a greengrocer.*

② look for

try to find somebody or something
☐ *He's decided to* look for *a new job.*
☐ *Why are the police* looking for *you?*

⑥ look forward to

await something eagerly or excitedly ☐ *The children are really* looking forward to *seeing you in October.*

---

① = ●●   ② = ●●○   ③ = ●○●   ④ = ●○●○   ⑤ = ●○● *or* ●●○   ⑥ = ●●●○   ⑦ = ●○●●○

⑥ ① **look in (on)**

pay somebody a short casual visit, especially when this does not require a long journey ❐ *Why don't we look in on John and Sally on the way home?*

② **look into**

investigate something ❐ *The police are looking into the disappearance of a five-month-old baby from its home in South London.*

① **look on**

stand and watch, without taking part ❐ *Do you mean to say that the two policemen just looked on without doing anything to stop the fight?*
N ❐ *A crowd of onlookers gathered to see the film being made.*

② ⑥ **look (out) on / onto**

provide a view of something
❐ *Her bedroom window looks out onto the back garden.*
N ❐ *The room has a very pleasant outlook.*

② **look on / upon (as)**

regard somebody or something in a certain way ❐ *I've always looked upon Mary as somebody I can trust.*

① **look out** ¹

be careful; often used in the imperative ❐ *Look out! There's a car coming!*
❐ *You're going to cut yourself if you don't look out!*

⑤ **look out** ²

search for or choose something
❐ *I'm sure I have a bicycle pump somewhere at home. I'll see if I can look it out for you.* ❐ *I've looked out a couple of books that I thought might interest you.*

⑥ **look out for**

keep watching attentively for somebody or something ❐ *If you're going to be at the party tonight, I'll look out for you.*
❐ *He advised us to look out for snakes if we were going into the jungle.*
N ❐ *Keep a look-out for Robert. We don't want to miss him.*

② **look over** ¹

do a tour of inspection around an office, factory, house, etc ❐ *I always enjoy looking over breweries when I'm on holiday in Germany.*

⑤ **look over** ²

1 examine or scrutinise somebody or something ❐ *The customs officers looked the car over very carefully before they let us go through.*
2 revise or check something, especially something that you have written ❐ *Don't forget to look over your work at the end of the exam.*

② **look through** ¹

1 read or scan something ❐ *I've looked through the newspaper twice, but I still can't find the weather forecast.*
2 ignore or seem to ignore somebody when you look at them ❐ *Ever since we had the argument, she looks straight through me as if I didn't exist.*

③ **look through** ²

examine something carefully, especially a formal written document ❐ *We'll have to look the last two paragraphs through very carefully before we sign the agreement.*

② **look to (for)**

approach somebody or something for help, support, comfort, etc ❐ *She has always looked to her parents for advice.*

---

① = ●●   ② = ●●○   ③ = ●○●   ④ = ●○●○   ⑤ = ●○● *or* ●●○   ⑥ = ●●●○   ⑦ = ●○●●○

⑤ **look up** [1]

1 search for something in a dictionary, encyclopedia or other reference book ❑ *If you don't know how to spell the word, why don't you* look it up*?*
2 visit somebody you have not seen for a long time ❑ *Now that we're in Cambridge, why don't we* look up *my old tutor?*

① **look up** [2]

improve, especially of business
❑ *Business must be* looking up *if he's got two more men working for him.*

② **look upon (as)**
see **look on/upon (as)**

⑥ **look up to**
admire or respect somebody
❑ *He's a born leader. Even at school the other boys* looked up to *him.*

① **loosen up**
do exercises in order to relax the muscles ❑ *I always* loosen up *for five minutes before a match.*

⑥ ① **lose out (on)**
suffer a loss or defeat, especially because of unfairness or bad luck
❑ *You often* lose out *when you bet* on *horse races.*
❑ *How much did we* lose out on *the deal?*

⑥ ① **lose out (to)**
be defeated, replaced or overtaken by somebody or something ❑ *We* lost out *in the election simply because the opposition had more money to run their campaign.* ❑ *Live entertainment is* losing out to *television.*

⑤ **louse up** *Informal*
spoil or disrupt something
❑ *The rescue work had been going very well until a sudden downpour* loused *the whole thing* up*.*

⑤ **lump together**
put two or more things together and treat them as a single item
❑ *Why don't you just* lump *the two bills* together *and pay with one cheque?*

---

① = ●● ② = ●●○ ③ = ●○● ④ = ●○●○ ⑤ = ●○● *or* ●●○ ⑥ = ●●●○ ⑦ = ●○●●○

M, m

② **make after**
chase or pursue somebody or something □ *She suddenly noticed that he had gone out without leaving her any money, and quickly made after him.*

① **make away / off**
leave or escape in a hurry □ *They ran out of the bank and made away in a stolen car.*

⑥ ① **make away / off (with)**
hurry away, especially after stealing something □ *The bank robbers made off with £6,000 in used notes.*

② **make for**
1 move towards something, especially in a determined way □ *As soon as they told me how much they would pay me, I got up and made for the door.*
2 rush towards somebody or something, in order to attack □ *We didn't want to open the garden gate in case their dog made for us.*
3 help cause something to happen or develop □ *Good communications normally make for better understanding.* □ *The drop in house prices made for an increase in the number of people buying their own homes.*

④ **make into**
cause somebody or something to change in some way □ *The headmaster is going to make me into a prefect.* □ *The two houses are being made into flats.*

④ **make of**
form an impression or understanding of somebody or something; often used with *what* and/or in the negative □ *She's a strange girl. I don't quite know what to make of her.*

① **make off**
see **make away / off**

⑥ ① **make off (with)**
see **make away/off (with)**

⑤ **make out ¹**
1 write or complete something, especially a cheque, bill, form, etc □ *The cheque was made out for sixty pounds.* □ *Make out a list and then you won't forget anything.*
2 manage to see, read, or distinguish something; usually used with *can* □ *It got darker and darker until we could no longer make out the names on the sides of the ships.*
3 understand somebody or something; usually used with *can* □ *Can you make out what he is saying? His voice is very low.* □ *Our daughter has changed a lot in the last five years. Nowadays, we just can't make her out.*

② **make out ²**
claim or assert something, especially something that is not true □ *He made out that he had never been married before. Then, one day, his first wife appeared on the doorstep.*

① **make out ³**
manage, survive or progress □ *How's your sister making out now that she's living on her own?*

① = ●● ② = ●●○ ③ = ●○● ④ = ●○●○ ⑤ = ●○● *or* ●●○ ⑥ = ●●●○ ⑦ = ●○●●○

⑦ ⑤ make over (to)
transfer ownership of something to another person, especially by signing a legal document
❒ *What will you do with the house that your father made over to you?*

⑤ make up ¹
1 invent a story, excuse, etc ❒ *Is he telling the truth, or making it all up?*
2 compose a tune, rhyme, etc
❒ *She's very good at making up poems.*
3 prepare something, especially medicine, by putting different things together ❒ *The chemist only took a minute to make up the prescription.* ❒ *If you want to give her something useful, get the shopkeeper to make up a basket of groceries.*
4 recover, repay or replace something that is owed, missing, or lost ❒ *Somehow the company has got to make up all the time we've lost through illness.*
5 make a number, total, amount, etc, complete ❒ *We need just one more player to make up a full team.*
6 add fuel to a fire, boiler, etc ❒ *He always makes the boiler up before he goes to bed.*
7 put sheets, blankets, etc, on a bed
❒ *You're welcome to stay the night. I can easily make a bed up.*
8 prepare a page or book for printing
❒ *Bob's report should have gone on the front page but unfortunately the page had already been made up.*
9 put the surface on a road ❒ *When will the road be made up?*

② make up ²
form or constitute something
❒ *How many countries make up the Common Market?*
N ❒ *The arrival of the new manager has changed the whole make-up of the team.*

①⑤ make up ³
1 put powder, lipstick, etc, on your face ❒ *You only have five minutes to make up before the show begins.*
N ❒ *She's worried that she won't have enough time to put on her make-up.*
2 become friendly again with somebody after a quarrel ❒ *The two boys soon made up once Timothy had been given his ball back.*

⑥ make up for
pay or compensate somebody for something ❒ *All the sunshine this week makes up for the rain we had last week.* ❒ *She's obviously trying to make up for all the trouble she has caused.*

⑥ make up to
try to gain the sympathy, favour, love, etc, of somebody by being very friendly and pleasant ❒ *She started making up to him the day she learnt that he was a millionaire.*

⑤ mark down
reduce the price of something
❒ *I wonder why these dresses have been marked down.*

⑦ mark out for
select somebody for special treatment ❒ *Within a week of joining the firm, James had been marked out for early promotion.*

⑤ mark up
1 decide the price at which to sell something ❒ *If we mark them up at that price, we'll never sell them.*
N ❒ *The mark-up is 100 per cent.*
2 raise the price of something
❒ *Everything in the shop will have to be marked up if the tax is increased.*

① = ●● ② = ●●○ ③ = ●○● ④ = ●○●○ ⑤ = ●○● *or* ●●○ ⑥ = ●●●○ ⑦ = ●○●●●

3 prepare a manuscript for printing ☐ *The manuscript contained so many mistakes that it took longer to mark up than the publisher had expected.*

② **marry above**

marry somebody higher than yourself in social rank ☐ *In spite of our advice, he married above himself.*

② **marry beneath**

marry somebody lower than yourself in social rank ☐ *In order to marry the girl he loved, he had to marry beneath himself.*

② **marry into**

become a member of a family, group, class, etc, by marriage ☐ *Her dream is to marry into the aristocracy.*

⑤ **marry off**

find a marriage partner for somebody, especially for your daughter ☐ *After all these years they have finally managed to marry her off.*

⑥ ① **measure up (to)**

display qualities, skills, etc, of a required standard ☐ *If she doesn't measure up to the job, she'll just have to leave.*

② **meet with**

encounter or experience problems, resistance, opposition, etc ☐ *The work has taken longer than expected because we met with one or two difficulties.*

① **mess about / around** ¹

1 spend time in a lazy way ☐ *Now and again it's lovely to spend the whole day just messing around.*
2 behave in a silly, playful or irritating way ☐ *If you'd stop messing about for five minutes, I might be able to hear what John is saying!*

③ **mess about / around** ²

upset or cause problems for somebody, especially by breaking a promise ☐ *At first they said they definitely wanted to buy our flat, but now they've started messing us about.*

⑥ ① **mess about / around (with)**

1 spend time on a hobby, interest, etc ☐ *Her husband loves messing around with car engines.* ☐ *Susannah would mess around in the kitchen all day if you let her.*
2 interfere with or use without permission something that does not concern or belong to you; have a casual sexual relationship with somebody ☐ *Who's been messing about with my tools? I can't find the hammer.* ☐ *He's been messing around with my wife.*
3 handle something in a clumsy or unskilled way ☐ *Why don't you stop messing about with the radio and take it to a proper repair shop?*

⑤ **mess up**

spoil something or do a job badly ☐ *The weather really messed up our holiday.* ☐ *If she messes it up again this time, I will not ask her to type any more letters for me.* **N** ☐ *He's made a complete mess-up of the arrangements.*

⑤ **miss out**

omit somebody or something, especially by mistake ☐ *Would you like to check the report in case I've missed out anything important?*

⑥ ① **miss out (on)**

fail to experience, profit from or take part in something
☐ *You'll miss out unless you get to the shop on the first morning of the sale.*
☐ *If you don't come to the party, you'll miss out on all the fun!*

① = ●●　② = ●●○　③ = ●○●　④ = ●○●○　⑤ = ●○● *or* ●●○　⑥ = ●●●○　⑦ = ●○●●○

④ **mistake for**

confuse the identity of somebody or something with that of somebody or something else ❐ *She looks so young that people often* mistake *her for her daughter.*

③ **mix up**

make somebody confused about something ❐ *You'll* mix *me* up *if you ask me to do two jobs at once.*

⑦ ⑤ **mix up (with)**

1 confuse the identity of somebody or something with that of somebody or something else ❐ *The two colours are so similar that I* keep mixing *them* up. ❐ *I think that you must be* mixing *me* up with *somebody else.*
2 cause something to be in disorder ❐ *Try not to* mix up *these examination papers* with *the ones that have been marked.*
N ❐ *I'm afraid there's been a bit of a* mix-up with *the tickets.*

⑥ ① **monkey about/around (with)**

play or interfere with something in a mischievous way ❐ *One of you is going to get hurt if you don't stop* monkeying around*.*

③ **mop up**

complete a task by doing the few minor things that remain; remove the few areas or resistance that remain after a major attack ❐ *All our problems are solved, except for* mopping up *the final details.* ❐ *The battle isn't over until the last of the enemy guns has been* mopped up*.*

①⑤ **move in**

transfer your possessions to where you are going to live, or do this for somebody ❐ *Our new neighbours are* moving in *tomorrow.*

⑥ ① **move in (on)**

approach, enter or attack an area when trying to get control of it, especially in business or military occupation ❐ *Our sales team have got two whole months before the competition* moves in*.*

⑥ ① **move on (to)**

1 change, progress or develop to something else, especially over a long period of time ❐ *Medical science has* moved on *a lot since I was a boy.*
2 change the topic of discussion, conversation, etc, to something else ❐ *If nobody has any further questions, perhaps we can* move on to *the next item on the agenda.*

①⑤ **move out**

remove your possessions from where you have been living, or do this for somebody ❐ *They're having to* move out *because they can't afford the rent.*

① **move over / up**

change your position to make room for another person ❐ *Would you mind* moving up *a bit so that I can sit down?*

⑤ **mow down**

murder somebody or kill people in large numbers ❐ *Our troops were* mown down *before they had even reached the bottom of the hill.*

③①⑥ **muck about (with)**

1 upset somebody, especially by changing a decision ❐ *He hates customers who* muck *him* about*.*
2 handle something playfully or in a clumsy way ❐ *Stop* mucking about with *the bananas if you're not going to eat one.*

① **muck about/around**
1 spend time in an aimless or idle way ❒ *If I were you, I'd stop mucking about and look for a job.*
2 behave in a silly, playful or foolish way ❒ *I'll send the pair of you to see the headmaster if you don't stop mucking about.*

⑥ ① **muck in (with)** *Informal*
share a task or activity with other people ❒ *You don't want people to think that you are too proud to muck in, do you?*

⑤ **muck out**
clean a place where animals are kept ❒ *I'm glad it's not my job to muck out the pigsty.*

⑤ **muck up**
spoil something or do a job badly ❒ *The hairdresser has really mucked my hair up this time. He's cut it much too short.* ❒ *Her mother arrived and mucked up the whole weekend.*
N ❒ *He made a complete muck-up of painting the front door.*

① **muddle through**
manage to do or complete something, despite lack of knowledge or skill ❒ *It always amazes me how Tom manages to muddle through.*

③ **muddle up**
cause somebody to become confused about something ❒ *Let's concentrate on one job at a time, or you'll muddle me up.*

⑦ ⑤ **muddle up (with)**
1 cause something to be in disorder ❒ *The photographs got muddled up with the postcards and it was difficult to sort them out.*

2 confuse the identity of somebody or something with that of somebody or something else ❒ *I've only met her brothers once, and I keep muddling them up.*

⑤ **mug up** *Informal*
learn something thoroughly, usually for an examination or test, by a short period of intensive study ❒ *I've forgotten nearly everything that I mugged up for the last exams.*

⑤ **mull over**
consider or think about something ❒ *He's asked for a bit more time to mull over my proposal.*

⑥ ① **muscle in (on)**
use force, influence, etc, in order to become involved in something and benefit from it ❒ *We don't want any of the big companies muscling in on the project.*

---

① = ●● ② = ●●○ ③ = ●○● ④ = ●○○● ⑤ = ●○● *or* ●●○ ⑥ = ●●●○ ⑦ = ●○●●○

N, n

⑤ **nail down**

1 make somebody express their position, opinion, etc ❑ *The more we try to nail her down, the more she refuses even to talk about the issue.*

2 make somebody agree to something, especially by strong persuasion ❑ *See if you can nail him down to accepting our offer.*

3 establish something firmly or formally, especially a written agreement; accurately define something ❑ *Our company has just managed to nail down a new contract worth £60,000.*

⑤⑦①⑥ **narrow down (to)**

reduce an issue, number or amount to something; may be reduced to something ❑ *The selection committee has narrowed down the original pile of applications to just these five.* ❑ *The whole question narrows down to who is going to pay for all the damage.*

① **nod off**

fall asleep unintentionally ❑ *Is it really so late? I must have nodded off.*

①② **nose about/around**

look inquisitively at other people's private possessions; used in a derogatory way ❑ *He hates the way her mother goes nosing around the house each time she visits them.*

N ❑ *There's nothing she enjoys more than a good nose-around when she thinks you're not watching.*

② **nose into** *Informal*

enquire inquisitively into somebody's private affairs; used in a derogatory way ❑ *She's always nosing into other people's business.*

⑤ **notch up**

achieve or record a victory, success, gain, etc ❑ *The team notched up another two points on Saturday with their seventh win in a row.*

⑤ **note down**

write something down ❑ *He noted down her address and telephone number in the back of his diary.*

O, o

② occur to

enter the mind or thinking of somebody, especially of an idea □ *It suddenly occurred to me that somebody might be able to lend us the money.*

② open onto

be next to or present a view of something □ *Nobody is going to buy a house whose front door opens onto a gas works.*

① open out

1 become wider, especially of a road, river, etc □ *We had to go slowly for a while, and then the motorway suddenly opened out and there were three lanes again.*
2 become visible over a wider area, especially of natural scenery □ *Just over the hill the countryside began to open out, and we had our first glimpse of the sea.*
3 become less shy or nervous in public □ *He's opened out a lot since he went to university.*

① open up ¹

1 become less shy or more talkative □ *Once she had got to know us, she began to open up and tell us about her problems.* □ *China has opened up a lot in recent years, and an increasing amount of information about the country is reaching the West.*
2 begin to fire, of a gun or gunner □ *We held our ears as the machine guns opened up.*
3 develop, arise or emerge, especially of possibilities, prospects, opportunities, etc □ *Quite unexpectedly a chance has opened up for Henry to go and work abroad.*

4 open a door; usually used in the imperative □ *Come on, open up! I can't wait here all day!*

⑤① open up ²

become or cause something to become more lively or exciting, especially of a match, contest, etc
□ *It was Kennedy's equaliser, just five minutes into the second half, that really opened the game up.*

⑤ open up ³

1 make something, especially land, available for use or development
□ *We are being forced to move because the council wants to open up the whole area for redevelopment.*
2 cause a gap, division, cut, etc
□ *The champion suddenly opened up a two-inch gash over the right eye of his opponent.*

⑥ ① opt out (of)

choose not to do or take part in something □ *Most of the group were willing to give blood, but Arthur opted out.*

③ order about/around

keep giving somebody orders or instructions, especially in an offensive way □ *Who does he think he is, ordering people about like that?*

⑥ ① own up (to)   admit responsibility for a crime, mistake, etc □ *The headmaster promised not to punish whoever broke the window if he owned up.*

P,p

②③ pack away

store something in a box, cupboard, etc ❐ *They packed away all their toys before they went on holiday.*

②③ pack in *Informal*

1 stop doing something, especially a job, habit, etc ❐ *You're coughing a lot. You should pack in smoking.* ❐ *That's a dreadful noise! Please pack it in!* ❐ *She had only worked in the shop for three months before she packed it in.*
2 end a relationship with a boyfriend or girlfriend ❐ *She went out with John for six months, but then she packed him in.*
3 attract large audiences to a theatre, concert, etc ❐ *The new pop group is really packing in the teenagers.*

⑦ ⑤ pack off (to)

send somebody away somewhere, especially quickly and without much care ❐ *His mother packed him off to school.* ❐ *She packed him off with a bottle of lemonade.*

① pack up

1 stop or abandon an activity ❐ *If you haven't learned how to drive after ten years, you may as well pack up.*
2 stop working or operating, especially of a machine ❐ *We had only just got the car out of the garage when the engine packed up.*

②③ pad out

make a sentence, story, etc, longer by adding unnecessary detail ❐ *Her letter to her aunt was not long enough, so*

she padded it out with information about the weather.

②③ paint in

add something to a picture by painting ❐ *He painted in a house to add some human interest.*

②③ paint out

cover something by putting paint over it ❐ *They painted out the old name of the street before they put in the new one.*

①⑥③⑦ pair off / up (with)

join or cause somebody to join another person to make a pair or couple ❐ *The teacher told the children to pair off.* ❐ *John paired up with Mary to play tennis.* ❐ *Jane's parents want to pair her off, but she refuses to get married.*

① pal up (with)

become friends with somebody ❐ *John and Bill palled up on their first day at school and they have been friends ever since.*

⑦ ⑤ palm off (on)

get rid of something you do not want by persuading somebody to buy or accept it ❐ *He palmed his old washing machine off on his aunt, even though he knew it was always breaking down.*

⑦ ⑤ palm off (with)

persuade somebody to accept something worthless or untrue ❐ *He tried to palm his boss off with the story that he had been to the dentist.*

② pander to
provide something for which there is a strong demand or desire, especially for the purpose of gain or profit ❑ *Far too many films* pander to *the public's love of violence.*

② paper over
conceal, disguise or repair something, especially a fault, mistake, disagreement, etc ❑ *They tried to* paper over *the differences between union and management, but the agreement did not last for long.*

②③ parcel out
divide something into parts, shares or portions ❑ *After his death, his land was* parcelled out *among his family.*

②③ pare down
reduce or minimise something, especially costs, expenditure, etc ❑ *If we're going on holiday, we must* pare down *all our other expenses.*

② pass as
see pass for/as

① pass away/on
die ❑ *Mr Smith* passed away *last night.*

③ pass by
ignore or pay no attention to somebody ❑ *She felt that life was* passing her by.

②③ pass down
hand or transfer a story, tradition, custom, etc, from one generation to another ❑ *The craft of candle-making has been* passed down *for many generations.* ❑ *The secret has been* passed down *from father to son over six centuries.*

② pass for/as
be mistakenly accepted or identified as somebody or something ❑ *You could* pass for *a teenager if you cut your beard off.* ❑ *Her dress was so soft it could* pass as *silk.*

① pass off
1 gradually disappear, especially of an illness or emotion ❑ *By the morning her fever had* passed off *and she was well enough to get up.*
2 take place ❑ *The organisers were pleased that the demonstration* passed off *without any police arrests.*

⑦ ⑤ pass off (as)
present somebody or something in a way that is meant to deceive ❑ *She tried to* pass *the knives* off as *silver.* ❑ *He tried to* pass *himself* off as *a doctor until he was caught.*

① pass on
see pass away/on

⑥ ① pass on (to) [1]
proceed to a new point, question, subject, etc, especially during a meeting ❑ *I shall now* pass on to *the next item on today's agenda.*

⑦ ⑤ pass on (to) [2]
transfer a price increase or decrease to customers, shoppers, etc, by making them pay more for something or letting them pay less ❑ *They* passed on *the tax increase to the customer.* ❑ *The profit can be* passed on to *the traveller who will pay even less next year.*

① pass out [1]
1 faint or lose consciousness ❑ *She thought she would* pass out *in the heat.*
2 leave or graduate from a military or police college ❑ *Thirty police cadets* pass out *every week.*

②③ pass out ²

distribute something ☐ *The salesman passed out cigarettes to everybody in the restaurant.*

②③ pass over ¹

1 not notice or avoid mentioning something ☐ *I passed over his unpleasantness without commenting on it.*
2 not promote or choose somebody who feels he should be promoted ☐ *Did you hear that they've passed over poor old Henry for a newcomer?*

② pass over ²

review or summarise something briefly ☐ *He quickly passed over the decisions which had been taken at the last meeting.*

② pass through

1 finish a course at a college, university, etc ☐ *He passed through medical school last year and is now a qualified doctor.*
2 experience or suffer something, especially a period of difficulty ☐ *She passed through a difficult time after her son left home.*

②③ pass up

not accept an invitation, opportunity, etc ☐ *He passed up the chance of going to New York for a year.*

②③ paste up

prepare a page, etc, for printing by sticking text and illustrations on to a sheet of paper ☐ *The printer pasted up the first chapter to show the author what his book would look like.*
N ☐ *The printer did a paste-up of the first chapter.*

②③ patch up

resolve or settle an argument, disagreement, etc ☐ *They soon patched up their disagreement.*

⑦ ⑤ pay back (for)

punish or take revenge on somebody ☐ *She paid him back for insulting her by refusing to speak to him.*

② pay for

suffer or be punished for something ☐ *They made him pay for his offence by giving him the sack.* ☐ *If you don't work now, you'll pay for it later when you fail your exams.*

②③ pay off ¹

1 pay everything that you owe somebody ☐ *He paid off the £500 that he owed his father.*
2 pay somebody their wages and then dismiss them ☐ *The whole ship's crew were paid off at the end of the voyage.*
3 give somebody money to stop them threatening you ☐ *He agreed to pay the gang off if they promised not to burn down his shop.*
N ☐ *He gave them £50 as a pay-off.*

① pay off ²

have a favourable or profitable outcome ☐ *His years of hard work paid off when they made him a director of the firm.*
N ☐ *The pay-off made all his work worthwhile.*

①②③ pay out ¹

pay a sum of money, especially regularly or in small amounts ☐ *I'm sick of having to pay out every time you have an accident.* ☐ *Their father must have paid out a fortune on school fees.*

---

②③ **pay out** ²
cause or allow a rope, cable, etc, to run through your hands
❒ *The kite climbed steadily higher until there was no more string to* pay out.

①②③ **pay up**
pay all the money you owe, especially unwillingly or under pressure
❒ *He eventually* paid up *when the firm threatened to take him to court.*

②③① **peel off**
remove some or all of your clothes
❒ *He was so hot that he* peeled off *his jacket.* ❒ *She* peeled off *and dived into the water.*

⑥ ① **peg away (at)**
work hard and steadily at something
❒ *He found maths difficult but he* pegged away at *it every evening and passed the exam.*

① **peg out** *Informal*
die ❒ *My grandfather finally* pegged out *at the age of ninety.*

⑤ **pen in / up**
shut animals or people in a small space
❒ *He* penned *the sheep* in *for the night.*

⑤/④ **pencil in / into**
make preparatory or tentative arrangements for something
❒ *Let me* pencil in *that date for the meeting and we can confirm it later.*
❒ *The minister's visit has been* pencilled into *the programme.*

⑤ **pension off**
dismiss somebody from a job after many years of service, and pay them a pension ❒ *He was* pensioned off *to make way for a younger man.*

⑤① **pep up**
become or make somebody or something more lively, interesting, etc
❒ *A holiday in the sun will* pep you up *and you'll soon feel better.* ❒ *He* pepped up *the fruit juice by adding some gin.*
❒ *Don't worry! You'll soon* pep up.

④ **pepper with**
hit somebody or something with a lot of small stones, questions, insults, etc ❒ *The bird had been* peppered with *lead shot.* ❒ *The journalist* peppered *the Prime Minister* with *questions.*

①⑤ **perk up**
become or make somebody more lively, cheerful, etc ❒ *She* perked up *when I suggested that we went to the theatre that evening.* ❒ *She was feeling depressed but a cup of tea soon* perked *her* up.

② **permit of** *Formal*
allow something to be possible, especially of a situation, agreement, etc; usually used in the negative ❒ *The travel arrangements do not* permit of *any change whatsoever.*

② **pertain to** *Formal*
be connected or associated with something ❒ *The other questions* pertaining to *this matter have yet to be answered.*

① **peter out**
steadily weaken or decrease, and come to an end ❒ *Her enthusiasm for dancing* petered out *and she stopped going to lessons.*

②③ **phase in**
introduce something gradually or in stages ❒ *They* phased in *the new course by accepting just five students in the first year, and ten in the second.*

---

① = ●●   ② = ●●○   ③ = ●○●   ④ = ●○●○   ⑤ = ●○● *or* ●●○   ⑥ = ●●●○   ⑦ = ●○●●○

②③ phase out

withdraw something gradually or in stages ☐ *British Leyland has announced plans to phase out some of its cars next year.*

②③ phone in

submit a question, complaint, comment, etc, by telephone to a radio or television programme ☐ *Listeners are asked to phone in their questions to the Prime Minister who will be in our studio for the next hour.*

N ☐ *Twenty housewives took part in the phone-in this morning.*

② pick at

1 eat very little of something, in an uninterested way ☐ *She picked at her dinner for a few minutes and then said she was not hungry.*
2 keep touching or scratching a cut, wound, etc ☐ *If you keep picking at that cut, it will never get better.*

②③ pick off

carefully and deliberately shoot people or animals one after the other ☐ *The gunman picked off each policeman as he tried to enter the house.*

② pick on

1 choose somebody, especially to do something unpleasant or boring ☐ *Why do you always pick on me to wash the kitchen floor?*
2 speak to somebody angrily and find fault with them ☐ *I wanted the teacher to stop picking on my daughter.*

②③ pick out

1 choose or select something from a number of similar things ☐ *There were a lot of blue dresses in the shop and I picked out one which was very pretty.*

2 recognise or identify somebody or something ☐ *Although he had not seen his sister for twenty years, he picked her out as soon as she got off the plane.*
3 play a tune on a musical instrument by guessing which notes to play and experimenting ☐ *As soon as she'd sung the first verse, he picked out the tune on the piano.*

②③ pick over

examine something by lifting and inspecting it, especially before making a decision to buy ☐ *She picked over the tomatoes, looking for the ripest ones.*

②③ pick up ¹

1 raise somebody or something from the ground or a surface ☐ *Please pick up the pieces of paper which you have just thrown on the floor.*
2 stop to buy or get something ☐ *I must remember to pick up some potatoes for dinner this evening.*
3 stop to collect somebody ☐ *The coach will pick you up at the corner of your road at nine o'clock.* ☐ *Whilst driving to Edinburgh he picked up two students who were hitching a lift.*
4 acquire or buy something, especially a bargain ☐ *He picked up a beautiful statue when he was in Rome.*
5 acquire knowledge of or proficiency in something, especially without lessons or tuition ☐ *She picked up French by living in Paris for six months.*
6 make the acquaintance of somebody casually or informally, especially for sexual purposes ☐ *I think she picked him up at a dance.*
N ☐ *He was surprised that she was such an easy pick-up.*
7 receive radio signals ☐ *With my new radio I can pick up stations all over Europe.*

8 rescue somebody from the sea or some other danger ☐ *They picked up the survivors in the lifeboat.* ☐ *The children who were stranded on the cliff were picked up by helicopter.*
9 earn something, especially an amount of money ☐ *He picked up £60 for two days' work.*
10 catch or arrest somebody ☐ *The police picked the burglar up as he was leaving the house.*
11 acquire information, especially by chance ☐ *She picked up some rumour that the king had died.*
12 continue or return to something after a break or interruption ☐ *I found it difficult to pick up the discussion again after lunch.*

① **pick up ² 1** improve or recover, especially of trade ☐ *Business has been very poor but we expect it to pick up again before Christmas.*
2 improve in health ☐ *He has picked up slowly since he came out of hospital.*
3 start to work properly again, especially of an engine ☐ *The car was very jerky but then the engine picked up and we had no more trouble.*

②③ **piece together**
1 join or gather bits, remnants, parts, etc, in order to make something
☐ *She pieced together any bits of material she had to make a cover for her bed.*
2 gather facts or pieces of information, especially to discover what happened, the whole truth, etc
☐ *After questioning everybody who was there, I eventually managed to piece the whole story together.*

①/② **pile in / into**
push, crowd, be pushed or crowded into a car, room, football ground, etc

☐ *It's not very far. I'm sure we can all pile into my car.*

①/② **pile on / onto**
push, crowd, be pushed or crowded onto a vehicle, stage, platform, etc
☐ *The children piled onto the bus.*

⑥ ① **pile out (of)**
push, crowd, be pushed or crowded out of a car, room, football ground, etc ☐ *We all piled out of the car when we got home.* ☐ *At the end of the football match, everybody piled out of the ground.*

① **pile up**
1 form into a heap or large mass
☐ *I've been on holiday for a month and my work has really piled up.*
2 crash into each other, especially of vehicles travelling too close together
☐ *Ten cars piled up in the fog this morning.*
N ☐ *There was another bad pile-up on the motorway this morning.*

②③ **pin down**
1 accurately define or determine something ☐ *It was impossible to pin down exactly what it was that he was trying to say.*
2 make somebody commit himself to a firm opinion or promise ☐ *I have been trying to pin him down to a date for a meeting next week, but with no success.*
3 trap somebody, especially of a heavy weight or gunfire ☐ *After pinning them down, it was only a short time before they surrendered.*

④ **pin on**
place blame or responsibility for something on somebody ☐ *You needn't think you can pin the robbery on me. I was out of the country at the time.*

---

① = ●● ② = ●●○ ③ = ●○● ④ = ●○○● ⑤ = ●○● *or* ●●○ ⑥ = ●●●○ ⑦ = ●○●●○

① pipe down
be quiet; often used in the imperative ❐ *Do* pipe down! *I'm trying to work.*

① pipe up
begin to speak, especially in a high, squeaky voice
❐ *Suddenly a little voice* piped up: *"Could I have a drink, please?"*

④ pit against
put somebody or something in a fight, contest, etc, against somebody or something else ❐ *He* pitted *his intelligence* against *my strength.*

⑥ ① pitch in (with)
join an argument, discussion, activity, etc, by saying something or offering help ❐ *If you see things going badly in the meeting, just* pitch in with *some good news.*

①/② pitch in / into
start to do something, especially to eat or work with enthusiasm or vigour ❐ *I am grateful for the way everybody* pitched in *and got all the work done.* ❐ *After walking on the hills all day, they could hardly wait to* pitch into *their dinner.*

② pitch into
attack somebody, either physically or verbally ❐ *The boys had to be separated once they had* pitched into *each other.* ❐ *The teacher* pitched into *her about her careless work.*

④ plague with
annoy or irritate somebody with endless questions, reminders, suggestions, etc ❐ *If you mention the exam to the students, you'll be* plagued with *questions all morning.*

⑥ ① play about / around (with)
behave in a silly, irresponsible way ❐ *The school told him that if he didn't stop* playing about, *he would fail all his exams.* ❐ *She is* playing around with *a man twenty years younger than she is.*

⑤ play along
keep somebody waiting for an answer or a decision ❐ *The Government have been* playing *the nurses* along *for six months in the pay talks.*

⑥ ① play along (with)
co-operate, conform or pretend to share somebody's ideas, beliefs, etc ❐ *He* plays along with *his boss all the time, but I'm sure he does not really agree with him.*

② play at
pretend to do something or do something in a half-hearted way ❐ *You must settle down and concentrate. You're only* playing at *doing your homework.*

②③ play back
play something which has been recorded on a tape-recorder, video-recorder, etc ❐ *We recorded our English lesson and then* played *it* back.
N ❐ *We studied the* play-back *carefully.*

②③ play down
try to make something seem less important or serious than it really is ❐ *She* played down *the fact that she had failed to get a degree.*

⑦ play off against
put somebody in competition with somebody else, so that you benefit from it ❐ *She was always* playing *her two brothers* off against *each other.*

② play on / upon

exploit something, especially somebody's feelings, weakness, etc ❐ *He played on her good nature and managed to borrow £20.*

②③ play out

1 finish something, especially a game, fight or struggle ❐ *In spite of the heavy rain they managed to play out the football match.* ❐ *The long struggle between management and trade unions is not yet played out.*
2 perform or conduct something ❐ *Their marriage was played out in a series of fights and arguments.*

②③ play up ¹

make something seem more important or serious than it really is ❐ *He loves to play up her bad qualities.*

⑤① play up ²

cause somebody trouble, unhappiness or pain ❐ *My leg always plays me up in winter.* ❐ *The new teacher didn't know what to do when the class started playing up.*

⑥ play up to

flatter or pretend to admire somebody, especially to gain favour, position, popularity, etc ❐ *She's always playing up to the men in the office.*

② play with

consider an idea, suggestion, possibility, etc ❐ *He's been playing with the idea of leaving his job and buying a farm, but he'll never do it.*

⑥ ① plod away (at)

work slowly and steadily, especially at something that you do not find interesting ❐ *He plods away at his studies every night, but he doesn't enjoy the work.*

⑦ ⑤ plough back (into)

reinvest profits in a company ❐ *He ploughed as much money back into the firm as he could because he wanted to expand.*

② plough through

read or work your way through something slowly and laboriously ❐ *He ploughed through the collected works of Charles Dickens.*

⑥ ① plug away (at)

keep working hard at something ❐ *He's been plugging away at his new novel for nearly a year.*

②③① plug in

connect something electrical to an electricity supply, by putting its plug into a socket ❐ *Plug in the kettle for me, please. I'd like a cup of tea.*

② plump for

choose something or somebody enthusiastically, especially after a lot of thought ❐ *We couldn't decide which car to buy, but we finally plumped for a Datsun.* ❐ *The appointments committee plumped for the older man with experience rather than the younger one with a degree.*

②③ plump up

make pillows, cushions, etc, soft and round by shaking and patting them ❐ *Every evening she plumps up the cushions before she goes to bed.*

①/② plunge in / into

begin work or an activity eagerly or abruptly ❐ *Instead of just plunging in, why don't you seek professional advice?*

① = ●● ② = ●●○ ③ = ●○● ④ = ●○○● ⑤ = ●○● *or* ●●○ ⑥ = ●●●○ ⑦ = ●○○●○

❏ *She plunged into her new assignment the moment she got it.*

④② plunge into
suddenly assume or cause somebody or something to assume a particular mood, condition, state, etc ❏ *She switched off the light and plunged the room into darkness.* ❏ *He was plunged into despair by the terrible news.* ❏ *Every month they plunged deeper into debt.*

④ ply with
keep supplying somebody with food, drink or questions ❏ *She plied all her visitors with cake until they could eat no more.* ❏ *They plied the speaker with so many questions that he had no time to answer them all.*

②③ point out
identify, indicate or draw attention to something ❏ *I pointed out the advantages of the plan.* ❏ *I asked him to point out the house where he was born.*

② point to
suggest or indicate something ❏ *All the evidence points to his guilt.*

②③ point up
emphasise or highlight something ❏ *The special enquiry is expected to point up the failure of the police to produce eye-witnesses.*

① poke about / around
move or disturb things while searching for something ❏ *Who's been poking about in my desk?*
N ❏ *Somebody's been having a poke-around in here by the looks of it.*

②③ polish off *Informal*
1 finish something, especially work,

food, etc ❏ *He polished off the last of the whisky.*
2 defeat or kill somebody ❏ *The champion soon polished off his opponent.*

②③ polish up
improve your knowledge of or proficiency in something, especially something you have partly forgotten ❏ *If I'm going to live in Paris, I'll have to polish up my French.*

① ponce about / around *Informal*
behave in a showy, often effeminate way ❏ *That new young salesman ponces around all day, getting in the way and never doing anything useful.*

① pop off *Informal*
die ❏ *I'm not going to pop off just yet, so you needn't worry.*

① pop up
appear, arise or emerge, especially suddenly or unexpectedly especially something written ❏ *He pops up all over the place, so you never know where to look for him.*

② pore over
study something carefully and with great attention ❏ *He is always poring over his books.*

① potter about / around
spend time doing small, unimportant jobs ❏ *He spent all morning pottering about in his greenhouse.*

② pounce on / upon
1 scold somebody or criticise something sharply ❏ *He pounced on my smallest mistake.*
2 grasp an opportunity eagerly ❏ *The children pounced on the chance of visiting the television studios.*

① pour down
fall hard and steadily, especially of rain ❐ *The rain poured down all day.*
N ❐ *There was a tremendous downpour.*

②③① pour out
say or tell something quickly and without stopping ❐ *Sobbing, she poured out the whole story.*

④ preclude from   *Formal*
prevent somebody from doing something ❐ *Non-residents are precluded from private ownership.*

④ predispose to / towards
cause somebody to behave in a certain way, especially of a past experience ❐ *His unhappy childhood predisposed him to spoiling his own children.*

② press for
keep demanding or insisting upon something ❐ *The nurses are pressing for a bigger increase in salary.*

① press on
continue to do something, especially without stopping, in spite of problems or difficulties ❐ *I know it's almost midnight, but we'd better press on and get the job finished.*

④ press on / upon ¹
force somebody to accept something ❐ *He tried to press his political beliefs on his wife, but she wouldn't listen to him.* ❐ *The old lady was always pressing money on him.*

② press on / upon ²
worry or trouble somebody ❐ *He looks as if all the worries in the world are pressing upon him.*

② presume upon / on   *Formal*
take unfair advantage of somebody's good nature, patience, feelings, etc ❐ *He presumed too much upon her generosity and she was forced to tell him so.*

② prevail upon/on   *Formal*
persuade somebody to do something ❐ *She prevailed upon her daughter to refrain from entering into conversation with complete strangers.*

② prey on / upon
1 exploit somebody or somebody's weakness ❐ *He was a very handsome man and lived by preying upon members of the fairer sex.*
2 attack and rob somebody or something ❐ *It was hard to believe that these little boats were being preyed upon by pirates.*
3 trouble or worry somebody, especially of sorrow, grief, fear, etc ❐ *His fears and worries preyed so much on his mind that eventually he comitted suicide.*

②③ print out
provide a printed record of information, especially of a computer
❐ *I asked the computer to print out every word beginning with 'b'.*
N ❐ *I asked for a print-out of phrasal verbs.*

⑦ ⑤ prise/prize out (of)
force information out of somebody
❐ *She prised the secret out of him by threatening to tell his father.*

② proceed against
take legal action against somebody
❐ *They have decided to proceed against the accused, despite the advice of their counsel.*

① = ●●   ② = ●●○   ③ = ●○●   ④ = ●○●○   ⑤ = ●○● *or* ●●○   ⑥ = ●●●○   ⑦ = ●○●●○

② proceed from
be the result of something
□ *His mistakes* proceed from *carelessness, not ignorance.*

② profit by/from
learn or benefit from something
□ *Has he* profited from *his year abroad?*

②③ prop up
support somebody or something that would otherwise fall or collapse
□ *The opposition parties decided not to* prop up *the Government any longer.*

② provide against
do something that lets you avoid foreseeable danger, hardship, distress, etc □ *She has* provided against *a bad winter by buying in lots of food.*

② provide for
1 support somebody or something by earning, producing or saving what is needed □ *He has always worked hard to* provide for *his family.*
2 make arrangements to overcome all foreseeable problems □ *In the space shuttle every possible electrical failure has been* provided for.

②③ puff out
1 make somebody short of breath
□ *Climbing stairs* puffs *me* out *these days. I must go and see a doctor.*
2 put out a flame by blowing on it
□ *She likes to* puff out *the candles.*

⑤ pull about / around
handle somebody or something roughly or clumsily □ *The baby doesn't like it when people start* pulling *him* about. □ *Their new puppy has been* pulling *the furniture* about.

⑥① pull ahead (of)
overtake somebody or something
□ *The winner of the men's 400 metres* pulled ahead *on the last bend.*
□ *The Rolls Royce* pulled ahead *of us and disappeared into the distance.*

③ pull apart
criticise somebody or find serious faults in an idea, plan, piece of work, etc □ *He* pulled *my argument* apart *and made me feel very stupid.*

② pull at / on
draw tobacco smoke from a pipe, cigarette, etc, into your mouth
□ *The old man sat in the corner,* pulling at *his pipe.*

① pull away
start to move, especially of a vehicle
□ *He leapt onto the train just as it was* pulling away.

⑥ pull away from
get further ahead of somebody or something □ *The car* pulled away from *the lorry as soon as they started going up-hill.* □ *She was an extremely intelligent child, and soon* pulled away from *the rest of the class.*

①②③ pull back
withdraw or cause somebody to withdraw from a position, especially of a group of soldiers □ *The platoon* pulled back *to safety.*

②③ pull down ¹
destroy or demolish something, especially a building □ *They* pulled down *my old house and built five new ones.*

③ pull down ²
cause somebody to feel weak and

---

① = ●● ② = ●●○ ③ = ●○○ ④ = ●○●○ ⑤ = ●○● *or* ●●○ ⑥ = ●●●○ ⑦ = ●○●●○

depressed, especially of an illness ☐ .
A really bad cold pulls you down and leaves you feeling very miserable.

②③ pull in
1 *Informal* earn money ☐ *He pulls in quite a lot as a milkman.*
2 take somebody to the police station because they are suspected of being a criminal ☐ *The men were pulled in on suspicion of having committed a burglary.*
3 attract a lot of people to a theatre, concert, etc ☐ *The Beatles always pulled in enormous crowds.*

①/② pull in / into
1 arrive, especially of a train at a station ☐ *The train from Edinburgh pulled in five minutes late.*
2 move to or towards one side, especially of a vehicle or driver about to stop ☐ *The lorry driver pulled into the side of the road and got out for a cup of tea.*

②③ pull off
complete or perform something successfully, especially a difficult or daring task ☐ *How did you manage to pull off the deal without offering them more money?*

② pull on
see pull at / on

⑥ ① pull out (of) ¹
1 move out of a line of traffic, especially to overtake another vehicle ☐ *The car in front was travelling very slowly, so I pulled out to overtake.*
2 leave, especially of a train from a station ☐ *The train pulled out exactly on time.*
3 recover from an illness, bad mood, etc ☐ *She's been very depressed recently, but I'm sure she'll soon pull out of it.*

①⑥⑤⑦ pull out (of) ²
leave or make somebody leave a place or situation where there is trouble ☐ *The foreign firm decided to pull out because of strikes.* ☐ *The government pulled the army out of the trouble-spot.*
N ☐ *There was a large pull-out of troops.*

①②③④ pull through
survive or help somebody survive an illness, accident, crisis, etc ☐ *He was very ill but he eventually pulled through.* ☐ *It was a miracle that they were able to pull her through the operation.*

① pull together
work as a team ☐ *People always seem to pull together in a crisis.*

①⑤ pull up ¹
stop or cause something to stop, especially of a vehicle or driver ☐ *The bus pulled up at the stop.* ☐ *He pulled up and we got out.*

①③ pull up ²
improve your position in a race, competition, class, etc ☐ *He's pulled up from seventh to second place.* ☐ *It must have been the history paper that pulled him up.*

③ pull up ³
scold or reprimand somebody ☐ *She was pulled up by the teacher for running down the corridor.*

③ push about / around
order somebody to do something in a rough or bullying way ☐ *I'm not going to be pushed about by anybody.* ☐ *She won't let anybody push her about these days.*

---

① = ●●   ② = ●●○   ③ = ●○●   ④ = ●○●○   ⑤ = ●○● *or* ●●○   ⑥ = ●●●○   ⑦ = ●○●●○

① push ahead/forward/on
advance or continue your journey, especially in a determined way
❐ *The infantry* pushed forward *until they came within range of the enemy guns.*
❐ *Although we were tired, we* pushed on *through the night.*

⑥ ① push ahead/forward/on (with)
proceed or continue to do something ❐ *Now that the plans have been accepted, we can* push ahead. ❐ *If you want to* push on with *the decorating, we can leave dinner until later.*

① push along
leave, especially of a guest, visitor, etc
❐ *It's getting late. We'd better be* pushing along.

②④ push for
keep insisting upon something or demanding something from someone ❐ *The miners are* pushing for *more money and less work.* ❐ *They're* pushing *the sales manager* for *better figures.*

②③ push forward ¹
1 try to bring something to somebody's attention ❐ *She* pushed forward *her plans for the new theatre.*
2 be assertive or forceful in order to be noticed ❐ *If only he had* pushed *himself* forward *at work, he might have been a director now.*

① push forward ²
see push ahead/ forward/on

⑥ ① push forward (with)
see push ahead/forward/on (with)

① push off
1 *Informal* leave or go away; often used in the imperative to express anger ❐ *Push off! Can't you see I'm busy!* ❐ *Tell him to* push off *if he starts annoying you.* ❐ *I'll be* pushing off *now. It's getting late.*
2 leave in a boat ❐ *We* pushed off *from the shore and were soon out to sea.*

① push on
see push ahead/forward/on

⑥ ① push on (with)
see push ahead/ forward/on (with)

⑤④ push through
1 gain acceptance of a bill, proposal, decision, etc, by somebody, using force or persuasion ❐ *Despite a lot of resistance, we managed to* push *the proposals* through.
2 cause somebody to pass or succeed in doing something ❐ *By giving him extra lessons we managed to* push *him* through *his exams.*

②③ push up
cause something to rise or increase
❐ *Wage increases keep* pushing up *the cost of living.* ❐ *The hot bath has* pushed *her temperature* up.

⑤ put about
spread or circulate a rumour, piece of news, story, etc ❐ *They've* put *it* about *that the Government's going to resign.* ❐ *Somebody's* putting *vicious rumours* about.

④ put across
deceive or trick somebody into believing or accepting something
❐ *You can't* put *anything* across *old Harrison. He's been around too long.*

⑤ put across / over
1 communicate an idea, message, argument, etc, so that it is clear,

① = ●● ② = ●●○ ③ = ●○● ④ = ●○○● ⑤ = ●○● *or* ●●○ ⑥ = ●●●○ ⑦ = ●○●●○

persuasive or understood ⊓ *He was too full of emotion to* put across *his ideas properly.*

2 project your personality or a song, story, etc, in a way that is liked or admired ⊓ *He just doesn't know how to* put *himself* across *at an interview.*

②③ **put aside**

1 save or reserve money, goods, time, etc ⊓ *Every month he* puts aside *£20.* ⊓ *Can't you manage to* put aside *five minutes to talk to your children?*

2 ignore or pay no attention to something ⊓ *During the war everybody* put *their political differences* aside *and worked together.*

④ **put at**

guess or estimate the weight, height, size, etc, of somebody or something ⊓ *I don't really know how old she is, but I would* put *her* at *about forty.*

②③ **put away**

1 *Informal* eat or drink, especially a lot ⊓ *He* put away *nearly half a bottle of whisky last night.*

2 confine somebody in prison or a mental hospital ⊓ *He became unstable and thought that he was a giant banana, so we had to have him* put away. ⊓ *They've* put *him* away *for thirty years.*

②③ **put away / by**

save something, especially money, for use in the future ⊓ *How much have you* put away *for your holiday?*

② **put away / down**

kill an animal, especially one that is old, ill or injured ⊓ *If the horse's leg is broken, it'll have to be* put down.

⑤ **put back**

1 move the hands of a clock or watch backwards so that it shows an earlier time ⊓ *Don't forget to* put *the clock* back *an hour tonight.*

2 move an event, appointment, etc, to a later time or date ⊓ *We had intended to get married in April but we had to* put *the wedding* back *to September.*

3 cause something to be delayed ⊓ *Heavy rains* put back *the harvesting of the corn this year.*

⑤ **put down** ¹

1 record something in writing ⊓ *He* put *the meeting* down *in his diary.*

2 stop and let a passenger get out, of a driver or vehicle ⊓ *Where would you like me to* put *you* down?

3 pay a deposit or make a down payment ⊓ *She* put down *£100 on some furniture.*

4 see **put away/down**

①③ **put down** ²

land or cause something to land, especially an aircraft ⊓ *The plane* put down *in a field.* ⊓ *The pilot* put *the plane* down *safely, despite the storm.*

③ **put down** ³

humiliate somebody ⊓ *He seems to enjoy* putting *his wife* down *in public.*

② **put down** ⁴

subdue a riot, rebellion, revolt, etc ⊓ *The army will soon* put down *the revolt.*

⑦ **put down as**

form a particular opinion of somebody or reach a certain explanation for something ⊓ *We* put *him* down as *a dreadful fool.*

---

① = ●●   ② = ●●○   ③ = ●○●   ④ = ●○●○   ⑤ = ●○● *or* ●●○   ⑥ = ●●●●   ⑦ = ●○●●○

⑦ **put down for**
1 write down somebody's name on a list because they are willing to give, buy or do something ☐ *How many raffle tickets can I put you down for?*
2 put somebody's name on the waiting-list for a school, club, team, etc ☐ *We put our son down for his father's old school when he was two years old.*

⑦ **put down to**
1 attribute something to a particular cause ☐ *She put his rudeness down to tiredness.*
2 charge something to a particular account ☐ *She put the dress down to her mother's account.*

②③ **put forward**
1 offer an idea, proposal, plan, etc, for consideration ☐ *We put forward our ideas on how the club should be run.*
2 recommend somebody or advance yourself for a job or position
☐ *He put himself forward for secretary.*
☐ *We put forward four names for the committee to consider.*
3 move the hands of a clock or watch forwards so that it shows a later time
☐ *We put the clocks forward in March.*
4 move an event, appointment, etc, to an earlier time or date ☐ *We had to put our holiday forward one month.*

②③ **put in** ¹
1 submit a request or application
☐ *If any of the goods arrive in a damaged condition, you must put in a claim within three days.*
2 spend a particular amount of time doing something ☐ *Altogether, he must have put in about four years' work on his thesis.*

3 elect a government ☐ *Voters put a Conservative government in at the last election.*
4 install, fit or supply something
☐ *We put central heating in when we moved into our new house.*

① **put in** ²
interrupt or interject ☐ *'Don't forget the work involved,' I put in.*

①⑥②③⑦ **put in (for)**
submit a request or application for something, especially for a job, promotion, rise, etc ☐ *The miners have put in a claim for a thirty per cent wage increase.* ☐ *You won't get the money if you don't put in for it.*

⑦ **put in for**
1 enter somebody or something in a competition ☐ *He put his beans in for the 'Best Vegetable' prize.*
☐ *She put herself in for the marathon.*
2 recommend somebody for a job, award, prize, etc ☐ *They put his name in for the Distinguished Service Medal.*

①/② **put in / into**
enter a port, used of a ship ☐ *The liner puts in at Bombay, Singapore and Hong Kong.* ☐ *We put into Amsterdam to unload.*

③ **put inside** *Informal*
put somebody in prison ☐ *He was put inside for murder.*

② ③ **put off** ¹
1 postpone something ☐ *He had to put off his trip to Japan for two weeks.*
2 distract, prevent or hinder somebody or something ☐ *The slightest noise puts me off when I'm concentrating.*

3 avoid seeing, meeting, talking, etc, to somebody □ *He put her off with the excuse that he had too much work to do.*
4 discourage somebody or cause them to lose interest in something □ *I tried to learn French but my teacher was so unpleasant that she put me off.*

③ ④ **put off** ²
1 cause somebody to lose their liking, desire or appetite for something □ *Don't let the price of the carpet put you off.* □ *The awful smell coming from the kitchen put me off my dinner.*
2 let or make somebody get out of a vehicle, especially a bus □ *The stupid conductor put me off at the wrong stop.*

② ③ **put on** ¹
1 cause electricity, gas or water to start flowing, by moving a switch or turning a tap □ *He opened the door and put on the light.*
2 gain weight □ *She put on a lot of weight last winter.*
3 provide extra trains, buses, etc □ *British Airways are putting on an extra flight to Rome every day.*
4 present or produce a play, exhibition, etc □ *They are putting on a new production of 'Romeo and Juliet'.*
5 move the hands of a clock or watch forwards so that it shows a later time □ *He forgot to put the clock on last night.*
6 assume or adopt a particular manner, tone, attitude, etc, especially to impress or deceive somebody □ *She always puts on a posh voice to talk to the vicar.* □ *He's not really angry. He's just putting it on.*

④②③ **put on** ²
1 add to the cost of something

□ *The rise in taxation will put pounds on the cost of living.*
2 bet or risk money on something, especially on a horse
□ *I put £5 on Black Beauty in the two o'-clock at Newmarket.*

② **put on / upon**
be a trouble or nuisance to somebody
□ *I don't want to put upon you, but could you possibly mind the baby for me for just ten minutes?*

⑦ **put on to**
1 give somebody information about somebody or something which will be interesting or useful to them
□ *My friend put me on to a very good restaurant.*
2 bring the attention of an authority to something or somebody, especially a criminal or suspect □ *We put the police on to them as soon as we discovered the gun in their room.*

⑤ **put out** ¹
1 cause a light or fire to stop burning, by moving a switch, etc □ *She put out the light and closed the door.*
2 extinguish a fire or flame, especially by using water □ *The firemen took an hour to put the fire out.*
3 publish, broadcast or circulate something □ *The government is about to put out a statement on its wages policy.*
4 dislocate a part of the body □ *You can imagine how painful it was when he put his shoulder out.*
5 cause figures, results, calculations, etc, to be wrong or inaccurate □ *The rise in transportation costs has really put our estimate out!*
6 cause somebody to become unconscious, especially with a drug or blow □ *His last words before they put*

① = ●●   ② = ●●○   ③ = ●○●   ④ = ●○●○   ⑤ = ●○● *or* ●●○   ⑥ = ●●●○   ⑦ = ●○●●○

him out *for the operation were: 'If only I'd listened to that life-insurance salesman!'*
□ *He* put out *his opponent in the seventh round.*

② put out ²
1 produce or manufacture something, especially of a factory □ *The company* puts out *900 cars a week.*
N □ *Our* output *is twice that of our nearest competitor.*
2 generate a particular amount of power
□ *The engine* puts out *thirty horsepower.*
N □ *What's the* output *of this engine?*
3 sprout new shoots, leaves, etc, especially of a tree or plant □ *She loves it when the trees start* putting out *their fresh green shoots in the spring.*

③ put out ³   **1** inconvenience somebody □ *You're not* putting *us* out *at all! On the contrary, we're glad to see you.*
2 annoy or anger somebody □ *You could tell that his rudeness had* put *her* out *by the way she slammed the door.*
3 remove somebody from a room by force □ *If you keep talking in class, I'll have to* put *you* out.

① put out ⁴
set sail or move away from the shore
□ *We* put out *at the crack of dawn.*

⑦ ⑤ put out (to)
1 transfer or subcontract a job to somebody □ *He* puts *a lot of his work* out *to other people, including carpenters and electricians.*
2 lend money to somebody in order to get interest on it □ *The banks have started* putting out *money to people wanting to buy their own homes.*

③ put over
  see **put across/over**

②③ put through ¹
successfully complete a plan, scheme, programme, etc □ *He* put through *an important business deal yesterday.*

④ put through ²
cause somebody or something to undergo or experience a test, upheaval, misery, etc
□ *All the students are* put through *an English test before starting their course.*
□ *Engineers are* putting *the new train* through *rigorous safety checks.*

④ put to
1 submit a question, belief, proposal, etc, to somebody for consideration
□ *I would like to* put *a question* to *the speaker, if I may.*
□ *I* put *it* to *you, Minister, that unemployment will continue to rise.*
□ *The plans for the new building were* put *to the committee last week.*
2 ask somebody to decide something; resolve something by voting or discussing it □ *May we* put *the proposal* to *the meeting?*
3 subject somebody to a lot of worry, trouble, distress, etc
□ *We've been* put *to a great deal of inconvenience by your irresponsible behaviour.*

②③ put together
construct or mend something by joining its parts together
□ *If you have some glue, I'll try and* put *the vase* together *again.*
□ *He* put *the story* together *by asking lots of people what had happened.*

---

① = ●●   ② = ●●○   ③ = ●○●   ④ = ●○●○   ⑤ = ●○● *or* ●●○   ⑥ = ●●●○   ⑦ = ●○●●○

②③ put up [1]
increase the price of something
❒ *Universities have just put up their fees.*

② put up [2]
1 give or lend somebody a sum of money needed for a project
❒ *He hopes that one of the major banks will agree to put up the bulk of the capital.*
2 offer a struggle, resistance, defence, etc ❒ *The losers certainly didn't put up much of a fight, did they?*
3 offer or submit something for consideration ❒ *Don't tell me they're going to put up yet another proposal: They've had four rejected already!*

⑤① put up [3]
provide food and a bed for somebody; stay somewhere overnight
❒ *I'm afraid we can't put you up tonight. We're full.*
❒ *Perhaps we could put up at this hotel.*

⑦③ put up (for) [1]
suggest or propose somebody for a job, official position, etc
❒ *We put him up for chairman, but he refused.*

①⑥③⑦ put up (for) [2]
offer yourself as a candidate for an election ❒ *He is putting up for Parliament next year.*

② put upon
see **put on/upon**

⑦ put up to
encourage or entice somebody to do something wrong or mischievous
❒ *He's not usually naughty. Somebody must have put him up to it.*

⑥ put up with
suffer or tolerate somebody or something patiently and without complaining
❒ *I'm not going to put up with their shouting and banging any longer!*

②③ puzzle out
find an answer or solution to something by thinking hard and carefully
❒ *He finally puzzled out how to use the dishwasher.*

② puzzle over
try to understand something difficult or confusing
❒ *He spent all day puzzling over his income tax form.*

Q, q

② quarrel with
dispute or disagree with something; often used in the negative

❏ *We're not* quarrelling with *the decision itself, just the timing of it.*

③① quieten down
become or cause somebody or something to become calm, especially after being anxious, busy, etc

❏ *There was nothing we could say or do to* quieten *her* down *while her husband was in hospital.*

❏ *The baby was very restless during the night, but* quietened down *after a feed.*

R, r

② rake through
search somewhere carefully

❏ *He* raked through *the attic trying to find the trunk.*

②③ rake up
1 mention or introduce a past event, especially an unhappy or unpleasant one, which was forgotten or hidden ❏ *Please don't* rake up *that awful quarrel.*

2 produce or find money, people, enthusiasm, etc, with a lot of effort ❏ *I'm busy* raking up *support for the cricket match.*

①② rally round
come together, especially of a group, to help and support somebody or something ❏ *When she was ill, all her family* rallied round. ❏ *The nation will* rally round *the flag in a time of crisis.*

②③ rattle off
say or repeat something quickly and easily from memory or by reading

❏ *The boy* rattled off *all the names of the England football team.*

② rave about / over
praise somebody or something in an excited and enthusiastic way

❏ *The girls* raved about *the rock concert.*

⑥ ① reach out (to)
extend a message, appeal, offer of help, etc, to somebody, especially to a particular group ❏ *Local church leaders are making a new attempt to* reach out to *the younger generation.*

② **read for**
study for a qualification, especially a university degree ❑ *When the children are older, she intends to* read for *a BSc at London University.*

④ **read into**
find more meaning in something than was expressed or intended ❑ *My book is widely misunderstood: people* read *things* into *it which aren't there.*

⑤ **read off**
read, often aloud, words or figures on an instrument, gauge, dial, etc ❑ *I peered at the dial and* read off *the numbers.*

⑤ **read out**
read something aloud, usually to a group ❑ *First the secretary* read out *the minutes of the last meeting.*

②③ **read over / through**
read a letter, document, etc, usually in order to check or judge it ❑ *The BBC* read *the script* over *before allowing the programme to be made.*

② **read up**
find out facts, details, information, etc, by reading ❑ *Out of curiosity, I* read up *all the details on the murder case.*

⑥ **read up on**
study something in detail, by reading ❑ *I had* read up on *the Renaissance before my trip to Italy.*

② **reason with**
try to persuade or convince somebody with logical arguments ❑ *I tried to* reason with *him, but it was no use.*

② **reckon on**
expect or depend on something happening ❑ *We are* reckoning on *increasing profits by 20 per cent next year.*

② **reckon with**
take something into account or consider something or somebody to be a serious obstacle or opponent ❑ *The hikers didn't* reckon with *the possibility of snow and fog when they set off.* ❑ *When he is angry he is a force to be* reckoned with.

② **reckon without**
fail to take something into account ❑ *The organisers had* reckoned without *a train strike on the day of the show.*

②③ **reel off**
say, repeat, or write something from memory, especially a list of things ❑ *When I asked him to recommend a good restaurant, he* reeled off *a long list of places.*

② **relate to**
form an understanding and establish a relationship with somebody or something ❑ *I don't get on with other people at work, but I can* relate to *David.*

①②③ **rev up**
push the accelerator of a motor vehicle, causing the engine to run fast while the vehicle is not moving ❑ *The youths* revved up *their motorbikes as they waited at the traffic lights.*

②③ **ride out**
come through a difficult situation, crisis, etc ❑ *The company faces severe financial problems, but we hope to* ride *them* out.

① **ride up**
move upwards out of its proper position, especially of clothing
❒ *This shirt keeps* *riding up* *and won't stay tucked in.*

②③⑦ **rig out (in / with)**
provide or equip somebody with something, especially clothes
❒ *He had* *rigged* *himself* *out in a dinner jacket and bow tie.* ❒ *They* *rigged him* *out* *with everything he needed for the journey.*

②③ **rig up**
arrange, assemble or construct something, usually temporarily
❒ *We* *rigged up* *the record-player in the dining-room for the party.* ❒ *The girls had* *rigged up* *a kind of bunk-bed using some planks and a few wooden boxes.*

①② **ring around / round**
make several telephone calls for a particular purpose
❒ *If you need to hire a car,* *ring round first* *and get the best price.* ❒ *Let's* *ring round* *a few friends and have a party.*

① **ring off**
finish a telephone conversation
❒ *I must* *ring off* *now. I'm in rather a hurry.*

① **ring out**
make a loud and clear sound, especially of a bell, voice, gunshot, etc
❒ *Their shouts* *rang out* *in the clear night air.*

⑤ **ring up**
record the amount of money paid for a purchase on a cash register
❒ *The shop assistant made a mistake and* *rang up £15 instead of £1.50.*

②③ **rip off**   *Informal*
1 steal something
❒ *Those kids* *ripped off* *two boxes of sweets while the shopkeeper wasn't looking.*
2 charge somebody a very high price
❒ *Don't buy a car from that garage! They'll* *rip you* *off.*
N ❒ *Sixty pounds for a pair of shoes! That's a real* *rip-off.*

① **roll about / around**
laugh, especially wildly or loudly
❒ *It was a really funny show. Everyone was* *rolling about* *with tears of laughter streaming down their faces.*

① **roll in** ¹
1 arrive or come home
❒ *What time did you* *roll in* *last night?*
2 arrive in large quantity at a steady rate, especially of money or people
❒ *When the hospital asked for donations, the cash* *rolled in* *from all over the country.*

② **roll in** ²
have plenty or more than you need of something, especially money
❒ *The Smith family are simply* *rolling in* *money.*

② **roll on**
hurry, of time, a date, etc; used to express a wish ❒ *Roll on, summer!* ❒ *Roll on five o'clock when I can go home!*

① **roll up**
arrive, especially late or in a particular manner ❒ *We waited for three hours for John to* *roll up.* ❒ *The Lord Mayor* *rolled up* *in a chauffeur-driven car.*

② **root for**
cheer or support somebody, especially in a contest ❒ *Dave was* *rooting for the Scottish football team in the World Cup.*

① = ●● ② = ●●○ ③ = ●○● ④ = ●○●○ ⑤ = ●○● *or* ●●○ ⑥ = ●●●○ ⑦ = ●○●●○

②③ **root out**

1 produce or find something after careful searching
❑ *When I get home, I'll see if I can root out a few of my old essays for you.*
2 destroy, remove or get rid of somebody or something
❑ *The Government is determined to root out MPs who criticise its policies.*

⑤/④ **rope in / into**

persuade somebody to take part in something, especially to join a group or give help ❑ *If they think you're interested in the club, they'll soon rope you in.*
❑ *Every year I was roped into helping with the school sports.*

②③ **rough out**

outline a plan, idea, scheme, etc
❑ *Let me rough out for you the design for the new wing.*

②③ **rough up**

use physical violence, especially to frighten somebody
❑ *The gang roughed up the doorman and then forced their way in.*

②③⑦ **round off (with)**

complete or conclude something in a suitable way❑ *The orchestra rounded off the concert with Brahms' Third Symphony.*

② **round on / upon**

1 turn and attack somebody or something unexpectedly
❑ *The dog suddenly rounded on the little boy who was playing nearby.*
2 turn against somebody unexpectedly in anger or annoyance ❑ *The old lady rounded on the ticket collector because the train was five minutes late.* ❑ *The Prime Minister rounded on his critics.*

⑤ **round out**

give something more content, body, details, etc ❑ *If you rounded out the story a bit, you could get it published as a novel.*
❑ *The board won't accept the scheme until we round it out with some figures.*

②③ **round up**

1 collect people or things together in one place, especially sheep or cattle
❑ *The farmer rounded up the cows for milking.*
2 bring a fraction to the nearest or most convenient higher whole number ❑ *The bill should have been £29.54 so I rounded it up to £30.*

① **rub along**

have a satisfactory relationship with somebody; live together in a friendly way ❑ *My wife and I have rubbed along all right for twenty-five years.*

⑤ **rub in**

talk repeatedly about something which somebody wants to forget or is embarrassed or angry about ❑ *I'm really surprised you failed your exams.'*
'OK. Don't rub it in.' ❑ *She kept rubbing in the fact that she was prettier than me.*

⑥ ① **rub off (on/onto)**

pass from one person to another as a result of close contact, especially of habits, qualities, attitudes, etc
❑ *Now that Sue and John are married, perhaps some of her intelligence will rub off on him.*

② **rule out**

1 prevent something from happening; make something impossible
❑ *It's pouring with rain, so that rules out tea in the garden.*

---

① = ●●   ② = ●●○   ③ = ●○●   ④ = ●○●○   ⑤ = ●○● *or* ●●○   ⑥ = ●●●○   ⑦ = ●○●●○

2 exclude, dismiss or decide not to consider a possibility, idea, suggestion, etc ❑ *We can't rule out the possibility of a nuclear war within the next decade.*

② run across / into
meet somebody or find something by chance or unexpectedly
❑ *I ran across an old school friend at the party on Thursday.*

② run after
pursue somebody, especially of the opposite sex, to gain their attention and affection ❑ *She loves money and is always running after rich bachelors.*

⑥ ① run around (with)
1 be very often in the company of somebody ❑ *I wish my son wouldn't run around with those hooligans.*
2 be unfaithful to your marriage partner, lover, boyfriend, etc
❑ *She's threatened to leave him if he doesn't stop running around.*

⑥ ① run away (from)
escape from somewhere or from the control of somebody, especially of a child ❑ *He hated his stepmother and eventually ran away from home.*

⑥ run away with
1 leave or escape from your home, husband, parents, etc, with somebody of the opposite sex
❑ *Did you know that her daughter has run away with the greengrocer?*
2 consume a great deal of something, especially fuel ❑ *His new car just runs away with the petrol.*
3 win a sports match or competition very easily ❑ *Argentina ran away with the World Cup a few years ago.*

4 become too strong and take control of somebody, especially of feelings, emotions, imagination, etc
❑ *When he saw his dead son, his grief ran away with him and he shot himself.*
5 steal something and escape with it
❑ *He ran away with the firm's money.*

⑥ run back over
review, repeat or discuss something again ❑ *Let's run back over the events that led up to the outbreak of the Second World War.*

①⑥② run behind (with)
fail to progress at the speed required by a schedule, programme, timetable, etc ❑ *The doctor missed lunch because he was running behind with his appointments.*
❑ *Hurry up! We're running behind schedule.*

⑤ run down ¹
1 knock something or somebody to the ground, especially of a car, bus, driver, etc ❑ *The train ran down several sheep on the track.* ❑ *Mr Smith ran an old lady down in the High Street.*
2 criticise or disparage somebody or something ❑ *You shouldn't run down members of your own family.* ❑ *She's always running down my work to the manager.*
3 catch or find somebody or something after a chase or search ❑ *The police eventually ran down the criminal on the moors.*

①②③ run down ²
1 lose or cause to lose power, strength, etc, especially because of age, use, or neglect ❑ *The clock has run down again. Did you forget to wind it up?* ❑ *If you leave the car lights on, they will quickly run the battery down.*

---

① = ●●   ② = ●●○   ③ = ●○●   ④ = ●○●○   ⑤ = ●○● *or* ●●○   ⑥ = ●●●○   ⑦ = ●○●●○

2 decline; cause something to decline or become less active, especially of a factory, school, organisation, etc
☐ *The local council is* run*ning down the Arts Centre over the next two years.*
☐ *The steelworks is slowly being* run down.

⑤ run in
1 prepare a new car engine for normal daily use by driving carefully and slowly ☐ *Don't drive at more than 50 m.p.h. when you are* running in *a new car.*
2 *Informal* arrest somebody, especially of the police ☐ *That's the second time he's been* run in *for speeding.*

④ run into ¹
crash a vehicle into something
☐ *Some crazy driver* ran *his car* into *the back of our taxi this morning.*

② run into ²
1 meet somebody unexpectedly or by chance ☐ *I* ran into *Mary in town this afternoon.*
2 crash into something, especially in the case of a car, bus, driver, etc ☐ *The taxi* ran into *the back of my new car.*

⑤ run off
1 print or make copies of a document, letter, article, etc, on a photocopier, duplicator or printing machine ☐ *When you've finished typing this letter, could you* run off *four copies for me, please?*
2 cause a liquid to flow or drain from a container
☐ *Before the beer is served, a few pints should be* run off *from the barrel.*

⑥ ① run off (with)
leave or escape from your home, husband, etc, with somebody of the opposite sex ☐ *His wife has* run off with *another man.*

⑥ run off with
steal something and escape with it; take something that isn't yours by mistake and leave with it ☐ *That silly girl has* run off with *my scissors.*

① run on
1 continue ☐ *The war could* run on *for another year yet.*
2 talk without pause ☐ *The old man* ran on *for hours about his childhood.*

① run out
1 be used, spent or consumed, especially of food, supplies, fuel, time, etc
☐ *Their food was* running out *fast so the climbers had to return.* ☐ *Hurry up! Time is* running out.
2 end, expire or cease to be valid, especially of a contract, lease, licence, etc ☐ *My employment contract* runs out *at the end of this month.*

⑥ ① run out (of)
have no more of something ☐ *The car* ran out of *petrol after ten miles.* ☐ *'Have you got any eggs?' 'Sorry. We've* run out.'

① run over ¹
overflow, especially of a container or its contents ☐ *Turn off the tap! The bath is* running over.

②③ run over ²
accidentally crash into and knock down a person or animal, especially of a vehicle or driver ☐ *The car* ran over *a duck crossing the road.* ☐ *Her little boy was* run over *on his way to school.*

② run over / through
say or read something again, especially notes, a speech, lines of a play, etc, for practice or as a check ☐ *I must* run over *this speech before the meeting tonight.*

---

③ **run through** [1]

1 review or give a summary of something ❐ *I'll run through the main points of the news again.*

2 rehearse ❐ *OK. Let's run through the whole thing again.*

N ❐ *This will be the final run through before the performance.*

3 spend money quickly and extravagantly ❐ *She could run through a year's salary in a week if you let her.*

② **run through** [2]

stab or wound somebody with a sword, knife, bayonet, etc
❐ *St George ran the dragon through with a golden spear.*

② **run to**

1 afford something; usually used in the negative ❐ *On my salary I can't run to a colour television.*

2 extend to or reach a certain amount ❐ *The book runs to 300 pages.*

② **run up** [1]

1 raise something, especially a flag or banner, by pulling on a rope
❐ *They ran up a flag in honour of the president's visit.*

2 incur a bill or debt, especially a big one ❐ *He ran up a huge overdraft at the bank.*

②③ **run up** [2]

make something quickly, especially a piece of clothing ❐ *Give me the material and I'll run up a dress in no time.*

⑥ **run up against**

encounter, meet or discover something, especially a difficulty, problem, obstacle, etc ❐ *Everything was going well until we ran up against opposition from the Government.*

②③ **rush out**

produce, make or publish a large number of things in a very short time

❐ *They rushed out half a million souvenir programmes for the Pope's visit to Britain.*

②③④ **rush through**

cause a proposal, order, document, etc, to be officially accepted, processed or dealt with as quickly as possible by a committee, parliament, etc ❐ *The Socialists want to rush this legislation through Parliament.*

❐ *The office rushed through his order and the goods were quickly delivered.*

⑤ **rustle up** **1** make or produce something quickly when required, especially a meal

❐ *Can you rustle up something for dinner in half an hour?*

2 search for and find somebody or something for a particular purpose or occasion

❐ *I'll rustle up a few more guests for the party tonight.*

---

① = ●● ② = ●●○ ③ = ●○● ④ = ●○○● ⑤ = ●○● *or* ●●○ ⑥ = ●●●○ ⑦ = ●○●●○

S, s

④ **saddle with**
give somebody something they do not want, especially an extra responsibility ❑ *He has saddled his wife with a house and five children to look after.*

⑤ **scale down**
decrease or reduce something in size, amount or scope, especially in proportion ❑ *He thinks that the project is much too ambitious, and that the whole thing should be scaled down.*

⑤ **scale up**
increase or expand something, especially in proportion
❑ *Taxes have been scaled up this year to keep pace with inflation.*

② **score off**
make yourself appear clever by making somebody else appear stupid ❑ *She enjoys trying to score off other people.*

⑤ **score out**
draw a line through something, especially a mistake ❑ *He scored out both calculations and did them again.*

⑥ ① **scout about / around (for)**
go and try to find something ❑ *He scouted around for a shop that sold milk.* **N** ❑ *I've lost my glasses. Have a scout-around for them, will you?*

⑥ ① **scrabble about (for)**
try to find or recover something in a hurried or clumsy way
❑ *She dropped the tickets on the floor and scrabbled about for them.*

⑥ ① **scrape along (on)**
manage to live on a small amount of money ❑ *When he was a student, he scraped along on what he earned as a waiter in the holidays.*

⑥ ① **scrape by (on)**
manage to live through a difficult time with very little money; have just enough of something for your needs ❑ *It won't be easy if you lose your job, but we'll scrape by somehow.*

①/② **scrape in / into**
just manage to get into a school, college or profession, especially with the minimum entrance qualifications ❑ *He just scraped into university, to the surprise of all his teachers.*

①② **scrape through**
pass a test or examination with the lowest marks possible ❑ *She scraped through her English exam with 50 per cent.*

⑤ **scrape together / up**
collect or save an amount with great difficulty ❑ *Can we scrape up enough to buy a new car?*

⑦ **screw out of**   *Informal*
obtain something, especially money, from somebody by using a lot of persuasion or pressure ❑ *He screwed ten pounds out of his grandmother, even though she could not really afford it.*

②③ **screw up**   *Informal*
do something badly; make a mess of something; used in a derogatory

---

① = ●●   ② = ●●○   ③ = ●○●   ④ = ●○●○   ⑤ = ●○● *or* ●●○   ⑥ = ●●●○   ⑦ = ●○●●○

way ❑ *We couldn't go on holiday because he* screwed up *all the arrangements.*

② see about

give your time and attention to something that needs to be done ❑ *I've got to* see about *the car. It's been making a funny noise recently.*

⑤ see off

1 cause somebody or something to stop troubling or attacking you and chase them away ❑ *Some boys were stealing my apples, but my dog soon* saw them off.

2 go to an airport, station, etc, to say goodbye to somebody ❑ *We* saw them off *the airport.*

②③ see out

last until the end of something ❑ *We have enough food to* see out *the winter.*

③④ see through[1]

help somebody survive a difficult time or crisis ❑ *She was very upset when her husband died but her friends* saw her through.

③ see through[2]

get to the end of something, especially a task of some kind ❑ *Before I leave, I would like to* see the project through.

② see through[3]

not be fooled by somebody or something ❑ *We easily* saw through *the man and his lies.*

② see to

give your time and attention to somebody or something ❑ *There is a lot to* see to *before you go on holiday.* ❑ *I'll cook the dinner if you* see to *Grandma.*

② seize on / upon

accept an idea or suggestion with eagerness ❑ *She* seized on *the chance of going to New York to work.*

① seize up

become stuck and stop working, especially of machinery ❑ *The car* seized up *on the motorway.*

⑥ ① sell out (to)

betray your principles or your friends, especially for money ❑ *He used to write serious novels but now he has* sold out *and writes thrillers.* ❑ *The workers' leaders* sold out to *their employers.* **N** ❑ *They were accused of a* sell-out *by their members.*

⑤ send down

expel a student from a university ❑ *He was* sent down *for gross indecency.*

②③ send out

emit something, especially a light or sound ❑ *The lighthouse* sent out *a very bright light.*

②③ send up

ridicule somebody or something, especially by imitating them ❑ *At the end of the session, the students wrote a play in which they* sent up *their teachers.* **N** ❑ *They did a good* send-up *of their teachers.*

② set about

1 begin to do something ❑ *He* set about *his work as soon as he had finished his meal.*

2 attack somebody verbally or physically ❑ *If those boys steal any more of my fruit, I'll* set about *them with my spade.*

① = ●●   ② = ●●○   ③ = ●○●   ④ = ●○●○   ⑤ = ●○● *or* ●●○   ⑥ = ●●●○   ⑦ = ●○●●○

④ **set against**
make somebody dislike a person
☐ *He set the children against their mother.*

⑦④ **set (off) against**
balance one thing against another
☐ *You can set the cost of a new car against the cost of repairing your old one.*

⑦③ **set apart (from)**
make somebody or something be or seem to be special or different from others ☐ *His intelligence set him apart from the other boys in his class.*

②③ **set aside**
1 dismiss or pay no attention to something ☐ *My objections to the plan were set aside by the other members of the committee.*
2 cancel or reject something
☐ *The Appeal Court set aside the prisoner's sentence.*
3 keep something for a special purpose ☐ *She set aside five hours a week to learn French.*

②③ **set back** ¹
delay or hinder the progress of something, especially by a certain amount ☐ *The snow this winter set back the building of our new house by two months.*
N ☐ *Our plans for moving received a setback when our buyer said he could not get a mortgage.*

③④ **set back** ²
cost somebody an amount of money, especially a large amount ☐ *Her new boots set her back seventy pounds.*

⑤ **set down** ¹
let somebody out of a bus or other vehicle ☐ *The driver will set you down just outside our house.*

⑤ **set down** ²
write something down ☐ *He was good at setting his thoughts down on paper.*

① **set forth / off / out**
begin a journey ☐ *We set off at nine o'clock and finally arrived at five.*

① **set in**
begin and last for a long time, especially of an illness, bad weather, etc ☐ *The snow set in in November and did not go until March.*

②③ **set off**
1 cause somebody to start laughing, crying, talking, etc ☐ *She had stopped crying but his shouting set her off again.*
2 cause something explosive to explode ☐ *Be careful that you don't set the fireworks off by mistake.*
3 make something look very good, especially by providing a contrast to it ☐ *That dress sets off her jewellery to perfection.*

① **set off**
    see **set forth/off/out**

⑦ **set off on**
cause somebody to start telling stories, talking about favourite subjects, etc ☐ *Don't mention Italy; you'll set him off on his holiday adventures again.*

④② **set on**
attack or cause a person or animal to attack somebody or something ☐ *He set his dog on the burglar.*

① **set out** ¹
1 decide upon and work towards an objective or ambition; followed by *to* and an infinitive ☐ *He set out to make a lot of money.*
2 see **set forth/off/out**

① = ●● ② = ●●○ ③ = ●○● ④ = ●○●○ ⑤ = ●○● *or* ●●○ ⑥ = ●●●○ ⑦ = ●○●●○

②③ set out [2]

arrange or organise something clearly
□ *He set out all the pieces on the floor.*
□ *My plans for the firm have been set out in this document.*

① set to

1 begin something eagerly and with determination □ *They set to and cleaned the whole house in two hours.*
2 begin arguing or fighting □ *The boys set to and the teacher could hardly separate them.*
N □ *We started talking quietly about the problem, but the discussion soon developed into a terrible set-to.*

⑤ set up [1]

1 establish a business, organisation, committee, etc □ *The Prime Minister set up an investigation into corruption in the police force.*
2 get something assembled or ready to use, especially a piece of apparatus
□ *It took him three hours to set his new stereo up.*
3 help somebody to open a shop, start a business, etc, especially by providing the money required □ *His father set him up in a restaurant.*
N □ *He's got an excellent set-up there.*

③ set up [2] 1 make somebody feel healthier, happier, etc □ *My holiday really set me up for the winter.*
2 claim that you or somebody is special in some way; followed by *as* or *to be* □ *He sets himself up as an expert in this field.*

② set up [3]

1 cause or produce something
□ *The heavy rain set up dangerous conditions on the motorway.*
2 achieve or establish something
□ *The French team set up a new record at tonight's meeting.*

① settle down

1 get married and establish a home
□ *You're 40 now; it's time you settled down like other people.*
2 give your whole attention to something □ *I really must settle down to my work this morning.*

② settle for

accept something which is not as good as you hoped for □ *She wanted to be a lawyer but she had to settle for being a secretary.* □ *He is so keen to sell his houses that he is willing to settle for less than the asking price.*

④ settle on

give money or property to somebody by signing a legal document □ *He settled £200 on each of his grandchildren.*

② settle on / upon

agree or decide about something, often after a lot of argument or discussion □ *We finally settled on Greece for our holiday.*

⑥ ① settle up (with)   pay a bill or debt □ *I asked for the bill and settled up.*
□ *You paid for the theatre tickets and the meal. I'd better settle up with you now.*

② settle with

take revenge on somebody
□ *I'll settle with him one day for telling people I am a thief.*

②③ sew up

complete, settle or finalise something □ *He was determined to sew up the deal before the meeting ended.*

⑥ ① shack up (with) *Informal*

live with somebody you are not married to □ *They shacked up just after leaving university.*

---

① = ●●　②= ●●○　③ = ●○●　④ = ●○○●　⑤ = ●○● *or* ●●○　⑥ = ●●●○　⑦ = ●○○●○

① shake down
become used to a new place of work, way of living, etc ❒ *It took the team a few weeks to shake down.*

②③ shake off
get rid of an unwanted companion, illness, bad habit, etc
❒ *Although he tried very hard, he could not shake off his assailants.* ❒ *It took him three months to shake off his illness.*

⑦ shake out of
make somebody change their behaviour or attitude by giving them a shock or surprise ❒ *He is so lazy. We must do something to shake him out of it.*

②③ shake up
1 make something, especially an institution or business, more efficient
❒ *I've a feeling that the new headmaster will soon shake the school up.*
N ❒ *There is to be a shake-up in the Government soon.*
2 cause somebody to be more lively, alert, disciplined, etc, especially by scolding or threatening them ❒ *The warning at the bottom of her school report really shook her up.*

②③⑦①⑥ shell out (for/on)
Informal
spend money reluctantly, especially because you have to do it regularly
❒ *I'm always being asked to shell out for my child's dancing lessons.*
❒ *It's not worth shelling out any more money on my car.*

② shin up
climb up something, especially a wall, tree or rope
❒ *The boy shinned up the tree to rescue a cat.*

②③ shoot down
criticise and dismiss an idea, suggestion, proposal, etc ❒ *The headmistress shot down my plan for making money for the school.*

①⑥⑤⑦ shoot out (of)
emerge or cause something to emerge quickly and suddenly from somewhere ❒ *The snake shot out its tongue.* ❒ *The dog shot out of the house and ran away.*

① shoot up
1 grow quickly, especially of children and plants ❒ *Mary shot up eight centimetres in one year.*
2 increase rapidly or by a large amount ❒ *Prices have shot up in the last year.* ❒ *When he was ill, his temperature shot up to nearly 39°C.*

① shop around
compare the prices and quality of goods in different shops before buying something
❒ *I need a new washing machine, but I'm going to shop around first.*

②③ shore up
1 support something, especially a house or wall, with lengths of wood or metal
❒ *They had to shore up the back of the church after it had been damaged by fire.*
2 strengthen or support something which is weak or in danger of collapse, especially by means of economic measures ❒ *The government took action to shore up the coal industry.*

②③ shout down
make it difficult to hear somebody by shouting loudly ❒ *The crowd shouted down the speaker who approved of nuclear weapons.*

① = ●●   ② = ●●○   ③ = ●○●   ④ = ●○●○   ⑤ = ●○● *or* ●●○   ⑥ = ●●●○   ⑦ = ●○●●○

① **shove off**   *Informal*

go away: often used in the imperative ❑ *I'm busy, so* shove off *and leave me alone!*

① **show off** ¹

try to impress people with your possessions or abilities

❑ *Nobody's watching you, so there is no point in* showing off.

N ❑ *She's an awful* show-off. *She loves it when people admire her clothes.*

②③ **show off** ²

1 display somebody or something that you are proud of ❑ *He enjoys* showing off *his new car to people.*
2 display something in a suitable or attractive way ❑ *The room is too small to* show off *the piano properly.*

①⑤ **show up** ¹

become or cause something to become clearly visible

❑ *The sun* shows up *the dirt on the windows.* ❑ *The scratches don't* show up *unless you look very closely.*

① **show up** ²

arrive, especially when you are late

❑ *We thought that you were never going to* show up.

③ **show up** ³

embarrass somebody by behaving badly when they are present ❑ *My friend always* shows *me* up *by laughing too loudly in the theatre.*

⑦③ **show up (as/for)**

reveal the nature or character of somebody, especially as being unpleasant, dishonest, etc ❑ *His behaviour* showed *him* up *for a cheat.*

②③ **shrug off**

dismiss something as not worth worrying about ❑ *He finds it easy to* shrug off *criticism.* ❑ *You can't* shrug off *all your responsibilities onto other people.*

②③⑦ **shuffle off (onto)**

try to rid yourself of responsibility for something by passing it onto somebody else ❑ *Although he had made the mistake himself, he tried to* shuffle *the blame* off onto *his son.*

①②③ **shut down**

stop operating or cause something to stop operating, either temporarily or permanently ❑ *The factory* shuts down *for three weeks every summer.* ❑ *The business was losing so much money that the owner had to* shut *it* down.
N ❑ *The* shut-down *in the steel industry lasted for two months.*

②③ **shut off**

stop or cease to operate, especially of a gas supply, electricity supply, etc, or an electrical or mechanical device; cause something to do this, especially by means of a switch ❑ *He always* shut off *his electricity and gas when he went on holiday.* ❑ *I've turned the key but the engine won't* shut off.

⑦③ **shut off (from)**

isolate yourself or cease to communicate with other people ❑ *She has threatened to* shut *herself* off from *the family.*

①⑤ **shut up**   *Informal*

stop or cause somebody to stop talking or making a noise; often used in the imperative to express anger or irritation ❑ *Oh,* shut up! *I'm trying to work.* ❑ *He* shut up *when he re-*

①= ●●   ②= ●●○   ③= ●○●   ④= ●○●○   ⑤= ●○● *or* ●●○   ⑥= ●●●○   ⑦= ●○○●○

alised nobody was listening to him.
❒ *Can't you shut those noisy children up?*

⑦ ⑤ shut up (in)
keep somebody or something locked in a room, box, safe place, etc
❒ *He shut the girl up in the house and refused to allow her to leave.* ❒ *She kept her jewellery shut up in a safe.*

⑥ shy away from
avoid something which you find unpleasant, difficult, etc ❒ *She shies away from anybody touching her.* ❒ *They shied away from buying a horse when they realised how much it would cost to keep it.*

② sicken of
become tired of somebody or something ❒ *She finally sickened of his behaviour and left him.*

② side with
give support to somebody, especially in an argument or quarrel ❒ *She always sides with her mother.* ❒ *He was careful to side with the winning team.*

⑥ ① sidle up (to)
approach somebody in a way which is not intended to attract attention
❒ *A man sidled up to me in the street and tried to sell me a watch.*

②③ sign away / over
formally give up rights, property, money, etc, by signing a document
❒ *He signed away his share of the house to his daughter.*

① sign in
record your arrival by writing your name and the time or date, especially at work or at a club ❒ *He signed in at 8 am.*

⑤/④ sign in / into
put your signature against someone's name in order that they may enter a club, etc, with you, especially of a member ❒ *If you'd like to come to Raffles with me one day, I'll sign you in.*

① sign off ¹
1 mark the end of a radio programme or of broadcasting for the day, especially by playing a piece of music ❒ *The announcer signed off by playing his signature tune.*
2 end a letter ❒ *I must sign off now. Love, Mary.*
3 stop work for the day ❒ *Because of the snow, we signed off at three o'clock.*

⑤ sign off ²
sign a piece of paper to say that somebody is too ill to work, especially of a doctor ❒ *The doctor signed me off for two weeks when I had influenza.*

①⑤ sign on ¹
sign or cause somebody to sign an agreement to work for a company, join a team, etc ❒ *He signed on for five years.* ❒ *We've signed on a hundred machine operators.*

① sign on ²
1 register as unemployed at an office of the Department of Health and Social Security (in Britain) ❒ *When the steel works closed, a thousand men had to sign on.*
2 begin a radio programme or broadcasting for the day, especially by playing a piece of music ❒ *The BBC signs on at six o'clock every morning.*

①⑥⑤⑦ sign out (of)
record your departure, especially from work or a club, etc, by writing your

name ❏ *We signed out of college on Friday evening and returned on Monday morning.*

②③ **sign over**
see **sign away/over**

①⑤ **sign up**
join or cause somebody to join a club, group, class, etc
❏ *The football team signed up three new players during the summer.*
❏ *He signed up for a course in French at the local college.*

① **silt up**
become or cause something to become blocked or filled with mud, sand, soil, etc
❏ *The mouth of the river has gradually silted up over the years.*

① **simmer down**
become calmer after being angry, excited, etc often used in the imperative ❏ *Simmer down, John! I can't talk to you when you are so angry.* ❏ *I told him to simmer down or go away.*

① **sing out** *Informal*
call out loudly ❏ *If you need anything, just sing out and I'll come.*

⑤ **single out**
select one person or thing from among many for special treatment
❏ *Why the critics singled me out, I'll never know. The whole cast was magnificent.*

① **sink in**
be absorbed, understood or acknowledged ❏ *It took a long time for the bad news to sink in.* ❏ *I think it has finally sunk in that she must be more careful: she won't forget her passport again!*

④ **sink in / into**
put a lot of money into a business, property, deal, etc ❏ *He sank all his savings into the firm.*

②③ **siphon off**
take something, especially money, gradually and illegally
❏ *He siphoned off a lot of the club's savings for his own use.*

① **sit about / around**
sit and do nothing, especially while other people are working
❏ *She sat around all day and watched me clean the house.*

① **sit back**
relax and do nothing, especially when your help is needed or when you have been working hard ❏ *He's happy just to sit back and let others take the decisions.* ❏ *It's marvellous to be able to sit back after a hard day's work.*

① **sit by**
observe but fail to act as needed
❏ *Even when his daughter was in trouble, he just sat by and did not help.*

② **sit for**
1 take an examination ❏ *His teachers said he should sit for university.* ❏ *He sat for a scholarship and got one.*
2 be a member of parliament for a certain place ❏ *He has sat for Worcester for twenty years now.*

① **sit in**
occupy a building or part of a building as a protest ❏ *The students have been sitting in for the last two weeks.*

N ❏ *They organised a very successful sit-in at the factory and prevented it from being closed.*

⑥① sit in (for)
take somebody's place at a meeting or on a committee, etc
☐ *The chairman is ill, so I am sitting in for him this evening.*

⑥ sit in on
attend a meeting or a course without taking active part in it
☐ *The professor said I could sit in on his linguistics lectures.*

② sit on
1 delay taking action on something
☐ *They have been sitting on my job application for weeks.*
2 serve as an official member of a committee, jury, etc ☐ *He has been sitting on the English committee ever since he came to university.*
3 quickly subdue somebody who behaves rudely or impertinently
☐ *Her brothers sat on her firmly whenever she was too noisy or silly.*

⑤ sit out
1 remain seated during a piece of dance music ☐ *I'm too hot to dance. Let's sit this one out.*
2 stay until the end of a meeting, film, performance, etc, especially when you are not enjoying yourself
☐ *I hated the play, but I sat it out to the very end.*

② sit through
stay in your seat while you attend, watch or listen to something, especially when you are not enjoying yourself ☐ *We had to sit through the first half of the film without any sound.*

① sit up
1 not go to bed ☐ *I sat up until four o'clock waiting for you last night.* ☐ *I'll be late tonight. Don't sit up for me.*

2 become alert and pay attention to somebody or something
☐ *You should have seen them all sit up as soon as I mentioned money.*
☐ *Coming bottom of the class certainly made Jill sit up and think about her work.*

② sit with
nurse or attend somebody who is ill
☐ *You go to bed for an hour. I'll sit with your mother while you are asleep.*

②③ size up
form an opinion or judgement of somebody or something
☐ *He sized up the situation and phoned the police immediately.*
☐ *I have difficulty in sizing people up.*

② skate over
treat a problem or serious matter lightly
☐ *He simply skated over the difficulties there would be if we moved to Singapore.*

① skip off / out
leave hurriedly and without attracting attention, especially to avoid something
☐ *He skipped off quickly when the waiter brought us the bill.*
☐ *She is always skipping out when there is washing-up to be done.*

⑤ slap down
firmly prevent somebody from doing something ☐ *He soon slapped her down when she wanted to speak.*

⑤④ slap on / onto
add an amount to the price of something, especially in a way that seems unfair ☐ *The builder slapped another £1000 onto the price of the house we had hoped to buy.*

① **sleep around**   *Informal*
have sexual relations with a lot of different people ☐ *She slept around a lot before she got married.*

① **sleep in**
1 sleep in the place where you work
☐ *They have two maids who sleep in.*
2 sleep until later than usual
☐ *I slept in and missed my bus.*

⑤ **sleep off**
get rid of a bad feeling or emotion by sleeping
☐ *He slept off the effects of all the drink he had at the party the previous night.*

② **sleep on**
have a night's sleep before making a decision about something
☐ *I can't decide what to do. I'll sleep on it and let you know tomorrow.*

① **sleep out**
sleep away from the place where you work
☐ *They have a gardener who sleeps out.*

① **sleep together**
have sexual relations
☐ *They've been sleeping together for a long time, but I don't think they're going to get married.*

② **sleep with**
have sexual relations with somebody
☐ *He has been sleeping with his girlfriend for two months.*

⑤ **slick down**
make hair smooth and shiny by using oil, water, etc
☐ *He slicked down his hair with haircream before he went to meet his girlfriend.*

⑤/④ **slip in / into**
mention something in a conversation or discussion in a casual way
☐ *She slipped the news of her wedding into the conversation.*

⑤/② **slip on / into**
put on an item of clothing easily and quickly ☐ *She slipped her shoes on.*
☐ *She slipped into her dress.*

⑥ **slip out of**
take off an item of clothing easily and quickly ☐ *She slipped out of her skirt.*

⑥ ① **slip up (over)**
make a mistake in something
☐ *They slipped up badly over the appointments for the new project.*
N ☐ *There was a slip-up in the university administration.*

② **slobber over**
show too much love or affection for somebody; used in a derogatory way
☐ *I hate the way she slobbers over her children.*

①② **slop about/around**
move about lazily, doing nothing
☐ *When my son is home from college, he just slops about the house and never does any work.*

① **slope off**
go away secretly or unobtrusively, especially to avoid something
☐ *He's always sloping off when I want him to help clean the house.*

② **smack of**
have a slight trace or suggestion of something, especially something unpleasant ☐ *His opinions smack of disloyalty to his firm.*

② **smell of**
strongly suggest something rather unpleasant ☐ *Don't listen to him. His ideas smell of dishonesty.*

②③ **smell out**
discover something by noticing certain signs ☐ *The teacher smelt out the culprit by the ink on his fingers.*

⑦ ⑤ **smoke out (of)**
force somebody out of hiding by using smoke or clever tactics ☐ *The police smoked the gunman out of the house.*

②③ **smooth away**
get rid of difficulties or problems ☐ *With a bit of effort, we will smooth away any problems we encounter.*

②③ **smooth over**
make problems, difficulties, etc, seem less important; resolve an argument or conflict ☐ *He tried hard to smooth over the quarrel.*

② **snap at**
accept something eagerly ☐ *She snapped at the chance of going to America.*

⑥ **snap out of** *Informal*
make yourself stop feeling miserable, depressed, bad-tempered, etc; often used in the imperative ☐ *You're so miserable today! Snap out of it before I lose my temper with you.*

②③ **snap up**
take or buy something quickly and eagerly ☐ *She snapped up a lot of bargains in the sales.* ☐ *If you don't marry me soon, I'll be snapped up by somebody else!*

② **snatch at**
try quickly and eagerly to seize or take advantage of something ☐ *She snatched at the chance of happiness she was being offered.*

② **sneeze at**
refuse to consider something seriously; usually used in the negative ☐ *Such a chance is not to be sneezed at.* ☐ *I wouldn't sneeze at the opportunity of working for such an interesting person.*

② **sniff at**
show contempt for something or consider something unworthy of attention; often used in the negative ☐ *His offer is certainly not to be sniffed at.* ☐ *You're silly to sniff at such a good opportunity.*

② **sniff out**
discover or detect something, especially a secret, criminal activity, etc ☐ *He tried to sniff out the reason for the unpleasant feelings between them.*

⑦ ③ **snow under (with)**
overwhelm somebody with a large amount of work or too many things to do; often used in the passive ☐ *I'm snowed under with work at the moment. I'm afraid I can't accept any more jobs.* ☐ *When we moved, we were snowed under with invitations to visit people.*

② **snuff out**
put an end to something ☐ *The Government quickly snuffed out the rebellion in the army.*

④ **soak in**
absorb as much of something as possible, especially by study; usually reflexive ☐ *For a whole year he soaked himself in the history of the Roman Empire.*

---

① = ●●   ② = ●●○   ③ = ●○●   ④ = ●○○○   ⑤ = ●○● *or* ●●○   ⑥ = ●●●○   ⑦ = ●○●●○

②③ **soak up** ¹

absorb, learn or remember something ❑ *I've never known a child who soaked up so much information.*

②③ **soak up** ²

something such as a sponge soaks up liquid when it absorbs it or takes it up into itself ❑ *Use the mop to soak up the water on the floor after you have a shower.*

①⑤ **sober down**

become or cause somebody to become calm or quiet, especially after being excited or jolly ❑ *Come on, children! Sober down or you will never get to sleep!*

①⑤ **sober up**

1 recover or cause somebody to recover from being drunk ❑ *He drank a lot of water to sober him up after the party.*
2 become or cause somebody to become serious ❑ *He soon sobered up when he heard the awful news.*

②③ **soften up**

1 weaken an enemy before a major attack ❑ *Our aeroplanes bombed the enemy and softened up their defences before the army landed and attacked.*
2 make it difficult for somebody to resist something, especially by using persuasion, seduction, etc ❑ *He sent her a huge box of chocolates to soften her up before he asked her to marry him.*

① **soldier on**

continue or persevere, in spite of difficulties ❑ *In spite of feeling ill, he soldiered on and finished the job.*

⑤ **sop up**

remove liquid by putting something absorbent in it, especially a cloth ❑ *He has spilt his orange juice. Sop it up quickly with a towel.*

②③ **sort out**

1 arrange things neatly or into groups ❑ *The child was sorting out the bricks into different colours.*
N ❑ *Your bedroom is very untidy. It could do with a good sort-out.*
2 resolve an argument ❑ *You will have to sort out your differences yourselves.*
3 organise somebody or something ❑ *He took just one month to sort out his new office and the secretarial staff.* ❑ *She told him to sort himself out or she would leave him.*
4 *Informal* attack somebody either verbally or physically ❑ *If you don't stop fighting, I shall come and sort you out.*

⑥ ① **sound off (about)** *Informal*

talk loudly and pompously, especially when expressing opinions; used in a derogatory way ❑ *He is always sounding off about how awful the Government is.* ❑ *Do we have to listen to her sounding off again about her holiday?*

②③ **sound out**

try to discover somebody's opinions, feelings, or plans in a cautious and tactful way ❑ *I'm not sure what he intends to do. Will you try to sound him out?*

②③ **soup up**

improve the performance of an engine, especially a car or motorcycle engine ❑ *He asked the garage to soup up his bike.*

②③ **space out**

place things apart from one another ❑ *Her family was well spaced out; she had 3 children in nine years.* ❑ *He carefully spaced out his rows of peas in the garden.*

②③ **spark off**

1 cause something to erupt or explode ❒ *Just one match sparked off a terrible forest fire.*

2 be the immediate cause of something violent or frightening
❒ *The whole war was sparked off by a minor disagreement.*
❒ *I have no idea what sparked their quarrel off this time.*

② **speak for**

1 express thoughts and opinions on behalf of somebody ❒ *I know I am speaking for everyone when I thank our hostess for a wonderful party.* ❒ *Just be quiet a minute and let John speak for himself.*

2 make a speech in support of something ❒ *He was asked to speak for the motion that nuclear weapons should be abolished.*

3 need no defence or justification; followed by itself or themselves
❒ *Our record on unemployment is so good that it speaks for itself.*

4 book or reserve something; usually passive ❒ *All the rooms in the hotel have been spoken for by the organisers of the conference.*

⑥ ① **speak out against**

give your opinions about something bravely and freely
❒ *She spoke out strongly against cruelty to animals.*

① **speak up**

1 speak more loudly
❒ *Please speak up so that the people at the back of the room can hear you.*

2 speak boldly about a subject
❒ *She spoke up in defence of her views on capital punishment.*

①②③ **speed up**

go faster or cause something to go faster ❒ *You're driving very slowly. Do speed up a bit or we'll never get to Edinburgh.* ❒ *The new government has speeded up the building of new houses.*
N ❒ *There has been a speed-up in the road building programme.*

②③ **spell out**

1 read something very slowly and with difficulty
❒ *He is eight now, but he still has to spell out nearly everything he reads.*

2 explain something in a very clear, simple way ❒ *He is so stupid. You have to spell out the most basic things to him.*
❒ *His speech spelt out the Government's plans for the army.*

①② ③ **spew up**   *Informal*
vomit ❒ *The dog spewed up all over the kitchen floor.*

① **spill over**

flow or spread beyond certain limits; used especially of people in urban areas ❒ *The housing estate spilled over into the very centre of the town.*
N ❒ *They built a new town to house Birmingham's overspill.*

⑤ **spin out**

make something last as long as possible ❒ *That's all the money there is, so you'll just have to spin it out for the rest of the week.* ❒ *He spun out his story for twenty minutes.*

⑤ **spirit away / off**

make somebody or something disappear quickly or in a mysterious way; often used in the passive
❒ *The pop star was spirited off through the back door.*

②③ spit out
say something angrily or sharply
◻ *He spat out an obscenity at the old man blocking his way.* ◻ *I'll never forget the way he spat out our names.*

③ splash about / around
spend money in an extravagant way; often used ironically ◻ *You won't have a penny left if you keep splashing your money about like that.*

① splash down
land in the sea, especially of a space vehicle which has returned to earth
◻ *The astronauts splashed down exactly on time.*
N ◻ *It was a perfect splash-down.*

①⑥② splash out (on)
spend a lot of money on something that you want but do not need
◻ *She splashed out all her month's salary on a beautiful fur coat.* ◻ *Let's splash out this evening. How about going to that new French restaurant?*

⑥ ① split away / off (from)
leave a group or organisation, especially in order to form a new one
◻ *Some of the members split away from the sports society and formed their own tennis club.*

② split on   *Informal*
give information to somebody in authority which will get somebody else into trouble; usually used by children ◻ *Don't split on me if I don't go to school tomorrow. It's swimming and I hate it!*

① split up
cease to live or work together, especially of a married couple, family,
group, etc ◻ *Did you know that John and Mary have split up?*

② spring from
1 appear suddenly from somewhere
◻ *He wasn't here a minute ago. Where on earth did he spring from?*
2 be the result or outcome of something ◻ *Her happiness springs from her love of her family.*

④ spring on
tell something to somebody so that they are surprised by it ◻ *She sprang the news on us without a warning.*

① spring up
suddenly appear, arise, or develop
◻ *New buildings are springing up all over the city.*

⑤ spruce up
make yourself, somebody else or something clean and tidy ◻ *Go and spruce yourself up, Mary, before we go to the party.* ◻ *She spruced up the children because their grandfather was coming.*

⑤ spur on
encourage somebody to try harder
◻ *Father spurred us on to do even better at school.* ◻ *The thought of winning the race spurred her on.*

② spy on
watch secretly what somebody else is doing ◻ *Our neighbours are always looking out of their windows, spying on us.*

② spy out
investigate an area, situation, etc, in a secret way, in order to get information about it ◻ *Go and see if you can spy out what the opposition is up to.*

---

① = ●●   ② = ●●○   ③ = ●○●   ④ = ●○●○   ⑤ = ●○● *or* ●●○   ⑥ = ●●●○   ⑦ = ●○●●○

⑥ ① square up (with)
pay somebody money that you owe them ❑ *Will you square up with the waiter while I go and get the car?* ❑ *If you tell me how much the meal was, we can square up later.*

⑥ square up to
1 stand as if ready to fight somebody ❑ *The boys squared up to each other, but the teacher stopped them.*
2 acknowledge or accept misfortune in a courageous way ❑ *He squared up to the possibility of losing his job.*

② squeal on
inform the police or somebody in authority about something illegal, especially of a criminal ❑ *One member of the gang squealed on the others and they were arrested while robbing the bank.*

②③ squeeze in
find time to do something, see somebody, etc ❑ *If I have a quick lunch, I might just manage to squeeze in a visit to the library.* ❑ *I know the professor is very busy, but could he possibly squeeze me in?*

⑦ ⑤ squeeze out (of)
obtain something from somebody by applying pressure ❑ *The government hopes to squeeze even more money out of the public by raising taxes.*

②③ stake off / out
mark an area of land with tall pieces of wood ❑ *He staked off the land where he was going to build his hut.*

④ stake on
bet or risk your money, reputation, life, etc, on something ❑ *He staked five pounds on the winning horse.* ❑ *I'll stake my life on his honesty.*

②③ stake out
1 see **stake off/out**
2 watch a place secretly, especially of the police ❑ *The police staked out the house where they thought the gunman was hiding.*

② stamp on
suppress something by acting decisively ❑ *We must stamp on any act of vandalism in the school.*

②③ stamp out
put an end to something by acting decisively ❑ *The Government quickly stamped out the rebellion.* ❑ *Many infectious diseases have been stamped out by the use of new drugs.*

① stand about / around
stand doing nothing, especially because of laziness ❑ *Don't just stand around. Help me cut the grass.*

① stand aside
move out of the way, especially to let somebody go past ❑ *The crowd were asked to stand aside to let the players go in.*

⑥ ① stand back (from)
1 be situated some distance from something ❑ *The house stands back from the main road.*
2 distance or detach yourself from something, especially to understand or appreciate it better ❑ *When he managed to stand back from his subject, the author realised he had misunderstood her motives.*

② stand between
be a barrier or difficulty between somebody and the thing that they want ❑ *Only one candidate stood between him and the job.*

---

① = ●●   ② = ●●○   ③ = ●○●   ④ = ●○●○   ⑤ = ●○● *or* ●●○   ⑥ = ●●●○   ⑦ = ●○●●○

① stand by ¹

1 watch something and do nothing
❒ *He could not* stand by *and watch the child being beaten.*
2 be ready for action, especially of the armed forces ❒ *The regiment is* standing by *to go to Northern Ireland.*
N ❒ *The army is on permanent* stand-by.
3 wait and be ready to act quickly
❒ *Stand by* to receive a telephone call from India.*

② stand by ²

1 defend or loyally support somebody ❒ *He is the sort of person who will always* stand by *a friend.* ❒ *The football supporters* stood by *their team, even when they were losing.*
2 be faithful to a promise, undertaking, agreement, etc ❒ *Even if I lose my job by complaining, I must* stand by *my principles.* ❒ *I* stand by *every word I said.*

① stand down

1 leave the witness box in a court of law ❒ *If there are no more questions, the witness may now* stand down.
2 withdraw from something, especially in favour of somebody else
❒ *He* stood down *as a candidate because he felt a younger man would be more suitable.*

② stand for

1 tolerate or accept something; usually used in the negative
❒ *I will not* stand for *behaviour of that kind in my house.*
2 represent, mean or be a symbol or abbreviation for something ❒ *I hate the woman and everything she* stands for.
❒ *What does 'BBC'* stand for?
3 be a candidate for something
❒ *She is* standing for *Parliament in the next election.*

⑥ ① stand in (for)

take somebody's place or job for a short time, especially of an actor or actress ❒ *Paul's understudy is* standing in for *him just for tonight's performance.*
❒ *I'm* standing in for *the secretary while she is sick.*
N ❒ *Her* stand-in *looks just like her.*

②③ stand off

dismiss workers, especially for a short time when there is no work to do ❒ *The management had to* stand off *a hundred men this week.*

① stand out

be noticeable or special in some way
❒ *Two of the girls* stood out *as being exceptionally good dancers.* ❒ *She* stands out *from other detective-story writers.*

⑥ stand out against

be firm in your opposition to something ❒ *The soldiers* stood out against *the enemy for as long as they could.*
❒ *We must* stand out against *any evidence of racism in our country.*

⑥ stand out for

wait stubbornly for something that you have demanded to be given or allowed ❒ *The union* stood out for *another twenty pounds a week for each member.*

② stand over

watch somebody very carefully
❒ *He never does his homework unless I* stand over *him.*

⑤ stand up

fail to keep an appointment with somebody
❒ *She* stood *him* up *because she was too tired to go out.*

---

① = ●● ② = ●●○ ③ = ●○● ④ = ●○●○ ⑤ = ●○● *or* ●●○ ⑥ = ●●●○ ⑦ = ●○●●○

⑥① **stand up (to)**
1 be accepted as true or be able to withstand an investigation
❒ *The charges against him will not stand up in court.*
❒ *His alibi stood up to all our questions.*
2 endure or withstand something
❒ *I could never stand up to another week like last week.*
❒ *Will the chair stand up to your weight?*

② **stand up for**
defend somebody or something against attack ❒ *He has got to learn to stand up for himself when he goes to school.*
❒ *It is important to stand up for your rights as a mother.*

⑤ **stare out**
look fixedly at somebody until they look away, blink, become silent, etc
❒ *The two boys decided to see which one could stare the other out.*

① **start back**
begin a return journey ❒ *What time do we have to start back?*

① **start off / out**
begin a journey ❒ *We started out at 8 am and arrived at 6 pm.*

①⑥③⑦ **start off (on)**
begin or cause somebody to begin doing something, especially talking in a way which other people find boring
❒ *Don't let him start off on his holiday stories again or we'll be here all night.*

⑥ **start out of**
wake quickly and suddenly from sleep, a daydream, etc
❒ *He started out of his dream when he heard the telephone ring.*

① **start up**
begin a career, business, working life, etc ❒ *He's thinking of starting up as a private consultant.* ❒ *She started up in dressmaking and then changed to typing.*

②③ **starve out**
force somebody to surrender or leave a hiding place by preventing food from reaching them, especially of an army or the police ❒ *It took just a week to starve the prisoners out.*

⑤ **stash away**   *Informal*
hide or put something in a safe place ❒ *The old man stashed his money away in a box in his cellar.*

② **stave off**
delay or prevent something from happening ❒ *He borrowed money from the bank to stave off bankruptcy.* ❒ *He ate a crust of bread to stave off his hunger.*

① **stay behind**
remain after other people have left, especially for a particular purpose
❒ *He stayed behind when the shop shut to tidy the shelves.*
❒ *Would somebody stay behind after the meeting and put the chairs away?*

① **stay down**
remain in the stomach, especially of food and drink ❒ *She kept being sick and nothing she ate would stay down.*

① **stay in**
1 remain at home ❒ *If you stay in for a few days, you'll soon feel better.*
2 remain in school after the other children have left, especially as a punishment ❒ *If you don't stop talking, you'll stay in for an hour after school.*
3 not be dismissed or defeated, es-

pecially of a batsman ❏ *He stayed in for two hours and scored seventy runs.*

①② stay off [1]
not go to work, school, etc
❏ *I don't feel very well. I think I'll stay off tomorrow and have a day in bed.*

② stay off [2]
not eat, drink, smoke, etc, things which may be bad for you ❏ *You'll have to stay off beer if you really want to lose weight.*

⑥ ① stay on (at)
remain at school, college, work, etc, after other people have left
❏ *I'll stay on this evening and help you if you like.* ❏ *He is staying on at school for another year.*

① stay out
1 remain out of doors or away from home ❏ *She lets her children stay out until ten o'clock in the summer.*
2 remain on strike ❏ *The miners threatened to stay out all winter if their pay claim was not accepted.*

① stay up
not go to bed ❏ *They stayed up until midnight watching television.*

① steal away
leave quietly and often secretly
❏ *He stole away while everyone else was watching the film.*

② steal over
slowly and quietly take hold of somebody, especially of feelings, emotions, etc
❏ *A feeling of happiness stole over the girl when she thought about the days ahead.*

⑥ steal up on
approach somebody slowly and quietly, especially in order to surprise them ❏ *Her friend stole up on her and made her jump.*

①②③ steam up
cover or become covered with steam
❏ *The car windows steamed up in the rain.*
❏ *The rain steamed up his glasses and he could hardly see.*

④ steep in
make yourself thoroughly familiar with something ❏ *He steeped himself in the traditions of the English countryside.*

② stem from
be traceable to or caused by somebody or something ❏ *Her interest in Italy stems from her uncle.* ❏ *Their hatred of him stemmed from fear.*

① step down
resign, especially from an important position
❏ *The chairman announced that he would step down at the next meeting.*

① step in
enter a discussion or argument
❏ *I stepped in to prevent John from saying something stupid.*
❏ *If the government does not step in, there will be no trains on Monday.*

① step out
1 start walking faster, especially by taking longer strides ❏ *When he realised how late it was, he stepped out to get home before dark.*
2 enjoy yourself socially
❏ *She's really stepping out these days: the theatre last night, dinner tonight and dancing tomorrow.*

②③ step up

increase something in size, number or speed ❒ *If we are to make all the cars we can sell, we must* step up *production this year by fifteen per cent.*

① stick about/around *Informal*

remain, especially waiting for something to happen ❒ *If you* stick around *long enough, he'll be sure to notice you.*

② stick at

continue to work hard and steadily at something

❒ *If you really* stick at *that essay, I'm sure you can finish it by Monday morning.*

② stick by

continue to help and support somebody ❒ *His wife* sticks by *him whatever he does.*

③ stick down *Informal*

put something down on the floor, etc ❒ *Just* stick *those books* down *over there. I'll put them away later.*

①⑤ stick out ¹

protrude or make something protrude or project ❒ *Her teeth* stick out. ❒ *Don't* stick *your tongue* out *at me.*

②③ stick out ² *Informal*

endure or tolerate something

❒ *Try to* stick out *the party for another hour and then we can go home.*

⑥ stick out for

wait stubbornly for something that you have demanded to be allowed or given ❒ *The students* stuck out for *three seats on the University Senate.* ❒ *The union are* sticking out for *a twenty per cent increase.*

② stick to

1 keep a promise, not change a plan, decision, etc ❒ *I'll* stick to *my promise whatever happens.* ❒ *Now we've made a decision, let's* stick to *it.*

2 concentrate on a particular point, subject, etc ❒ *I hate listening to him; he never* sticks to *the point.* ❒ *Why doesn't he* stick to *the subject of the lecture?*

① stick together

remain united, especially when threatened ❒ *If we all* stick together, *there won't be any trouble.*

②③ stick up *Informal*

rob somebody, a bank, etc, with the aid of a gun ❒ *If you are so desperate for money, you could always* stick up *the post office.*

N ❒ *This is a* stick-up! *You've got two minutes to empty the safe!*

⑥ stick up for

speak or act in defence of somebody or something ❒ *You have got to* stick up for *your rights.* ❒ *My mother always* sticks up for *me against my brother.*

② stick with

stay close or loyal to somebody or something ❒ *If you* stick with *us, you will come to no harm.* ❒ *He* stuck with *the Labour party all his life.*

②③ stir up

cause or encourage trouble, hatred, bad feelings, etc; make somebody angry or agitated ❒ *Please don't* stir up *trouble between them.* ❒ *I think she enjoys* stirring *him* up *now and then.*

⑥ ① stock up (with)

store a large amount of supplies, especially for a particular purpose or occasion ❏ *She stocked up with food and drink for the Christmas party.*

①⑥⑤⑦ stoke up (with)
1 put fuel on a fire ❏ *Don't forget to stoke up before you go to bed.*
2 *Informal* fill yourself with a great deal of food ❏ *She stoked up with chocolates as if she would never eat again.*

② stoop to
lower your standard of behaviour; often followed by *-ing*
❏ *He even stooped to stealing money from his own children.* ❏ *He would stoop to anything to get what he wanted.*

② stop at
stay in a hotel, etc ❏ *For two days we stopped at a nice little inn in the mountains.*

⑥① stop away (from)
be absent from something ❏ *Why did you stop away from the meeting? We expected to see you there.*

① stop behind
remain after other people have left, especially for a particular purpose ❏ *He stopped behind to ask the speaker some questions.*

①⑥② stop by (at)
visit or stop somewhere for a short time, especially on your way to somewhere else ❏ *We were passing your house, so we thought we would stop by for a few minutes.*

② stop for / to
stay somewhere to share a meal, etc
❏ *You will stop to dinner, won't you?*

① stop in
1 stay at home ❏ *I'm stopping in tonight to wash my hair.*

2 remain at school late as a punishment ❏ *If there is any more trouble, you will all stop in for two hours.*

① stop off
interrupt a journey, especially to visit friends, shop, rest, etc ❏ *They stopped off for a meal.* ❏ *We'll stop off at Oxford and see them on our way to London.*

⑥① stop on (at)
remain at school, college, etc, especially after other people have left ❏ *She stopped on at school until she was 19.*

① stop out
1 remain out of doors or away from home ❏ *She stopped out until 1 o'clock and her father was furious.*
2 remain on strike
❏ *The workers decided to stop out until their conditions of work were improved.*

① stop over
interrupt a journey by air for a short time and then continue it
❏ *He stopped over in Paris for a day.*
N ❏ *They decided on Brussels for their stop-over.*

② stop to
see stop for/to

① stop up
not go to bed ❏ *We shall be home late, so please do not stop up for us.*

①/② storm in / into
enter a room or building noisily and often angrily ❏ *He stormed into the manager's office, shouting and swearing.*

① stow away
hide secretly on a ship or plane in order to travel on it free ❏ *He stowed away on a ship going to New York.*

N ❐ *There was a* stowaway *on the ship.*

⑤ **straighten out**

1 resolve a problem or difficulty
❐ *My daughter was having problems at school but we soon managed to* straighten *them* out.

2 cause somebody to stop being confused, anxious, critical, etc
❐ *He doesn't seem to understand what I'm trying to do. Perhaps if you talked to him you could* straighten *him* out.

② **strain at**

pull hard on something, especially a rope ❐ *The sailors* strained at *the rope, but couldn't lift the anchor.*

③④② **strain off**

remove liquid from something by using a sieve ❐ *She* strained *the water* off *the beans and put them on the table.*

⑤ **strap in**

fasten a seat-belt, especially in a car or plane ❐ *Don't forget to* strap *yourself* in. ❐ *The plane will not take off until everybody is* strapped in.

⑤ **strap up**

fasten something with straps, bandages, etc ❐ *Your ankle is swollen. You'd better* strap *it* up. ❐ *They* strapped up *their luggage and took it downstairs.*

①②③ **stretch out**

1 extend your body or part of it, especially to relax, take something, or greet somebody ❐ *He* stretched out *on the grass in the sunshine.* ❐ *She* stretched out *her hand and took the ice cream.*

2 be enough or cause something to be enough ❐ *You should have phoned me. I don't think I can* stretch out *the food to feed three more people.*

② **strike at**

try to hit somebody or something
❐ *She* struck at *him with a hammer.*
❐ *This* strikes at *the heart of democracy.*

⑤ **strike down**

make somebody unable to lead a full, active life ❐ *He was* struck down *by a heart attack at the age of forty.*

④② **strike into**

penetrate or cause something to penetrate, especially of fear, cold, etc
❐ *The headmaster* struck terror into *the new teacher by telling her about his pupils.*
❐ *Her cold words* struck into *his heart.*

③④② **strike off** [1]

remove something, especially a name from a list; end somebody's membership of a professional group ❐ *The doctor was* struck off *for prescribing illegal drugs.* ❐ *He was* struck off *the register.*

② **strike off** [2]

print copies of something ❐ *They* struck off *5000 copies of the election leaflet.*

② **strike on / upon**

discover something suddenly and unexpectedly ❐ *He* struck on *a way of making diamonds.*

① **strike out**

start to do something new and different, especially on your own
❐ *He decided to leave his father's firm and* strike out *on his own.*

① **strike out / through**

remove or draw a line through a piece of writing
❐ *She* struck out *the sentence she had just written and added a new one.*

---

① = ●● ② = ●●○ ③ = ●○● ④ = ●○●○ ⑤ = ●○● *or* ●●○ ⑥ = ●●●○ ⑦ = ●○●●○

⑥ ① **strike out (at)**
try to hit somebody in a wild or un-controlled way ☐ *The little boy was frightened and struck out madly.*

⑥ ① **strike out (for/towards)**
move quickly in a certain direction, especially by swimming ☐ *He dived off the boat and struck out for the island.*

①② **strike up**
begin playing a piece of music or singing a song ☐ *The orchestra struck up the National Anthem.* ☐ *People won't get up to dance until the band strikes up.*

② **strike up (with)**
begin a friendship with somebody, especially in a casual, unplanned way ☐ *They struck up an acquaintance with each other on the beach and soon became very friendly.*

② **strike upon**
see **strike on/upon**

③ **string along**
deceive somebody, especially by giving them false hopes ☐ *She's been engaged to Jim for five years, but she'll never marry him. She's just stringing him along.*

⑥ ① **string along (with)** *Informal*
accompany or be friendly with somebody, especially for as long as it suits you ☐ *We're going to John's party too. You can string along with us if you like.*

①②③ **string out**
be spread or spread something at intervals in a line ☐ *The police strung out across the field looking for clues.* ☐ *She was stringing out the clothes on the washing line when it started to rain.*

⑤ **string together**
combine words, sentences, etc, in a meaningful way ☐ *He says he can speak fluent German but I have never heard him string more than three words together.*

②③ **string up**
1 hang something high, especially as a decoration ☐ *They strung up pretty lights all over the room.*
2 *Informal* kill somebody by hanging ☐ *They strung up the captured terrorist for everybody to see.*

②③ **strip down**
take something to pieces, especially an engine, machine, etc ☐ *He is never happier than when he is stripping down the car.*

① **strip down / off**
take your clothes off ☐ *She stripped off and went for a swim.*

④ **strip of**
take something valuable from somebody ☐ *The convicted spy was stripped of all his public honours.*

②③ **stub out**
stop a cigarette burning by pressing it against something hard ☐ *He stubbed out his cigarette in the ash-tray.*

② **stumble across / on / upon**
discover or meet somebody or something unexpectedly ☐ *They stumbled across the entrance to an old tunnel.* ☐ *Coming out of the airport, he stumbled on an old friend.*

② **stumble over**
hesitate and make mistakes when you are speaking or reading ☐ *The little girl stumbled over nearly every word until the teacher told her to stop reading.*

---

① = ●●   ② = ●●○   ③ = ●○●   ④ = ●○●○   ⑤ = ●○● *or* ●●○   ⑥ = ●●●○   ⑦ = ●○●●○

④ **subject to**

1 bring a country or person under your control, especially by the use of force ☐ *The Romans never succeeded in subjecting the Scots to their rule.*

2 make something have to undergo a test, treatment, etc ☐ *All cars are subjected to various tests before they leave the factory.*

3 expose somebody to something, especially to something unpleasant ☐ *The audience subjected the speaker to a lot of difficult questions.*

② **subscribe to**

1 agree with something that is said or done ☐ *I could never subscribe to torture, no matter what the reason.*

2 pay regularly in order to receive a newspaper, magazine, etc ☐ *Many teachers subscribe to that periodical.*

④ **subsume under** *Formal*

place something in a particular group or class; usually used in the passive ☐ *Sugar, tea and coffee can be subsumed under the heading 'groceries'.*

③ **suck down / under**

pull somebody or something below the surface of a liquid or something similar to liquid ☐ *He was sucked under by the river's strong current.*

⑥ ① **suck up (to)**

try to make somebody like you, especially by using flattery ☐ *She is always sucking up to her teachers but they do not like her for it.*

④ **suit to**

choose or adjust something so that it is appropriate for a particular situation or purpose ☐ *It is important to suit the punishment to the crime.*

①②③ **sum up** ¹

1 summarise or give the main points of an argument, lecture, etc

☐ *The chairman summed up the speaker's talk and asked for questions.*

☐ *To sum up, for the reasons I have just given, I think my plan is better.*

N ☐ *He was congratulated on his excellent summing-up.*

2 summarise and comment on the main points of a legal case ☐ *The judge summed up for twenty minutes.*

N ☐ *His summing-up lasted 20 minutes.*

⑤ **sum up** ²

form a judgement or opinion of somebody or something

☐ *She summed the man up as incompetent.*

☐ *He could sum up situations at a glance.*

② **summon up**

gather the necessary courage, strength, patience, etc, to do something ☐ *He had to summon up all his courage before he dared enter the room.*

☐ *He found it impossible to summon up enough strength to finish the marathon.*

②③ **suss out** *Informal*

discover or find out something, often in a secret way

☐ *I'm not sure how she will vote. See if you can suss her out.*

②③ **swallow up**

consume or absorb something quickly, especially money or natural resources ☐ *New clothes for the children seem to swallow up all her money.*

☐ *My new car swallows up petrol.*

④ **swamp with**

overwhelm somebody with a great amount or excess of something

☐ *They were swamped with replies to their advertisement.*

② **swarm with**
be full of or crowded with people, animals, etc ☐ *The whole town is swarming with tourists during July.*

④ **swathe in**
wrap something or somebody tightly in a cloth, bandage, etc ☐ *He came out of hospital swathed in bandages from head to foot.*

② **swear by**
praise or recommend something, especially as an aid to health ☐ *She swears by aspirin as the best remedy for a headache.*

⑤ **swear in**
make somebody take an oath to be truthful, loyal, obedient, etc ☐ *They will swear the jury in for the murder trial this morning.* ☐ *The new president was sworn in last week.*
N ☐ *The whole senate was present for the swearing-in of the president.*

② **swear to**
say you are certain of something; often used with *can/could, will/would* and a negative ☐ *I can't swear to it, but I don't think he would lie to me.* ☐ *I am prepared to swear to his honesty.*

②③ **sweat out**
get rid of an illness by sweating ☐ *He went to bed with a hot-water bottle and sweated out his cold.*

②③ **sweep aside**
dismiss comments or objections ☐ *He swept aside all criticism and continued to explain his plan.*

②③ **sweep away**
abolish or get rid of something ☐ *The government promised to sweep away all tax privileges.*

②③ **swill down**
drink something rapidly in large quantities ☐ *He swilled down six whiskies in half an hour.*

⑤ **swill out**
wash or rinse something with a lot of water ☐ *She swilled the saucepan out with plenty of clean water.*

⑦ **swindle out of**
get money from somebody by cheating them ☐ *He swindled the old lady out of fifty pounds.* ☐ *He swindled fifty pounds out of the old lady.*

① **swing round**
turn round quickly ☐ *He swung round to see who had pushed him.*

① **swing to**
close or almost close, especially of a door, gate, etc ☐ *The gate swung to with a bang.*

②③ **switch off** ¹
stop the flow of light, water, gas, electricity, etc, by moving a switch ☐ *Don't forget to switch off the electricity before you go away.*

① **switch off** ²
stop listening, responding or being attentive ☐ *Whenever Bill starts talking, Jim simply switches off.*

②③ **switch on**
1 start the flow of water, light, gas, electricity, etc, by moving a switch ☐ *She switched on all the lights to make the house seem welcoming.*
2 *Informal* make somebody become lively, excited or responsive ☐ *Parties really switch her on: she becomes a completely different person.*

①②③ **swot up**
learn something thoroughly, usually for a test or examination, by a short period of intensive study ☐ *He swotted up his history the night before the exam.*

T,t

⑤/④ tack on/onto
add or join something to the end of something else
❒ *He tacked on another paragraph at the end of the letter.*
❒ *The publisher tacked some notes onto the book before it was printed.*

⑥ ① tag along (with)
accompany somebody somewhere, especially because you have no other plans
❒ *We're going to the pub. Do you want to tag along?*
❒ *I had nothing better to do, so I tagged along with the others.*

① tail away / off
fade or become gradually quieter until the sound stops, especially of a voice, music, sound, etc ❒ *Their voices tailed away down the corridor.*

① tail off
gradually decrease in quantity, especially of trade or business
❒ *Demand for new cars has tailed off since the fuel crisis.*

③ take aback
surprise, astonish or shock somebody; usually preceded by *completely, somewhat, rather,* etc ❒ *I was rather taken aback by her rudeness.* ❒ *The violent reaction of the crowd quite took him aback.*

② take after
be similar to a parent or other relation in character, appearance or behaviour
❒ *He's a very solemn boy. He takes after his mother in that respect.*

③ take apart
1 criticise somebody or something severely ❒ *When the play was first shown the critics took it apart.*
2 defeat somebody easily, especially a team, army, opposition, etc
❒ *United defended well for the first twenty minutes, but after the first goal City began to take them apart.*

②③⑦ take away (from)
subtract one number from another
❒ *Five take away three equals two.*
❒ *If you take £5 away from the total, you're left with £10.*

②③ take back
admit that something you said was wrong or that you should not have said it
❒ *I was very unfair to you just now. I'm sorry. I take it all back.*

⑦ ③ take back (to)
cause somebody to remember something which happened much earlier in their life
❒ *Hearing that song takes me back a few years.*
❒ *The old photograph took him back to his days at school.*

⑤ take down
1 write down or make notes on what somebody is saying, especially of a secretary, student, etc
❒ *The clerk will take down the details of the accident.*
❒ *The students were taking down notes on the lecture.*
2 dismantle or remove something
❒ *At the end of the week we have to take the fireplace down.*

④ **take for**

1 judge somebody's character in a particular way, usually incorrectly
❏ *I took him for a fool, but I was wrong.*
❏ *I won't hurt you. What do you take me for?*

2 assume or believe wrongly that somebody or something is somebody or something else ❏ *I'm sorry. I took you for the secretary.*

⑤ **take in** ¹

1 alter an item of clothing to make it smaller ❏ *The trousers are slightly too big but I can take them in.*

2 understand and absorb something ❏ *She warned him about the danger but he didn't take it in.*

3 fool, deceive or cheat somebody ❏ *I hope you weren't taken in by the advertisement.*

② **take in** ²

1 include something
❏ *The UK takes in Scotland, Wales and Northern Ireland.*

2 undertake work, especially washing, laundry, sewing, etc ❏ *She takes in laundry to earn a bit of extra money.*

3 provide accommodation or food for somebody
❏ *He took in one or two down-and-outs as a sign of his generosity.*

⑤ **take off** ¹

1 imitate or copy the speech or appearance of somebody, especially in order to make people laugh
❏ *It's very funny when Giles takes off the headmaster.*

2 remove something from service, especially a bus or train
❏ *The London-Edinburgh express service has been taken off.*

③④ **take off** ²

1 remove somebody from a job or task ❏ *Because he is so inefficient, we have taken Mr Jones off the job.*

2 remove a particular item from a menu in a restaurant ❏ *'Duck á l'orange' has been taken off tonight.*

3 have a holiday or period of time away from work, school or college
❏ *When I broke my leg I had to take three weeks off.* ❏ *When I was ill I had to take time off.*

① **take off** ³

1 rise up from the ground into the air, especially of an aeroplane or space-rocket ❏ *The plane is scheduled to take off at 17.30.*
N ❏ *The astronauts were getting ready for take-off.*

2 become very successful or popular ❏ *Despite a few early difficulties, the idea really took off.*

3 increase very quickly, especially of sales, profits, etc ❏ *In the last few years, sales of microcomputers have really taken off in a big way.*

②③ **take on** ¹

employ or give a job to somebody ❏ *The steelworks took on 300 extra workers last month.*

2 have a fight or quarrel with somebody; accept somebody as an opponent ❏ *He said he would take on anybody who stood in his way.*

3 accept a job or responsibility
❏ *Her health has begun to suffer since she took on the extra work.*

② **take on** ²

acquire or be seen to have a new or different quality, meaning, appearance ❏ *The novel takes on a new meaning when you know more about the author.*

---

① = ●● ② = ●●○ ③ = ●○● ④ = ●○●○ ⑤ = ●○● *or* ●●○ ⑥ = ●●●○ ⑦ = ●○●●○

②③ **take out** [1]

obtain or pay a fee for an official document or a service, especially an insurance policy, subscription, legal summons, etc ❐ *I'd like to* take out *a subscription to "The Times".*

③ **take out** [2]

take somebody somewhere for recreation, pleasure or exercise ❐ *Let me* take *you* out *to a night club on Saturday. You'll enjoy it.*

⑦ **take out on**

get rid of an unpleasant feeling such as anger or frustration by making somebody else suffer ❐ *You may have had a difficult day at the office, but there's no need to* take *your anger* out on *me now you're home!*

②③ **take over**

get control of something, especially of one company getting financial control of another ❐ *The state airline has* taken over *two small airline companies this year.* **N** ❐ *The* take-over *is worth many millions of pounds.*

①⑥⑤⑦ **take over (from)**

take responsibility for or control of something from somebody else ❐ *Dave* took over *the driving while his mate slept for a few hours.* ❐ *I'm retiring at the end of this year. Mr Clark will* take over from *me.*

② **take to**

1 quickly develop a liking for somebody or something ❐ *He* took to *Sally from the moment he met her.*
2 begin to do something regularly or as a habit ❐ *I've* taken to *playing tennis once a week.*

3 go away somewhere, especially to escape or hide from somebody or something ❐ *The criminal* took to *the hills when she heard that a police hunt had begun.*

② **take up** [1]

start doing some activity regularly, especially a job, sport, hobby, etc ❐ *I* took up *squash only a few months ago.*

⑤ **take up** [2]

1 occupy or fill time, space, room, etc ❐ *Move over! You're* taking up *far too much room. John can't sit down.*
2 shorten a dress, skirt, curtains, etc ❐ *Anyone who can sew can* take up *a skirt.*
3 become soaked with a liquid ❐ *A paper tissue will soon* take up *that spilt coffee.*
4 accept or agree to do something, especially an invitation, offer, challenge, etc ❐ *I had an invitation to the dinner, but I didn't* take *it* up.
5 resume or return to something ❐ *I* took up *the story where Helen had left off.*

⑦③ **take up (on)**

argue with somebody about something they have said ❐ *The lecturer was talking excitedly until someone* took *him* up on *one of his wilder observations.*

②③⑦ **take up (with)**

raise an issue, matter, complaint, etc, for discussion with somebody ❐ *If you have any complaints,* take *them* up with *the manager.*

⑦ **take up on**

accept somebody's offer, challenge, invitation, etc ❐ *If he has said that he will pay for you, why not* take *him* up on *his offer?*

① = ●● ② = ●●○ ③ = ●○● ④ = ●○○○ ⑤ = ●○● *or* ●●○ ⑥ = ●●●○ ⑦ = ●○●●○

⑥ take up with
become friendly with somebody and be frequently in their company
❐ *She has taken up with an unpleasant fellow she met in London.*

③ talk down
1 make it difficult to hear somebody by talking loudly ❐ *The objectors talked the speaker down.*
2 give instructions to a pilot to guide the landing of an aircraft ❐ *The control tower talked the plane down.*

⑥ ① talk down (to)
speak to somebody in a way that makes them feel less intelligent or of a lower social position than yourself
❐ *He's so arrogant: he is always talking down to people.*

④ talk into
persuade somebody to do something
❐ *The salesman talked the customer into buying a new suit.*

⑦ talk out of
persuade somebody not to do something ❐ *Her friends talked her out of getting married.*

⑤ talk over
discuss something, especially a problem, in a relaxed and informal way
❐ *When we've got time, we must talk the whole thing over.*

③ talk round
persuade somebody to agree to something, especially despite their reluctance ❐ *He said he wasn't interested in helping out, but I'll try to talk him round.*

①⑤ taper off
gradually decrease or cause something to decrease in size, number or intensity ❐ *The stick tapered off to a point.* ❐ *Sales of new cars have been tapering off since October.*

②③ tart up   *Informal*
try to make somebody or something look attractive or smart; used in a derogatory way ❐ *She always tarts herself up before she goes out in the evening.*
❐ *The house had obviously been tarted up before it was offered for sale.*

⑥ ① team up (with)
start working with somebody as a team ❐ *John and Susan teamed up to produce a book.*

② tear into
attack somebody or something violently, either physically or verbally
❐ *The teacher tore into the poor girl for being late for class.*

②③ tear up
you tear something up when you destroy it completely by ripping it into pieces ❐ *Did you tear up the letter because you were angry?*

⑤ tell off
scold or reprimand somebody
❐ *The little boy's mother told him off for being naughty.*

② tell on
1 have a bad effect on somebody's health or appearance ❐ *These late nights are beginning to tell on me.*
2 reveal a secret about somebody to somebody else ❐ *Don't tell on me when Dad comes in!*

---

① = ●● ② = ●●○ ③ = ●○● ④ = ●○●○ ⑤ = ●○● *or* ●●○ ⑥ = ●●●○ ⑦ = ●○●●○

①⑤ thaw out
become or cause something to become unfrozen
❒ *You must leave the chicken to thaw out completely before cooking it.*

①②③ thin out
become or cause something to become less dense, packed or crowded
❒ *The crowds in town thin out when the shops close.* ❒ *A good gardener will thin out the plants regularly.*

⑤ think out / through
consider or think carefully about something ❒ *I can't make a decision until I've thought the matter out.*

⑤ think over
take time to consider something carefully ❒ *You've got a few weeks to think the matter over.*

②③ think up
invent or produce a new idea, plan, scheme, etc ❒ *The manager thought up a scheme to increase sales while reducing the number of staff.*

⑤ thrash out
1 solve a problem by intense discussion and argument ❒ *The management and union leaders thrashed out their disagreement.*
2 produce a plan, agreement, document, etc, by intense discussion
❒ *The committee thrashed out a proposal for a new children's hospital.*

③ throw about / around
be very generous or wasteful with something, especially money
❒ *Since John was promoted, he's been throwing his money about.*

⑤ throw away
1 discard, reject or waste something, often foolishly or thoughtlessly
❒ *You had a marvellous opportunity and you threw it away.*
2 speak words casually or carelessly
❒ *You threw away the last line and nobody could hear what you said.*

⑤ throw back
delay the progress of something
❒ *The fire has thrown production back badly.*

⑦ throw back at
remind somebody of something they have done wrong in the past
❒ *Whenever he tried to get a job, his time in prison was thrown back at him.*

⑦ throw back on
force somebody to depend more on something ❒ *The failure of all her plans threw her back on her own resources.*

⑤ throw in
1 include something extra, usually unexpectedly, in the price of something else ❒ *The car is only £10,000 and I'll throw in delivery and a year's road tax.* ❒ *It was £10 for the coach trip, with a free meal thrown in.*
2 add a comment, suggestion, remark, etc, to a conversation or discussion ❒ *Can I just throw in a few ideas on what's been said so far?*
3 resign from a job or abandon a course, project, etc ❒ *He threw in the job after only two weeks.*

④ throw into
involve yourself enthusiastically in a job or task ❒ *The team really threw themselves into the project, and it was soon finished.*

---

① = ●●   ② = ●●○   ③ = ●○●   ④ = ●○●○   ⑤ = ●○● *or* ●●○   ⑥ = ●●●●   ⑦ = ●○●●○

②③ throw off [1]

1 escape from somebody who is following you □ *The two men threw off their pursuers after a dangerous car chase.*
2 reject or get rid of something, especially something unpleasant □ *He's had a heavy cold for weeks but at last he's beginning to throw it off.*

②③④ throw off [2]

upset or disconcert somebody; disturb somebody's work or routine
□ *The loud noise threw off my concentration.* □ *The sudden disturbance threw me off just as I saw the answer.*

⑤ throw out [1]

1 reject or discard something
□ *I threw out a lot of old junk from the garage.* □ *The committee threw out the Finance Officer's proposals.*
2 cause figures, results, calculations, etc, to be inaccurate or wrong
□ *Errors in the computer have thrown out the inflation figures for this month.*
3 spoil or disrupt something
□ *The arrangements were thrown out by the bad weather.*
4 be a source of light, heat, etc
□ *This radiator throws out a good heat.*

③ throw out [2]

upset or disturb somebody or their work or routine
□ *I'd like to bring the family to see you on Sunday, as long as it doesn't throw you out too much.*

② throw out [3]

say or write something, especially a suggestion, idea, plan, etc, in a casual way
□ *Tom wasn't serious. He was just throwing out a few suggestions for discussion.*

⑦⑤ throw out (of)

1 dismiss or expel somebody from a company, school, club, etc, especially because of bad work or behaviour □ *He was thrown out of the school for bullying.* □ *The team lost every match until they threw Jim out.*
2 make somebody leave a room, bar, restaurant, etc, especially by using physical force □ *His teacher threw him out for talking.*

⑤ throw together [1]

produce or construct something in a rush or without care
□ *I threw together a quick meal for a few unexpected guests.*

③ throw together [2]

cause two people to meet
□ *Fate threw them together during the war and they got married soon after.*

①⑤ throw up [1] *Informal*

vomit something
□ *He got terribly drunk and was throwing up for most of the evening.*
□ *The dog threw up its dinner.*

② throw up [2]

produce or give rise to somebody or something, especially a famous person or an interesting idea, etc
□ *This decade has thrown up very few notable architects.*
□ *The conference has thrown up a number of interesting problems.*

⑤ throw up [3]

1 build something quickly □ *They threw up a new cabin in a couple of hours.*
2 abandon, reject or resign from a career, opportunity etc □ *John threw up his job to go to Africa as a missionary.*

②③ **tick off** ¹
scold or reprimand somebody
❒ *The headmaster* ticked *the boy* off *for disobedience.*

②③④ **tick off** ²
place a mark alongside somebody's name or an item on a list, usually to indicate that the person or item has been treated, included, checked etc
❒ *When you have paid me, I'll* tick *you* off *the list.* ❒ *As the goods were unloaded, the foreman* ticked *them* off*.*

① **tick over**
1 operate or run slowly and smoothly, especially of the engine of a vehicle ❒ *I've left the car* ticking over *outside, so we can go straightaway.*
❒ *Is everything at work* ticking over *OK?*
2 live or work at a steady rate without achieving much ❒ *He's just* ticking over *in the job until he finds something more interesting.*

③ **tide over**
be sufficient for somebody for a period of time, especially of money
❒ *Can you lend me £20 to* tide *me* over *until I'm paid?*

③ **tie down**
restrict or limit somebody's freedom with responsibilities or duties ❒ *She wouldn't marry him because she didn't want to* tie *him* down*.* ❒ *We were both* tied down *with a family and a full-time job.*

①⑥③⑦ **tie in (with)**
be or cause something to be compatible with something else ❒ *The book is designed to* tie in with *the series of TV programmes.* ❒ *Tim is very depressed. I hear his wife is very ill, so that* ties in*.*

① **tie up** ¹
fit together or be logically compatible, especially of two or more testimonies, reports, accounts, etc
❒ *The police got two eye-witness accounts but they didn't* tie up *at all.*

⑤ **tie up** ²
1 keep somebody busy
❒ *This report will probably* tie *me* up *for about a week.* ❒ *I'm* tied up *at the moment. Can I see you later?*
2 complete or finish making arrangements for something ❒ *Have you* tied up *the arrangements for the trip to London yet?*

⑦⑤ **tie up (in)**
invest money, capital, savings, etc, so that the money cannot be used for anything else ❒ *Jane would have bought the car if she hadn't* tied up *all her money* in *the house.* ❒ *The Government has a lot of money* tied up in *European development.*

⑤ **tighten up**
make rules, regulations, laws, etc, more strict or harsh ❒ *The company has* tightened up *the rules governing overtime.*

⑥① **tighten up (on)**
become more severe and firm about something, especially of a group or person in authority ❒ *The police are really* tightening up on *drunken driving this Christmas.*

⑤ **tip off**
warn somebody that something is going to happen; inform the police of a crime which is going to be committed ❒ *Scotland Yard had been* tipped off *about the bank robbery.*

N ❒ *I got a* tip-off *that the company was in trouble, so I sold my shares.*

⑤ **tire out**
make somebody very tired or exhausted ❒ *Looking after the children* tires *me* out. ❒ *After a day at the office she comes home* tired out.

①⑥③⑦ **tog up (in)** *Informal*
dress yourself or somebody else in formal or unusual clothes
❒ *The people entering the theatre had really* togged *themselves* up.
❒ *The army* togged *us* up *in full battle-gear and sent us off to the desert.*

②③ **tone down**
make something less strong, loud or shocking ❒ *If he* toned down *his arguments, people would be more sympathetic.*

①⑥③⑦ **tone in (with)**
be or cause something to be compatible or in harmony with something, especially in terms of appearance ❒ *The new buildings in the village* tone in *nicely* with *the older ones.*
❒ *It would be nice to* tone *the curtains* in with *the green carpet in the lounge.*

⑤ **tone up**
make something, especially your body, skin, muscles, etc, more vigorous, strong or healthy-looking
❒ *This exercise will* tone up *flabby tummy muscles.* ❒ *Daily jogging will* tone *you* up *and help you to lose weight.*

⑤ **top up**
1 fill to the top a container which is partially empty
❒ *The car radiator should be* topped up *with water each week.*

2 fill somebody's glass with more drink ❒ *More sherry, John? Let me* top *you* up.
N ❒ *Would you like a* top-up, *Mary?*

⑤ **toss off**
produce or create something, often something artistic, quickly, and with little effort
❒ *The composer was able to* toss off *a complete sonata in two days.*

① **toss up**
spin a coin to decide a matter, especially which team will bat, kick off, etc, in games like cricket and football
❒ *The referee* tossed up *to decide which team was to play against the wind.* ❒ *We can't both go out tonight. We'll* toss up *to see who goes.*

②③ **tot up**
calculate the total of something
❒ *When we've* totted up *the votes, we'll announce the result of the election.*
❒ *I'll just* tot up *the cost of my holiday in France this summer.*

① **touch down**
land on the ground, especially of an aircraft
❒ *TWA flight 402 is scheduled to* touch down *at 17.25.*

② **touch off**
1 cause some violent action or reaction to take place
❒ *Police harrassment* touched off *a wave of inner-city riots.*
2 cause gunpowder, a bomb, a firework, etc, to explode
❒ *The slightest spark will* touch off *the whole ammunition dump.*

② **touch on / upon**

mention or talk briefly about something □ *Later in the lecture, I will touch on the issues of free will and determinism.*

⑤ **touch up**

1 improve the appearance of something by adding small areas of paint, etc □ *You'd better touch up those rust spots before you sell the car.*

2 *Informal* make sexual advances by touching somebody

□ *Mr Smithers is vile! He touches me up whenever I go near him.*

⑤④ **tout about / around**

offer something for sale somewhere, especially something which has been dishonestly obtained

□ *There are always people touting tickets around during the Wimbledon tennis championship.*

⑦⑤ **trace back (to)**

find evidence of the origin of something in the past

□ *He traced his ancestors back to the mid-sixteenth century.*

□ *We must find out when the fault occurred. Can you trace it back?*

⑤ **track down**

find somebody or something by collecting evidence and clues

□ *The police tracked the murderer down after a three-week hunt.*

□ *I've tracked down that book I was looking for.*

⑤ **trade in**

give something second-hand and used in partial payment for something newer

□ *He traded his old car in for a new hatch-back.*

② **trade on / upon**

use somebody's good nature, kindness, etc, for unfair advantage or benefit

□ *He's trading on his wife's generosity by selling the house.*

① **trail away / off**

gradually become quieter, especially of a voice

□ *As the figure in black moved past the window, Jim's voice trailed off into silence.*

②③ **trigger off**

cause some event, action or series of events to take place

□ *The minister's remarks triggered off a fierce debate in the daily papers.*

① **trip up** ¹

1 stumble and possibly fall because your feet or legs hit some obstacle

□ *I didn't see the step and I tripped up.*

2 make a mistake or be inefficient

□ *I tripped up with the arrangements for the party, and forgot to buy any wine.*

⑤ **trip up** ²

1 cause somebody to stumble and possibly fall by putting some obstacle in their way

□ *The boys think it's funny to trip up the girls in the playground.*

2 deliberately cause somebody to make a mistake

□ *The interviewer tried to trip me up with his questions.*

② **trot out**

produce or say something in a casual way, without careful thought

□ *Frank trotted out the same feeble excuse for not attending the meeting.*

② **trump up**

invent a charge, accusation, story, etc, especially in order to send somebody to prison
❒ *The police trumped up false evidence in order to get the man convicted.*

⑤ **truss up**   tie or bind something firmly with rope, string, etc
❒ *The prisoners had been trussed up and left to die.*

⑤ **try on**

put on an item of clothing to see whether it fits and looks nice
❒ *Would you like to try on a larger size, sir?*

⑦ ③ **try on (with)**

do something deceitful, unlawful, improper, etc, to see if it will be allowed or tolerated
❒ *If you try your old tricks on with the new headmaster, you'll soon be in trouble.*

⑤ **try out**

test a new invention, scheme, product, etc ❒ *The design of the new car seems excellent, but we haven't tried it out on the road.*
N ❒ *We could always give the idea a try-out to see if it works.*

⑦ **try out on**

test the effect of something, especially a new drug, on somebody or something
❒ *The manufacturers tried out the drugs on rats and mice.*

⑤ **tuck away**

1 put something in a drawer, cupboard or safe place, especially in order to hide or store it
❒ *When she heard his voice, she tucked the money away under her pillow.*

2 eat something quickly or eat a lot
❒ *You should see him tuck away a steak! Like lightning!*

①② **tuck in / into**

start to eat something, especially a meal, in a hungry way
❒ *Dinner's ready at last. Do tuck in, everybody!* ❒ *They tucked into the cake as if they were starving.*

⑤ **tuck up**

wrap sheets and blankets around somebody, especially a child, to make them comfortable and warm
❒ *Mummy will read you a story and tuck you up in a minute.*

⑥ ① **tune in (to)**

adjust a radio so that it receives the broadcast from a particular radio station ❒ *Tune in at the same time next week for another edition of your favourite programme!*

①⑤ **tune up**

adjust a musical instrument so that the notes produced are correct or in tune with other instruments
❒ *The musicians need a few minutes to tune up before the concert can start.*

⑦ ③ **turf out (of)** *Informal*

ask or force somebody to leave or resign from somewhere ❒ *The landlord will turf you out if you get too drunk.*
❒ *Poor Andy was turfed out of the cricket club for trying to bribe the umpires.*

②④ **turn against**

become or cause somebody to become hostile or opposed to another person or thing
❒ *Why on earth should I want to turn your son against you?*

① = ●●   ② = ●●○   ③ = ●○●   ④ = ●○○○   ⑤ = ●○● *or* ●●○   ⑥ = ●●●○   ⑦ = ●○●●○

❐ *After ten years of friendship, Susan suddenly* turned against *Alice for no apparent reason.*

②③ **turn away**
refuse to admit or give help to somebody
❐ *The show was sold out. Hundreds of people were* turned away *at the door.* ❐ *A doctor can't simply* turn away *a dying man.*

⑤ **turn down**
1 adjust the volume control of a radio, record-player, tape-recorder, etc, to reduce the noise ❐ *Turn that radio* down! *I'm trying to go to sleep!*
2 adjust the controls of a cooker, heater, oven, etc, to reduce the heat ❐ *If you're too hot, I'll* turn the fire down *a bit.*
3 refuse an offer, request, invitation, etc ❐ *This opportunity is too good to* turn down. ❐ *Chris offered to lend me his car but I had to* turn it down.

① **turn in** ¹
go to bed ❐ *It's late. I think I'll* turn in.

⑤ **turn in** ² 1 deliver somebody to or put somebody under the control of the police, authorities, etc ❐ *I promise never to do it again! Please don't* turn me in.
2 produce and submit an essay, report, etc ❐ *The teacher says that Paul is* turning in *some excellent pieces of homework.*

②④ **turn into**
change or cause somebody or something to change into somebody or something different ❐ *He used to be a nasty little boy but now he's* turned into *a charming young man.* ❐ *I've discovered how to* turn iron into *gold.*

⑤ **turn off** ¹
1 stop the supply of gas, water or electricity, by turning a tap or moving a switch ❐ *Turn the tap* off! *The basin is overflowing!*
2 stop a machine or appliance, especially a radio, record-player, television, etc, by moving a switch or button ❐ *If you don't like the programmes, you can simply* turn the television off.

④③ **turn off** ² *Informal*
cause somebody to dislike or lose interest in somebody or something
❐ *Television debates are guaranteed to* turn anybody off *politics.* ❐ *That man is so arrogant! He really* turns me off.

②③ **turn on** ¹
1 start the supply of water, gas or electricity, by turning a tap or moving a witch ❐ *He* turned the water on.
2 start a machine or appliance, especially a radio, television, engine, etc, by moving a switch or button
❐ *He* turned the radio on *to listen to the midday news.*

② **turn on** ²
attack somebody suddenly and unexpectedly, either physically or verbally ❐ *What made the dog suddenly* turn on *him after all these years?*

③ **turn on** ³ *Informal*
excite somebody, especially sexually
❐ *The silk dress she was wearing really* turned *him* on.

⑤ **turn out** ¹
1 make something, especially a light or fire, stop burning by moving a switch ❐ *Will the last person to leave please* turn out *the lights?*

---

① = ●●   ② = ●●○   ③ = ●○○   ④ = ●○●○   ⑤ = ●○● *or* ●●○   ⑥ = ●●●○   ⑦ = ●○●●○

2 produce, manufacture or construct something, especially of a factory, company, machine, etc

❑ *This factory turns out thirty cars a day.*
3 empty or remove the whole contents of something ❑ *He turned out all his pockets trying to find the ring.*

②① **turn out** ²

prove or eventually be seen, felt, or judged to be something ❑ *After a bad start, the party turned out to be a great success.* ❑ *It turned out that she had known their intentions right from the start.* ❑ *Let me know how things turn out, won't you?*

① **turn out** ³

leave your home and go outside
❑ *I'm not turning out in this rain!*
❑ *People turned out in their thousands to see the new president.*
N ❑ *For such an important election, the turn-out was very low.*

⑦ ⑤ **turn out (of)**

ask or force somebody to leave or resign from somewhere or something
❑ *The manager turned the youth out of the cinema for being noisy.*

② **turn over**

sell goods or do business worth a particular amount
❑ *This company has the potential to turn over a million pounds per year.*
N ❑ *Our London branch has a much larger turn-over.*

⑦ ⑤ **turn over (to)**

deliver somebody or give control of somebody to the police, authorities, etc ❑ *The customs officials turned the man over to the French police.* ❑ *At the request of Scotland Yard, the French police turned over their prisoner.*

⑦ **turn over to**

transfer control of something to somebody else
❑ *When I retire I'll turn the family business over to my son.*

① **turn up** ¹

1 arrive, appear or be found
❑ *He's always late. Yesterday he didn't turn up until six.*
❑ *I lost my wallet in town last week and today it turned up at the bus station.*
2 arise or become available unexpectedly, especially of an opportunity, chance, job, etc
❑ *I'm still unemployed but I'm hoping something will turn up next week.*

②③ **turn up** ²

1 discover, reveal or expose something ❑ *While I was digging the garden I turned up a lovely Victorian brooch.*
❑ *I went to the library and turned up a few more facts about the private life of Louis XIV.*
2 adjust the controls of a radio, TV, fire, etc, to increase the sound, brightness or heat
❑ *Turn the record-player up. I can't hear it properly.*
❑ *She felt cold and turned the heating up a little.*

① = ●●   ② = ●●○   ③ = ●○●   ④ = ●○●○   ⑤ = ●○● *or* ●●○   ⑥ = ●●●○   ⑦ = ●○●●○

U, u

③ urge on 1
force or encourage a person or animal to move or continue to move forward

❏ *If the group leader hadn't urged them on, they would have been stuck in the forest for the night.*

2 encourage or try to persuade somebody to do or to continue to do something

❏ *The book would never have been written if the editor hadn't urged the writer on.*

⑤ use up
finish a supply or remainder of something

❏ *Why don't you use up the rest of the chicken in a soup? It's a shame to waste it.*
❏ *If I'd known that you'd used up all the milk, I'd have bought some more.*

⑤ usher in
introduce or mark the beginning of a new period, fashion, generation, etc

❏ *The invention of the telescope ushered in a new way of thinking about the universe.*

V, v

② verge on/upon
come very near to being in a certain condition, especially one which is undesirable

❏ *Several of his paintings verge on the obscene.*
❏ *His poor wife seems to be verging on senility.*

② vie with
compete with somebody, especially in order to win something or show yourself to be superior

❏ *The two children vied with each other for their father's attention.*

② vouch for
1 guarantee the truth, reliability, etc, of something

❏ *I certainly wouldn't like to vouch for the accuracy of these figures, unless I had checked them myself.*
❏ *We can't vouch for the chair remaining at this price for much longer, you know.*
2 declare your support for or confidence in somebody

❏ *How can I vouch for you when I hardly know you?*

---

① = ●●   ② = ●●○   ③ = ●○●   ④ = ●○○●   ⑤ = ●○● *or* ●●○   ⑥ = ●●●○   ⑦ = ●○●●○

W, w

② wade into
attack somebody, either physically or verbally
❒ *The boys waded into each other, kicking and punching.*
❒ *The teacher waded into the girl for not doing her homework.*

② wade through
read or work through a large amount of material slowly and laboriously
❒ *If you expect me to wade through 200 pages of this nonsense, you're mistaken.*

① wait about / around
remain somewhere, usually doing nothing, especially because the person that you are meeting is late
❒ *Where have you been? I've been waiting around here for two hours.*

① wait behind
remain somewhere after other people have left
❒ *I'd like to ask you something in private. Could you wait behind for a couple of minutes, please?*

② wait on/upon
1 serve somebody with food and drink in a restaurant, etc
❒ *We were waited on by a pretty girl in a pink pinafore.*
2 take care of somebody's needs and wants
❒ *The old man expected his entire family to wait on him.*

⑥① wait up (for)
not go to bed until somebody comes home ❒ *I'll be very late tonight, so don't wait up for me.*

①⑥⑦ wake up (to)
become or cause somebody to become aware of a problem, situation, etc ❒ *She woke up to the problems of growing old.* ❒ *If only we could wake them up to the dangers of the situation.*

⑥ walk away / off with
win a prize, race, contest, etc, very easily ❒ *He is so clever he walked off with all the prizes at school.*

② walk into
1 get a job, position, place on a course, etc, very easily
❒ *He did so well at university that he walked into the first job he applied for.*
2 enter a trap or difficult situation, especially because you have not been warned ❒ *He walked straight into the same mistake that we all made.*

②③ walk off
get rid of weight, a headache, a bad mood, etc. by walking
❒ *He is determined to walk off some of his fat this week.*

⑥ walk off with
1 take something which belongs to somebody else, either by mistake or on purpose
❒ *The burglars walked off with all my jewellery.*
2 see **walk away/off with**

① walk out

leave a factory or place of work and go on strike

❏ *The men walked out when they were asked to work for lower wages.*

N ❏ *They staged a walk-out over their working conditions.*

①/⑥ walk out / out of

leave a meeting, conference, etc, as a protest

❏ *When the new member began to speak, everybody got up and walked out.*

N ❏ *The talks ended abruptly with an angry walk-out by union leaders.*

⑥ walk out on

leave, abandon or desert somebody or something, especially when you are needed or expected to stay

❏ *He walked out on his wife and children and went to live in Australia.*

② walk over

1 defeat somebody very easily in a race, contest, etc ❏ *Our candidate will walk over the opposition. You'll see.*

N ❏ *His election was a complete walk-over.*

2 treat somebody with contempt

❏ *I can't understand why she allows her children to walk over her as they do.*

⑤ wall in

enclose somebody or something with a wall or some barrier

❏ *He was walled in by the crowd.*

② wallow in

enjoy or indulge in something more than you should

❏ *She wallowed in the praise she received.*

⑥ waltz off with

win something, especially a prize, by defeating other people easily ❏ *He*

waltzed off with six gold medals.

② want for

lack or be in need of something; always used in the negative

❏ *Her little girl never wants for anything: she has everything she could possibly need.*

② ward off

prevent something, especially a blow, illness, emotion, etc, from hitting or overwhelming you

❏ *She moved out of the way to ward off his blow.* ❏ *What can you recommend for warding off a cold?*

② warm to

gradually become more interested in or enthusiastic about something

❏ *She began to warm to her subject after a few minutes and spoke with real enthusiasm.*

② warm to / towards

gradually begin to like somebody and to feel interested in them

❏ *I warmed to the girl as soon as she came into the room.* ❏ *She warmed towards him when she realised he was lonely too.*

① warm up [1]

prepare for a contest or strenuous physical activity by doing exercises

❏ *The footballers warmed up for half an hour before the match.*

N ❏ *They had an hour's warm-up before the match.*

①②③ warm up [2]

become or cause somebody or something to become more interested or lively ❏ *The magician warmed up his audience with a few quick tricks.*

❏ *The game suddenly warmed up when the other side scored a goal.*

③④ warn off

try to prevent somebody from going somewhere or doing something, especially by threatening them
☐ *We wanted to have a picnic in the woods, but a large notice* warned *us* off.

⑦ ⑤ wash down (with)

help something be swallowed by having a drink
☐ *This bread's rather dry.* Wash *it* down *with a cup of tea.*

⑤ wash out

cause an outdoor game, contest or event to be cancelled, postponed or abandoned, especially of bad weather
☐ *The match was* washed out *by the heavy rain.*
N ☐ *The match was a complete* wash-out.
N ☐ *His idea turned out to be a total* wash-out.

② wash over

have no effect on somebody's attitude, understanding or behaviour
☐ *He is so used to receiving complaints that they just* wash over *him nowadays.*

① wash up ¹

wash the dishes, glasses, cutlery, etc, after a meal
☐ *Her husband* washed up *while she put the children to bed.*
N ☐ *Whose turn is it to do the* washing-up?

②③ wash up ²

bring something onto the shore, especially of the sea
☐ *The waves* washed *the oil* up *onto the sand.*
☐ *A lot of rubbish was* washed up *by the high tide.*

① waste away

lose weight and strength, especially of a part of the body or somebody who is ill ☐ *We could see him* wasting away *because of his illness.*

① watch out

be careful, especially to avoid a dangerous situation or upsetting other people; often used in the imperative
☐ *Watch out! This is a very busy road.*
☐ *If you do that again you'll be in trouble, so you had better* watch out.

⑥ ① watch out (for)

remain alert, attentive or observant, so that you notice somebody or something
☐ *He asked me to* watch out for *his uncle who would be wearing a green suit.*
☐ *The doctor told me to* watch out for *any sickness or high temperature.*

② watch over

protect and be responsible for somebody or something
☐ *She asked me to* watch over *her daughter on the journey.*
☐ *He has been appointed to* watch over *the interests of the disabled.*

②③ water down

1 dilute a liquid by adding water to it
☐ *I'm sure this whisky has been* watered down.
2 make something weaker, less intense, less severe, etc
☐ *He agreed to* water down *his criticisms of the Government.*

②③ wave aside

dismiss or refuse to consider a comment, remark, suggestion, etc ☐ *She* waved aside *his objections to her plan.*

①⑤ wear away

gradually disappear or cause something to disappear, because of use or friction ❒ *This staircase is so old that some of the steps have almost* worn away. ❒ *Over the centuries, the sea has* worn away *the rocks.*

②③① wear down

1 gradually become or cause something to become lower, thinner or reduced because of use or friction ❒ *You must buy a new tyre. This one has been* worn right down.

2 weaken or cause somebody or something to be weakened gradually by continuous pressure or opposition ❒ *He was sure he would eventually* wear down *her objections to marrying him.*

① wear off

become less intense or no longer felt, especially of a pain or drug ❒ *Now that you have taken a pill your headache will soon* wear off.

① wear on

pass tediously or slowly, especially of time ❒ *She became more and more tired as the evening* wore on.

①⑤ wear out ¹

become or cause something to become unusable because of continuous use or wear ❒ *Her little boy* wears *his shoes* out *every two months.* ❒ *His shoes* wear out *very quickly.*

⑤ wear out ²

tire or exhaust somebody or something ❒ *Looking after four children* wears *her* out.

②③ weed out

get rid of the weakest, worst, etc, in a group or collection ❒ *He looked through the applications for the job and* weeded out *the most unsuitable ones.*

② weigh against

cause people to judge or regard somebody unsympathetically ❒ *His years in prison will* weigh against *him when he tries to get a job.*

⑤ weigh down

1 cause somebody or something to bend, especially of a heavy load ❒ *She was* weighed down *by her shopping.* ❒ *The snow* weighed down *the branches of the trees.*

2 make somebody feel sad and depressed ❒ *Problems of money* weighed *her* down.

② weigh on

cause worry and anxiety to somebody ❒ *The pressures of her job* weighed *heavily on her and she decided to find a new one.* ❒ *You can tell that something is* weighing *on his mind.*

②③ weigh up

1 consider something carefully, especially before reaching a decision, making a judgement, etc ❒ *He* weighed up *the situation and decided he was unlikely to be successful.*

2 form an opinion about somebody's character ❒ *My wife is very quick at* weighing *people* up.

② welch / welsh on *Informal*

fail to pay a debt, keep a promise or agreement, etc ❒ *He* welched on *his debts.* ❒ *She* welshed on *her employer and the promises she had made him.*

⑦ **wheedle out of**
obtain something from somebody by using persuasion and flattery
❏ *She wheedled a new car out of her father.*

②③ **while away**
pass time lazily and pleasantly
❏ *He whiled away his holiday reading and listening to music.*

② **whip up**
1 prepare something quickly, especially food
❏ *It won't take her long to whip up a meal.*
2 arouse interest or feelings
❏ *He tried to whip up some support for his plan.* ❏ *I can't whip up any enthusiasm for going out this evening.*

⑤ **whisk away / off**
suddenly remove somebody or something, especially in a vehicle
❏ *The police whisked the politician away as soon as the crowd became violent.*

② **whistle for** *Informal*
ask for something, especially payment, with no hope of getting it
❏ *We won't be able to pay them until next year. They'll just have to whistle for their money.*

②③ **whittle away**
reduce something gradually
❏ *The high cost of living has been whittling away our savings for a long time now.*

②③ **whittle down**
reduce something in stages, especially the size of a group, collection, list, etc ❏ *Eventually they whittled down the number of applicants to three.*

⑤ **win back**
regain something, especially affection or support
❏ *What can I do to win my girlfriend back?*

⑦ ⑤ **win over (to)**
succeed in getting somebody's support, agreement, etc, especially by persuasion ❏ *She soon won him over to her way of thinking.*

① **win through / out**
succeed, especially after a difficult period ❏ *He had a long fight against illness but eventually he won through.*

① **wind down** ¹
1 work, move or take place with less and less speed, energy, frequency, etc, especially before stopping completely
❏ *School activities start winding down about two weeks before the end of term.*
2 relax and become calmer ❏ *It took her a week to wind down after her exams.*

②③ **wind down** ²
gradually reduce the activity or intensity of something, especially before final closure or termination
❏ *The company wound down its affairs in South Africa.*

①②③ **wind up** ¹
end or bring something to an end, especially a meeting or business operation ❏ *He wound up the afternoon by thanking everybody for coming.*
❏ *What will happen to all our jobs if the company winds up?*

⑤ **wind up** ²
cause somebody to become tense or excited ❏ *If there's any bad news nowadays, I simply don't tell him. It only winds him up.*

---

① = ●● ② = ●●○ ③ = ●○● ④ = ●○○● ⑤ = ●○○ *or* ●●○ ⑥ = ●●●○ ⑦ = ●○●●○

①② wind up ³
find yourself in a certain place or state, as the result of a previous action ❑ *If you insist on working so hard, you'll wind up in hospital.*

②③ wipe down
clean a table, wall, car, etc, with a slightly wet cloth
❑ *Before you paint a room you should wipe down the walls and ceiling.*

②③ wipe off / out
cancel a debt
❑ *You've helped me so much that I'm willing to wipe off the £20 you owe me.*

②③ wipe out   1
clean the inside of something by using a cloth ❑ *Don't forget to wipe out the bath after you've used it.*
2 kill, destroy or get rid of somebody or something, especially in great numbers
❑ *A whole regiment was wiped out in the battle.* ❑ *Doctors hope that they will be able to wipe out malaria very soon.*

②③ wipe up ¹
remove something which has been dropped or spilled by using a cloth
❑ *Please wipe up the coffee you have just poured all over my carpet.*

②③① wipe up ²
dry dishes, glasses, cutlery, etc, that have just been washed
❑ *Whose turn is it to wipe up?* ❑ *I dropped the glass while I was wiping it up.*
N ❑ *You can help me do the wiping-up if you like.*

④ wish on / onto
want somebody or something to become somebody else's responsibility or property, usually used with *would* and a negative ❑ *The child gets naughtier every day. I wouldn't wish him on my worst enemy.*

②③ wolf down
eat something quickly and greedily like a wolf ❑ *If you wolf down your food like that, you'll be sick.*

② wonder at
be very surprised by something; usually used with a negative ❑ *You can hardly wonder at her leaving home. She should have done it years ago.*

② work against
hinder or impede something ❑ *His laziness works against his basic intelligence.*

⑤④ work in / into
include something in a story, conversation, etc, especially in a deliberate or contrived way
❑ *He always manages to work in a reference to the money I still owe him.*

②③ work off
get rid of weight, tension, emotions, etc, especially by work or physical activity ❑ *He worked off his anger by concentrating on all the letters he had to write.* ❑ *He hoped to work off his extra weight by swimming and playing tennis.*

⑦ ⑤ work off (on)
get rid of an unpleasant feeling or emotion by making somebody else suffer ❑ *You needn't think you can work your frustration off on me!*

②③ work out ¹
1 calculate or solve something
❑ *Can you work out how much money we will need for our holiday?*

2 plan, invent or devise something
❏ *He worked out all the details of the attack.* ❏ *They decided to work out new rules for the game.*
3 understand somebody's character or reasons; usually used with a negative ❏ *I can't work out why he behaves as he does.* ❏ *He's a strange child. I can't work him out.*

① work out ²
1 have a definite answer
❏ *Surely your maths teacher wouldn't give you a sum that didn't work out!*
2 have a favourable/happy outcome
❏ *I hope your plans for the future work out.* ❏ *Things do not seem to be working out for them as they had hoped.*
3 do physical exercises, especially of a boxer, dancer, etc
❏ *He spent the morning working out at the gym.*
N ❏ *He had a long work-out before his fight.*

⑥ work out at / to
have a final cost or total after all calculations have been done
❏ *His salary works out at £10,000 a year.* ❏ *The whole journey worked out to 310 miles.*

③ work over *Informal*
beat somebody in a deliberate and calculated way, especially as a punishment or to extract information
❏ *The gang worked him over until he told them where the money was hidden.*
N ❏ *They gave him a working-over.*

② work towards
try to achieve something
❏ *All the teachers were working towards the introduction of new syllabuses.*

② work under
do a job under the guidance or supervision of somebody
❏ *He was lucky to work under a professor who was always willing to help young members of staff.*

②③ work up
1 gradually develop something, especially a business
❏ *It's amazing how he has managed to work up the business from almost nothing.*
2 arouse feelings, interest, appetite, etc ❏ *I can't work up any enthusiasm for studying today.* ❏ *He walked 20 kilometres and worked up a good appetite for dinner.*

⑦ ③ work up (into/to)
get or cause somebody to get very excited or upset about something
❏ *If you want the men to agree to strike action, you'll have to work them up a bit first.* ❏ *She worked herself up into a terrible state of panic.*

⑥ work up to
gradually approach or prepare to mention a subject, especially an important or embarrassing one
❏ *I haven't asked her if she can lend me the money yet, but I'm working up to it.*

⑦ worm out of
get information, a secret, etc, from somebody by using persuasion and cunning
❏ *It took me a long time to worm the truth out of him.*

① wrap up ¹
1 put on warm clothes
❏ *It's cold outside, so make sure you wrap up well.*

2 *Informal* stop talking; often used in the imperative to express anger or irritation ▢ *Wrap up, Mary, for goodness' sake! I'm trying to work.*

② **wrap up** ²
1 conclude a meeting, discussion, investigation, etc ▢ *His instructions were to wrap up the meeting by three o'clock.*

2 finalise an agreement, business deal, etc ▢ *To wrap up the deal, their sales team offered us a £1000 reduction on each model.*

⑥ **wriggle out of**   *Informal*
avoid a duty or difficult situation, especially by being cunning or by making excuses
▢ *You promised that you would cut the grass today, so don't try wriggling out of it.* ▢ *How does he always manage to wriggle out of his share of the work?*

⑥ ① **write away / off (for)**
send an order for something, especially for a free gift or something that you cannot buy locally ▢ *I have written away for a copy of the new English dictionary.* ▢ *If you write off within two weeks, we'll send you a free record.*

⑥ ① **write in (to)**
send a letter to a magazine, newspaper, radio station, etc, to complain, make a request or express an opinion
▢ *He wrote in to the newspaper to complain about the previous day's headline.*
▢ *The presenter of the programme asked listeners to write in with their suggestions.*

⑤ **write in / into**
include something deliberately in a legal or official document ▢ *Make sure that the clause about medical expenses is written into the contract.*

⑤ **write off**
1 accept or decide that somebody or something is no good
▢ *He wrote off the team without giving them a proper chance.*
▢ *The critics wrote him off as a conductor after just one concert.*
2 damage something badly, especially a car
▢ *You're lucky to have written off the old car and not the new one.*
N ▢ *His car was a complete write-off.*
3 accept that something, especially an amount of money, is lost and cannot be recovered
▢ *The firm had to write off the man's debt when they heard that he was bankrupt.*

⑦ **write off as**
form a certain judgement or opinion about somebody or something, especially one that reveals your disappointment or displeasure
▢ *Within days she had written him off as an idiot.*

⑥ ① **write off (for)**
  see **write away/off (for)**

⑦ ⑤ **write out (of)**
remove a character from a television or radio series
▢ *She was eventually written out of the serial after playing the part for ten years.*

⑤ **write up**
produce a full written account of something, especially on the basis of a set of notes
▢ *I've got to stay in tonight and write up this afternoon's experiment.*
▢ *If I don't write up my notes almost immediately, I simply can't understand them.*

① = ●●   ② = ●●○   ③ = ●○●   ④ = ●○●○   ⑤ = ●○● *or* ●●○   ⑥ = ●●●○   ⑦ = ●○●●○

Z, z

⑥ ① zero in (on)

1 approach or discover the exact position of something, especially of guns

❒ *The tanks zeroed in on our defences with the most deadly accuracy.*

2 concentrate your efforts or focus your attention on something

❒ *We should zero in on this opportunity to win public approval before it's too late.*

⑤ ① zip up

help somebody dress by fastening the zip on their clothing; fasten by means of a zip

❒ *"Will you zip me up, please?" she asked.*

❒ *She hates dresses that zip up at the back.*

⑥ ① zoom in (on)

make the subject of a photograph appear to come closer by the use of a zoom lens

❒ *Occasionally the camera would zoom in on the old lady's hands.*